BUFFY AND THE ART OF STORY SEASON THREE PART 1

WRITE STRONGER PLOTS, CHARACTERS, AND THEMES BY WATCHING BUFFY

WRITING AS A SECOND CAREER

L. M. LILLY

SPINY WOMAN PRESS

Copyright © 2023 by Lisa M. Lilly

All rights reserved.

No part of this book may be reproduced in any form or by any electronic or mechanical means, including information storage and retrieval systems or through use of or by artificial intelligence, without written permission from the author, except for the use of brief quotations in a book review.

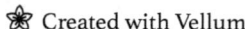 Created with Vellum

CONTENTS

Introduction	xi
1. ANNE S3 E1	1
Quick Opening Conflict	1
Looking For A Story Spark	3
Possible Story Sparks In *Anne*	4
More Conflict And Exposition	5
Subtle Foreshadowing	7
Exposition, Pacing, And The One-Quarter Twist	7
Identity As A Theme	10
Eggshell Buffy Commits At The Midpoint With A Look	12
Showing Emotions	14
Buffy As Herself	17
The Three-Quarter Turn In Demon Fighting	17
More On Identity	19
More Themes Happen On The Way To The Climax	20
Falling Action And Lily's Choice	22
Protagonist Goals, Stakes, And Where The Demon Plot Falters	23
Pilots	25
Lily Becomes Anne, Foreshadowing Mr. Faithful	25
Wish Fulfillment	26
Identity Themes For Season Three	26
Angel And The Underworld	26
Questions For Your Writing	27
2. DEAD MAN'S PARTY S3 E2	28
Opening Conflict And Story Sparks	28
Showing Emotion Through Action	30
Character Consistency	31
The One-Quarter Twist Of *Dead Man's Party*	32
Storytelling Through Dreams	33

Conflict Between Joyce And Buffy	34
Metaphors And Universal Themes	35
Midpoint Reversals In *Dead Man's Party*	36
Eavesdropping As A Plot Device	38
Why The Zombie Plot Feels Slow	39
False Conflict In An Emotional Three-Quarter Turn	39
Zombie Plot Turn Or Not?	41
Out Of Character Or In?	43
Reconnecting Through Fighting Leads To The Climax	44
Falling Action	46
Spoilers And Foreshadowing	47
Giles And Buffy	47
Eavesdroppers	48
Questions For Your Writing	48
3. FAITH, HOPE & TRICK S3 E3	50
Opening Conflict And Exposition	51
Story Spark	52
Dream Scene Story Spark	53
A One-Quarter Twist And Giles's Concerns	55
Faith And The One-Quarter Twist	57
Everyone Loves Faith	59
Midpoint Reversal In *Faith, Hope & Trick*	60
Real Conflict Between Faith And Buffy	61
A Three-Quarter Ring And A Vampire Turn	63
Vamp Plot Climax	65
Buffy's Emotional Plot Climax	66
The Game Changer	67
Comparison To *Dead Man's Party*	68
Plot And Characters In Faith, Hope & Trick	69
Unanswered Story Question	70
Snyder's Conditions	70
Faith Foreshadowing	70
Giles's Roles, The Council, And Communication	71
Questions For Your Writing	72

4. BEAUTY AND THE BEASTS S3 E4 — 73
　Opening Conflict And Voiceover — 73
　The Chase, A Theme, And The Story Spark — 74
　Guidance And Themes — 76
　A Later But Powerful One-Quarter Twist — 79
　Two Possible Midpoints — 81
　Misleads And Cheats — 83
　Buffy's Commitment And Reversal With Platt — 84
　Three-Quarter Turn And Cold-Blooded Jelly Donuts — 85
　Troubling Metaphor And Theme — 88
　The Climax — 89
　Falling Action Ending With Voiceover — 91
　The Cost When Characters Get What They Want — 93
　Love And Loss, Faith And Buffy — 94
　Oz's Inner Wolf — 94
　Questions For Your Writing — 95

5. HOMECOMING S3 E5 — 97
　Opening And Unspoken Conflicts — 98
　A Story Spark From Scott — 100
　A Layered Villain — 101
　The One-Quarter Twist — 102
　Spike, Trick, And On Being An Antagonist — 104
　Giving Willow What She Most Wants — 104
　Midpoint Reversal, Commitment, And Montage — 106
　Integrated Action-Based And Emotional Plots — 107
　Slayerfest Three-Quarter Turn — 109
　Xander Getting What He Wants — 111
　The Climax — 113
　Falling Action And Story Questions — 114
　Angel And Giles — 116
　Jonathan — 116
　The Mayor — 116
　Questions For Your Writing — 117

6. BAND CANDY S3 E6 118
   Opening Conflict Commentary, Theme, And
      Foreshadowing 119
   Story Sparks 121
   Strong Scene Transitions 121
   Internal Conflict For Buffy Over Angel 123
   The One-Quarter Twist And Conflict With And
      Without Evil 124
   The Adults Change At The Midpoint 127
   Exposition And The New Character 128
   Universal Themes 129
   The Three-Quarter Turn 132
   The Climax And Multi-Purpose Dialogue 133
   Falling Action In *Band Candy* 134
   Moving The Season Arc 136
   The Council 136
   Joyce And Giles 137
   Buffy And Cars 137
   Questions For Your Writing 137

7. REVELATIONS S3 E7 139
   Three Opening Conflicts 139
   Three Story Sparks 141
   The Demon Plot And A Universal Theme 142
   Plot Questions, Guilt, And Angel 144
   More Guilt At The One-Quarter Twist 145
   Plot Manipulation? 146
   Timing Question 148
   An Intervention That Fits The Characters 149
   Midpoint Reversal And A Human Giles 150
   Plot Question: Faith's Exclusion 152
   Bonding And Secrets 153
   The Three-Quarter Turn In *Revelations* 155
   Isolation As A Theme: Angel And Giles 156
   The Climax 157
   Falling Action, Arcs, Bookends, And Subplots 157
   Trust And Faith 159
   Faith, Buffy, And Willow 160

Future Watcher, Future Rebellion	162
Questions For Your Writing	163

8. LOVERS WALK S3 E8 — 164
- Opening Conflict — 164
- A Spike Spark And A Story Spark — 166
- Subplot, Exposition, And Theme — 169
- Dealing With Too Many Characters — 169
- Linking Scenes — 170
- The One-Quarter Twist Of *Lovers Walk* — 171
- Angel and Buffy: Real Or False Conflict? — 173
- Who Is The Protagonist? — 175
- Midpoint Commitment: Willow Stands Up For Herself — 176
- The Three-Quarter Turns And Twists — 181
- A Big Fight At The Climax — 182
- Falling Action — 183
- Plot Or Subplot For Spike? — 184
- Friends And More Falling Action — 184
- The Most Healthy Character? — 187
- The Wish, The Mayor, And The Season End — 188
- *Angel* Crossovers — 189
- Mortality And Magic — 189
- What Else Spike Sees — 190
- Questions For Your Writing — 191

9. THE WISH S3 E9 — 193
- Opening Conflict — 194
- Cordelia's Scary Story Spark — 195
- Callbacks And Building Toward The Twist — 197
- The One-Quarter Twist Of *The Wish* — 199
- Midpoint Of *The Wish* — 202
- Story Questions — 203
- The Climax Begins — 207
- The Falling Action — 210
- Can Your Protagonist Die Mid-Story? — 210
- Faith, Buffy, And Theme — 211
- The Antagonist In *The Wish* — 213
- Insights From The Script About Anya And Story Structure — 213

Future Anya And Willow	215
Faith And Buffy	215
Evil As The Antagonist	216
Questions For Your Writing	216

10. AMENDS S3 E10 — 218
Opening Conflict	219
Story Spark And Subplots	221
Setting, Character, And The One-Quarter Twist	223
Dreams And Ghosts Of Christmas Past	225
The Gang Comes Through And A Subplot Twist	226
Angelus And Christmas Past	227
The Midpoint Of *Amends*	227
The Protagonist And Antagonist	228
Oz And Willow Subplot Midpoint And Turns	231
Plot and Subplot Three Quarter Turns	232
The First's Goals	234
The Climax, An Incorporeal Antagonist, And The Pilot	236
Deus Ex Machina?	239
The Falling Action	239
Forces For Good And Evil	240
The Series *Angel*	241
Oz, Willow, And The Wolf	242
Angel And Buffy	242
The Final Villain	243
Questions For Your Writing	244

11. GINGERBREAD S3 E11 — 246
Opening Conflict	247
A Different Story Spark	248
The One-Quarter Twist	250
Major Midpoint Reversal And Theme	253
Reuniting And A Mission Statement	255
Sheila And The Three-Quarter Turn	257
Minor Character Arcs	259
The Climax	260
The Falling Action	261
The Effect Of *Gingerbread*	262
Change Or No Change	264

Amy The Rat And Willow	265
More On Willow's Magic	265
Bad Girls	266
Class Protector	266
Questions For Your Writing	267
12. RESOURCES	269
Notes	271
About the Author	273
Also by L. M. Lilly	275

INTRODUCTION

If you love *Buffy the Vampire Slayer* and love diving into how and why it works (and very occasionally doesn't), this book is for you.

There's so much to learn from every episode of *Buffy*, and each is so much fun to revisit, that a few years ago I started a podcast about it. This book covers Episodes 1-11 of Season Three. (The podcast is now up to Season Six.) Along with identifying the major plot points and turns as I recap each episode, I look at other aspects of storytelling. These include how the writers weave in backstory without slowing the plot, create compelling characters who suffer, rejoice, grow, and change, build suspense, explore key themes without preaching, and more.

While you may enjoy watching each episode before reading the chapter about it, I go through each in depth, so you don't need to.

If you prefer, you can skip reading this book and listen to the *Buffy and the Art of Story* podcast, on which the book is based. Here, though, the discussions are edited for better flow and organization. You'll also find a list of topics at the start of each chapter and questions at the end to think about for your writing.

Who Am I?

If you haven't read my fiction or my books for writers, you might wonder who I am and why I'm sharing storytelling advice. So here it is:

First, as you might guess, I am a big fan of **Buffy the Vampire Slayer**. When it aired on network TV, I loved every episode. (Okay, almost every episode.) But it was only after the DVDs came out and I watched full seasons within a shorter timeframe that I saw how well constructed it is.

That started me rewatching the entire series in order, which I've now done more times than I can count. When I decided to start a podcast, combining my love of fiction writing and **Buffy** seemed natural. I learned so much from the show over the years. Why not delve into it in a more deliberate way?

As for fiction writing, as Lisa M. Lilly, I'm the author of the bestselling four-book Awakening supernatural thriller series. Books in the series have been downloaded over 100,000 times in over 100 countries. The second book in my current series, the Q.C. Davis Mysteries, **The Charming Man**, was a 2019 Finalist in The Wishing Shelf Book Awards. Windy City Reviews called the fourth book, **The Troubled Man**, one of the best Chicago mysteries, favorably comparing it to the work of Louise Penny (one of my idols) and Jo Nesbo. As I write this introduction, the sixth Q.C. Davis Mystery, **The Forgotten Man**, just released.

I also write non-fiction books for writers under L. M. Lilly (I was a writing major in college), work as an attorney, and teach legal writing to law students. I founded WritingAsASecondCareer.com to share information with people juggling writing novels with working at other jobs or careers. Not that I know anything about that….

Introduction

Story Structure

The major plot points and turns I focus on in each episode are listed below. They are drawn from what I've learned over decades of writing and studying fiction. Nearly every good story I read, watch, or listen to includes these points in order:

- **Opening conflict** (draws the viewer in fast)
- **Story Spark** or Inciting Incident (sets the main plot rolling)
- **One-Quarter Twist** (the first major plot turn that occurs about one-quarter through any story and spins the plot in a new direction, often while raising the stakes)
- **The Midpoint** (when the protagonist commits fully to the quest, suffers a major reversal, or both)
- **Three-Quarter Turn** (the last major plot turn that arises from the protagonist's actions at the Midpoint and spins the plot yet again)
- **Climax** (self-explanatory I hope)
- **Falling Action** (where subplots resolve and open questions are answered)

If you find this story structure helpful, you can download a free story structure template to use with your own writing at WritingAsASecondCareer.com/Worksheets.

A Quick Note On Spoilers

Each chapter focuses on a single episode with no spoilers until a section on Foreshadowing at the end. There, I talk about how the episode foreshadows later events in *Buffy* and occasionally *Angel*. If you aren't familiar with the whole of the Buffyverse, proceed with caution.

Introduction

Ready? Let's dive into the Hellmouth.

CHAPTER 1
ANNE S3 E1

THIS CHAPTER TALKS ABOUT *ANNE*, Season Three, Episode One, where Buffy tries to live anonymously in Los Angeles but demons find her. Written and directed by Joss Whedon. Original air date: September 29, 1998.

Along with the episode breakdown, topics include:

- Using minor conflict among friends to reveal exposition in a fun way
- How a slow start and unclear plot turns affect pacing
- Themes that sometimes shape and sometimes muddle the story
- How well Buffy, a wounded protagonist with negative goals, works for the episode

Okay, let's dive into the Hellmouth.

Quick Opening Conflict

A story's opening conflict is there to draw the audience in quickly. It may or may not relate to the main plot. Before I get to that initial conflict, though, overall *Anne* is the first *Buffy* season pilot episode that didn't draw me in as much as I expected, though I'd been anticipating it all summer. (I watched *Buffy* as it aired on network TV.) Breaking it down for the podcast helped me understand why. But there is a lot to appreciate, too, in this episode.

Anne starts with plenty of conflict in a classic location: the cemetery. A hand comes out of the dirt. A young woman stands over the grave, waiting. But as soon as we hear her voice, we know it's not Buffy.

Willow: That's right, Big Boy, come and get it.

The vampire emerges. He does some stunning acrobatics. (Later we learn he was on the tumbling team when he was alive.)

Xander, Willow, and Oz struggle to subdue him. The fight builds until the vamp runs away. Oz throws a stake after him. The stake twirls in the air and bounces off a tombstone. And the vampire gets away. Xander turns to Willow.

Xander: Come and get it, Big Boy?

Willow explains that the Slayer always uses puns and wise cracking and Willow thinks it throws the vampires off. But it's not as easy as it looks. Xander comments that he was always amazed by Buffy's fighting, but he feels like they took her punning for granted.

Willow: Xander. Past tense.

He awkwardly says he only meant that in the past they took it for granted, but they won't when Buffy gets back.

That opening provides a great example of how to reveal exposition about Buffy through conflict. We learn more when Willow says she hopes that Buffy will just show up for school tomorrow. Xander responds that Buffy can't just show up. She got kicked out.

Now we know Buffy's gone, she's been away for a while, school is starting, and Buffy got expelled. That's a lot to find out in less than 3 minutes. And it all comes out through engaging minor conflict between our friends. No one just tells one another (or the audience) what happened. The opening also includes foreshadowing. Oz looks troubled when Willow mentions the first day of school. Willow reassures him she'll still have plenty of time to see him.

The scene cuts to Buffy. She stands in a pretty sundress on the beach. Ocean waves roll behind her. It's sunny. We discover it's a dream when Angel appears and puts his arms around her from behind.

Buffy: Stay with me.

Angel: Forever, that's the whole point. I'll never leave. Not even if you kill me.

Buffy's face shows how much that upsets her. It also reminds the viewers what happened at the end of the last season. And the scene teases fans with the hope of Angel returning and weaves in story questions that kept them tuning in.

When I watched *Buffy* as it aired, each glimpse of Angel was heartbreaking. It brought back all Buffy's feelings and filled me as a viewer with a longing to know the answers. Was Angel coming back? How? When would he be part of a storyline rather than a dream or flashback? It was both exciting and frustrating.

The camera zooms in on Buffy's face. She blinks. The sound of the surf blends into street noises. The camera pans back and Buffy is in a small one-room apartment on a busy street.

Looking For A Story Spark

The switch to the room happened at 4 minutes, 17 seconds, about 10% through the episode. Normally around there, or a bit earlier, we see a Story Spark (also known as the Inciting Incident). That's the plot point that gets the main plot rolling.

So far, though, I don't see anything that truly starts the main plot.

Instead, we've gotten backstory and learned a few new things. Buffy's living alone somewhere. Her friends don't know where she is. She's still devasted over Angel.

The scene switches to a diner. At 5 minutes, 13 seconds, Buffy walks in wearing a waitress uniform. (I can't help seeing this as an homage to *Terminator* —the original film —where Sarah Connor begins as a waitress in a similar environment and uniform.) Buffy takes an order from a couple guys who make crude comments. One slaps her butt as she leaves the table. She pauses. Ominous music plays. But Buffy walks away.

At the next table a young couple sits side-by-side with their arms around one another. The young man, Ricky, calls Buffy by the name on her name tag, which is Anne, and asks what they can get for their handful of change. Ricky's girlfriend, Lily, wants cake. But Ricky says No to cake because they need to eat healthy. How about pie? The two show Buffy their interlocking tattoos. Each has half a heart with the other's name on it. Buffy says it's nice. And permanent.

Ricky: Forever. I mean, that's the whole point.

The episode is now 6 minutes, 41 seconds in. Ricky's words, though, don't serve as a Story Spark. They don't drive the story in any way, though the echo of what Angel said in the dream sets off an emotional reaction in Buffy. After taking the order, she asks another waitress to cover for her and leaves.

Possible Story Sparks In *Anne*

Before Ricky's line, Lily looks at Buffy and asks if she knows her. Buffy says she doesn't think so. That exchange could be a Story Spark, as later we'll see that Lily does in fact know Buffy and she seeks Buffy's help when Ricky goes missing. But Lily thinking she recognizes Buffy doesn't truly trigger the main plot. If Ricky never goes missing, there's no main storyline. At least, there's not if we see the main plot as Buffy fighting demons and freeing other humans.

On the other hand, the main plot can be seen as Buffy transitioning from isolating herself to reconnecting — not just with her friends and family but with herself and with people overall. Reconnecting is what ultimately sends her home.

If that is the main plot, Lily recognizing her does drive the story. That still puts the Story Spark quite a bit past 10%, meaning that it takes a long time to begin. It's one reason the episode didn't grab me. I kept waiting for the story to start.

While any pilot requires scenes to get the audience into the world (or catch them up), the story itself needs enough hooks to make sure they stay there.

More Conflict And Exposition

Students swarm the library. Giles checks out books and tells Willow he hopes they're being careful when trying to slay vampires. She reassures him that "don't get killed" is part of their mission statement.

Cordelia walks in complaining about her summer at a nightmare resort that made you have organized fun and ordered you around. She asks if Xander is around and if her hair looks okay. She also wants to know if he met anyone over the summer. Then Cordelia answers her own question by saying who could Xander meet when there are only monsters in Sunnydale. Still, she has a moment of doubt because he's always been attracted to monsters. She asks Willow again how her hair is. This conflict brings out more exposition and sets off a minor subplot about Cordelia and Xander reuniting.

Oz appears. Willow thinks he came to visit her on her first day at school until she sees he's carrying books. She's confused because Oz was a senior last year. He should have graduated.

Oz: Remember when I didn't graduate?

Oz reminds her he got an incomplete. Willow points out that's what summer school was for.

Oz: Remember when I didn't go?

Oz hopes Willow will find it all sort of endearing and quirky. She tells him she's trying to get there, but is more on the concerned side. Xander appears and asks the two of them if they've seen Cordelia. He's excited to see her.

Xander: How's my –

Willow: Your hair is fine.

Then Larry, a side character we met last season, adds some humor.

Larry (to a football teammate): If we can focus, keep discipline, and not have quite so many mysterious deaths, Sunnydale is going to rule.

This line is both a wink to the audience and a way to tell anyone new to the show about the general atmosphere of Sunnydale High. It also tells viewers students are aware of the danger.

Cordelia and Xander finally see each other. After all their excitement, their conversation is flat, along the lines of *Hey. Hey. Good summer? Whatever.* And they walk away from each other.

Normally in dialogue it's good to leave out greetings like, *Hello, how are you?* and conversation endings like *See you* or *Goodbye.* They take up space without advancing the plot or developing characters. As a result, these exchanges, while realistic, tend to bore readers and slow your story.

But here they serve a purpose. We've seen Cordelia and Xander separately, and each is so excited to see the other. And concerned that the other might not share their feelings. The result when they finally meet is bland greetings that don't convey any of that emotion. The audience knows that they're both trying to play it cool, but the characters don't. We feel for them, grasping how disappointed each is that the other seems unaffected by the reunion.

Subtle Foreshadowing

At about 10 minutes 41 seconds, Buffy passes a guy giving out flyers in the street. He hands one to a kid on a curb. An old man huddles in a doorway. As Buffy walks past the old man says (twice), *I'm no one.*

The first time I watched the episode, I thought these moments were just part of the street ambiance. But both are key to the main plot and help Buffy unravel the mystery later. It's ideal when these types of clues not only foreshadow later developments but set tone or add texture to a scene. That way, the writers don't give away too much, but the audience finds the plot twists down the road believable. I love the way that's done here.

Exposition, Pacing, And The One-Quarter Twist

At about 11 minutes, more exposition through conflict occurs. After a phone call, Giles rushes out of his office. He tells Willow and Xander that a friend of his in Oakland heard about a girl fending off vampires a week ago. Xander asks what makes this different from the last nine leads. Giles falters a bit and says there's a meal on this flight. But he and Willow agree that he needs to try. He leaves.

Willow: Don't you think maybe he'll find her?
Xander: I think he'll find her when she wants to be found.

This minor conflict between Giles and the friends catches us up on how hard Giles has been looking for Buffy. I love knowing that Giles is taking every flight and going everywhere. But that information could have been quickly worked into a line or two of dialogue earlier. As it is, the scene happens past the one-quarter point of the 44-minute episode. It feels like something bigger should be happening. The scene adds to my sense of waiting for the story to start.

If you've read any of my writing books or listened to the podcast, you know I call the first major plot turn in any story the One-Quarter Twist. It most often occurs about 25% through a novel or movie, though sometimes as late as one-third through a television episode. It should come from outside the protagonist and spin the story in a new direction. It also sometimes raises the stakes (no pun intended).

At nearly 12 minutes, so about 27% into the episode, Buffy again walks alone at night. Lily, behind her, calls out to "Anne." When she gets no response, she says, "Buffy." And Buffy stops. Lily reminds her how they met. Lily was part of that club Buffy's former friend Ford organized to worship vampires. She was calling herself Chanterelle at the time. Buffy's concerned about Lily knowing her identity and Lily reassures her that she's not going to turn her in. She knows what it's like when you have to get lost.

Buffy says she chose Anne because it's her middle name. Lily says Ricky picked her name from a song. Then Lily tells Buffy about a rave. If Buffy has any money, they could go. Buffy awkwardly says she doesn't think so. She wants to be alone. She tries to give Lily money. Lily seems offended at that. She was trying to connect, not get money.

On many watches of *Anne* (including the one for the podcast), I didn't see anything that turned the story here. But if the main plot is not fighting evil but Buffy's shift from isolation to reconnection, this does spin the story. Lily comes from outside of Buffy and connects with her. Though Buffy is a bit reluctant, she engages with Lily. She shares why she chose her name and asks about Lily. And we get the sense that this is the first time Buffy has done this since leaving Sunnydale.

Next there's a slight turn in the demon-fighting plot. An old man with thinning gray hair bumps into Buffy. She asks if he's okay.

Man: I'm no one.

He runs into the street. At 15 minutes, 6 seconds, a car almost hits him, but Buffy runs and shoves him out of the way. She gets hit. This occurs well past the one-quarter or even one-third point in the story. Taken with a couple later developments, it spins the story. For now, the man's *I'm no one* comment is a clue.

The driver who hit Buffy jumps out of the car. Buffy's a little overwhelmed by everyone asking her how she is. She runs off around the corner and almost runs into the guy we saw earlier with the flyers. This moment definitely spins the story, but it's more like a Story Spark for Buffy. Though she doesn't know it, and neither does the audience, she's just encountered the villain, Ken.

He acts concerned and asks what she's doing there. He tells her she has the look of the kids around there who had to grow up too fast. And he gives her a flyer for a family home and tells her she might find something she's missing. When she claims she's okay, Ken asks why she's there if that's true. It's not a good place for a kid. They get old fast. Despair drains the life out of them. It's the last stop for many.

Plaintive music plays under scenes of young people living on the street. In a way, this is camouflage for the fact that Ken is evil. On first watch, it feels like he's there to segue into this montage and make a point about kids living on the street. The montage, though, never quite works for me. I'm unsure how it fits with the theme of the episode. The number of people living on the street, particularly teenagers, is an important issue. But the episode doesn't do a lot with that. These young people are part of the demon storyline, but there's no follow up and no grappling with the issue.

The music playing during the montage continues in the

next scene at the Bronze.

Xander: Boy, I'm glad we showed up for depressing night.

Xander and Willow slump in a couple of couches. Willow wonders what "she's" doing now. Xander talks about Cordelia and how she probably met someone else over the summer. Willow gives him a look. And he says it's possible she's talking about Buffy. Xander comments that the slaying is also not going well as Oz brings over drinks. Oz says he thinks they're getting a rhythm down. Xander disagrees because they're still losing half the vampires.

Oz: Yeah, but rhythmically.

Then Xander gets an idea. What they need is bait. This idea is a good hook for the demon plot as the story shifts back to Giles.

Identity As A Theme

At 18 minutes, 38 seconds, Joyce hurries to her front door. She's clearly disappointed that it is Giles, not Buffy. He tells her Oakland didn't pan out. Joyce says she can hardly leave the house. She's afraid Buffy will call and need her. (There were cell phones at that time, but most people did not have them.) Giles tries to reassure Joyce.

Giles: Buffy is the most capable child I've ever known.

This is not the first time in the series that Giles refers to Buffy as a child. As I commented in earlier seasons, that's part of why we never have any sort of creepy or uncomfortable vibe about Giles hanging out with these kids all the time or being a mentor to this young woman. Calling Buffy a child here reemphasizes that. It also highlights the struggle Buffy has with being a child or teenager on the verge of adulthood, yet needing to shoulder so much adult responsibility, including having to make terrible choices.

Joyce expresses regret about how the last thing she and

Buffy did was fight.

Giles: Don't blame yourself.

Joyce: I don't. I blame you.

Joyce goes on to say, her voice breaking, that Giles was a huge influence on Buffy. He had this relationship with her behind Joyce's back. She feels like Giles has taken Buffy away from her.

I love the way the actress plays it and the way it was directed. It could have seemed accusatory. And there is some blame and accusation there. But it is more that my heart breaks for Joyce as she recognizes how much about her daughter she did not know. And how close Giles and Buffy were, the role that Giles played, and Joyce didn't know about it and wasn't able herself to serve in that role for her daughter.

Giles is very still when she speaks. And by that stillness, I can tell it breaks his heart too.

Giles: I didn't make Buffy who she is.

Joyce: And who exactly is she?

So here we have the theme of the episode made explicit, or at least the intended theme, of identity. We already saw it in the names. Buffy is not using her own name. She's being Anne. Lily is a name that Ricky chose for her. And Lily tells Buffy she had a couple other names before that. Though Buffy asks, she doesn't share her name from birth. And then we have the older man saying over and over *I'm no one*.

While this identity theme recurs, I have some questions about how well it plays out.

In the next scene, Buffy fills salt shakers. Lily comes into the diner. Ricky is gone, and she wants Buffy's help. Buffy asks if she tried the police or looked in his usual places. Lily can't go to the police because Ricky skipped out on parole. She could just be causing trouble for him. She asks Buffy to help find Ricky. Buffy says she can't.

Lily: But that's who you are and stuff. You help people.

(**Buffy says she's sorry.**) **You know how to do stuff.**

Buffy claims she doesn't anymore. And Lily responds that she doesn't know what to do.

We are midway through the episode, yet this, as with a couple earlier scenes, still feels a lot like the Inciting Incident or Story Spark that sets the story off. Or maybe a One-Quarter Twist that sends it in a new direction, because now the story is about finding Ricky.

Eggshell Buffy Commits At The Midpoint With A Look

Despite what I said about it starting the story, the diner scene includes a classic Midpoint for the demon-fighting plot. Normally at the Midpoint of a well-structured story, you'll see the protagonist fully committing to the quest (also seen as throwing caution to the wind) or suffering a major reversal. Or both.

Here at 21 minutes, 15 seconds, Buffy — who has been avoiding Lily's gaze by looking down at the salt shakers — looks up and makes eye contact with Lily. That happens right after Lily says she doesn't know what to do. And we know Buffy is going to help.

Often, Buffy's Midpoint Commitments are large and groundbreaking. Sometimes they're significant on a cosmic scale. At the very least, they are quite dramatic. But here Buffy looks up and agrees to help, something that she did almost reflexively in Season Two.

That shows something important about the nature of a Midpoint Commitment. What makes it large in scope and strong enough to drive the rest of the story isn't how significant it is on an objective scale or compared to other similar stories. It's how big is it for that protagonist at that moment in life. For Buffy right now, with her emotional state after killing Angel and leaving Sunnydale, this is a huge commitment.

In my other life as a lawyer, we talk about something called the eggshell plaintiff. The plaintiff there is the person who brings a lawsuit to recover for an injury. If that plaintiff had a lot of physical issues before, maybe they hurt their back before or already had tendinitis, that doesn't get a defendant who hurts them off the hook. If, for instance, you run a red light and hit a plaintiff like that with your car and their injuries are more serious because of previous problems, you are responsible for all those greater injuries. You don't get to claim that if that person had been healthier when you hit them, this wouldn't have been a big problem. That's the eggshell plaintiff.

And you can have an eggshell protagonist. Buffy is not physically injured and vulnerable, but she is emotionally broken and barely pieced back together. For her, that simple act of looking up, meeting Lily's eyes, and agreeing to help, is a massive step. She's throwing caution to the wind because she has been keeping herself separate and protecting herself.

If you write about a protagonist who has this sort of injury or is limited in the scope of what they can do emotionally, it could be a big deal simply to yell at someone or walk out of a room.

Lily and Buffy go to a clinic where Lily says she and Ricky often donate blood. The nurse there remembers Ricky, but he hasn't been in lately.

Buffy (to Lily): Uh, this'll probably go faster if we split up.
Lily: Can I come with you?
Buffy: Okay, when did I lose you on the whole splitting up thing?

This exchange goes to another theme I see in the episode, intended or not: self-reliance. Lily says often that Ricky takes care of her. Now she's gone to Buffy for help, a good choice, but she wants to stay with Buffy. She doesn't want to be left on her own even temporarily. Her default is to ask *Can I go with you?*

We already have an identity theme, and now we add self-reliance. Maybe they are two sides of the same coin. They connect later when Lily chooses another new identity for herself, one where she does take care of herself. But this is part of why the episode falters a bit for me. I'm unclear what it is about at its core, both as to plot and theme.

The two split up. Buffy searches alone in a dark warehouse. She finds the body of an old man with the name Lily in half a heart tattooed on his arm. It is the exact tattoo Ricky had.

So very shortly after the Midpoint where Buffy commits, she suffers a major reversal. It took a long time to get the search-for-Ricky/demon-fighting story moving. But once it started, a commitment and reversal occurred quickly. Right after the hook of the tattoo, the episode cuts to a commercial.

Showing Emotions

On return, at 23 minutes, 30 seconds, Lily waits at Buffy's apartment holding a little stuffed duck. I love this element because Buffy has a history with stuffed animals. She had Mr. Gordo, her stuffed pig. When Kendra named her stake, Buffy told her to remind her to get Kendra a stuffed animal. And now we see that despite the sparseness of Buffy's life now, she either brought with or bought herself this little stuffed duck.

Lily holding this small stuffed animal for comfort also shows her worry.

Buffy returns and tells Lily that she thinks that Ricky is dead.

Lily: But he takes care of me. We're going to get a place.

This line shows Lily's grief through denial. It's the way many of us react to tragic news. We can't take it in. Buffy tells Lily something else going is on. The man she found was old, about eighty. Lily argues that's not Ricky, but Buffy is sure. Something drained him of life, but it wasn't a vampire because vampires can't accelerate aging. This makes Buffy think of blood and ask when Ricky last donated. Lily, though, still struggles to take this in.

Lily: But he didn't do anything wrong.

Buffy tells her that's not the point, that things happen. You can't close your eyes and just hope they'll go away. It seems she's partly talking to herself.

The "close your eyes" line calls back to that heartbreaking moment when Buffy told Angel to close his eyes and she killed him. Angel, as opposed to Angelus, didn't do anything wrong. Buffy may be thinking of that or of herself. She didn't do anything wrong, but these things still happen. Or this may resonate with Buffy because she's in denial herself, unwilling to deal with her grief and her sadness.

As if to stress that, Lily asks if all this happened because of Buffy. She knows about these things and she could have brought something with her to Los Angeles. Now Buffy gets angry. She says she didn't bring anything with her. She didn't ask Lily to come to her for help. All she wanted was to be left alone.

Buffy: If you can't deal, then don't lay it on me.

Her anger also fits someone who is talking to herself. But I'm unclear who Buffy is most angry at. I talked in *Becoming Part Two* about Buffy being angry at her friends for that "kick his ass" message she thought Willow sent. And angry at her mom for not supporting her and more or less kicking her out when she found out who Buffy was.

But it's not clear that's what Buffy "brought with her." That may refer more to all those feelings of anger and grief and guilt that she can't flee and leave behind in Sunnydale.

Lily leaves. Buffy sighs, looking sad.

Out on the street, Lily encounters Ken, who is again giving out flyers. He sees she's upset and asks if she's okay. She mentions Ricky. He tells her whoever said Ricky was dead is wrong.

Ken: He's no more dead than I am.

That line turns out to be true in a way. He tells her Ricky is "with us" now.

Next, Buffy breaks into the clinic. She's looking through the records.

Buffy (to herself): Candidate for what?

From the shadows, the nurse asks what she's doing. And I love Buffy's answer, which is much more like herself. It shows a progression of Buffy coming back, not just to helping people, but to her in-your-face attitude.

Buffy: Breaking into your office and going through your private files. Candidate for what?

The nurse says Buffy's getting herself into a lot of trouble. Buffy says she doesn't want trouble. She just wants to be left alone and quiet in a room with a fireplace and a tea cozy.

Buffy: And I don't even know what a tea cozy is, but I want one.

Buffy's comment is one that anyone who has been through significant trauma, or a difficult extended time, can empathize with. That feeling of just needing things to stop. To be alone, to sit by a fire and not do anything and maybe feel safe.

The nurse finally tells Buffy that she gives them the names of the healthy ones.

At 28 and a half minutes, Ken tells Lily she looks nice. She wears a gown that looks like it might be burlap for the cleansing, which Ken says is like a baptism. He promises she'll see Ricky right after it. They're in a dark room with lit candles and tiny lights and a small, rectangular pool.

In the graveyard, Cordelia is supposed to be bait, but she and Xander start bickering. Willow listens from the other side of a hedge and rolls her eyes. A vampire looms behind Willow, but nobody notices.

I enjoy seeing our friends again, but it's not clear how Cordelia being bait can help them kill vampires. One person alone might lure the vampires out. But the gang's problem hasn't been finding vampires to slay. It's the slaying part.

We know Xander wants to bring Cordelia into the group again, and she wants to be part of the group again, though they're both denying it. So maybe the others go along for the ride.

Buffy As Herself

Lily stands at the edge of the pool in an inner room. Buffy knocks on the door of the center. She's trying to finagle her way in by, in stilted language, telling the guy what she thinks he needs to hear.

Buffy: You know, I just....I woke up, and I looked in the mirror, and I thought, hey, what's with all the sin? I need to change.

She rattles off some things, ending with that loud music kids listen to nowadays. The guy looks skeptical.

Buffy: I just suck at undercover. Where's Ken?

This scene fits the identity theme. Buffy embraces more of who she is, and in the process, recognizes she's no good at pretending to be someone else (something the audience knew from earlier seasons).

Lily reaches her hand into the pond just as Buffy bursts into that inner room. She demands that Ken tell her how he makes them old. Does he feed on youth? But it's too late for Lily, who is pulled into the pool from below. She yells.

The Three-Quarter Turn In Demon Fighting

Buffy tries to dive in after Lily, but Ken grabs her. Buffy struggles. Her momentum pitches both her and Ken into the pool.

This is the Three-Quarter Turn. That's the last major plot turn. It grows from the Midpoint but takes the story in another new direction. Here, at 31 minutes, 17 seconds, Buffy and Lily land on a concrete floor underground. Ken is a ways away from them. He peels off his face.

Ken: Do you have any idea how hard that is to glue on?

Underneath, he is a demon. He calls for the guards who take Buffy and Lilly into this vast, dim underground area. There are sparks from welding and fires in spots. It looks like it's some kind of an iron or steel mill. Everyone working wears rough gowns or outfits like Lily's.

Ken: Welcome to my world.

He knocks Buffy out with a club and we go to a commercial.

This story turn came from that commitment Buffy made at the Midpoint to help Lily. It also arose from the reversal of finding Ricky dead, which Ken used to lure Lily in. And this event turns the story. Buffy and Lily are brought to a new world. We learn that Ken is a demon, but not merely a soul-sucking one as Buffy thought, but one who is part of some sort of larger enterprise.

On the return from the commercial, Xander and Cordelia bicker, he asks how long it took her to forget him.

Cordelia: Oh, Mr. Faithful probably met up with some hot little Inca mummy girl. Yeah. I heard about that.

The vampire attacks Willow, who screams. She and Oz fight. Xander jumps in and the vampire grabs him and throws him to the ground. Cordelia stakes the vampire from behind. It dusts and she falls forward onto Xander who is lying on his back. Romantic music plays as they kiss.

This drastic switch from a dark underworld to this heightened, comic melodrama felt jarring to me, though I usually enjoy tone switches in *Buffy*. I think this one didn't land because typically the tone shift happens with the same characters and within the same scene. So Buffy quips as she fights or Xander makes a clever comment during a tense scene and Giles yells at him for it. It's funny in the midst of fear or tragedy. But here we're flipping from scene to scene. It highlights how isolated Buffy is from her friends. But that doesn't make me love it.

More On Identity

Buffy wakes up locked in a cage, still in her street clothes. Lily is in the next cage and says she (Lily) belongs here, it's hell. Buffy says it's not.

But Ken is lurking. And he tells them it is hell. Because hell is the absence of hope, and Lily's been heading here all her life, just like Ricky was. He also tells Lily Ricky forgot her eventually, though it took years. They're confused, but he explains time moves differently here. A hundred years is only a day on earth. Lily will die of old age before anyone looks for her. Not that anyone will. That's why Ken chose her. Buffy says he didn't choose her.

Ken: No. But I know you, "Anne." So afraid. So pathetically determined to run away from whatever it is you used to be. To disappear. Congratulations, you got your wish.

A guard brings the group of new humans out in a row, including Buffy and Lily. He tells them all they're allowed to do is work, not complain or laugh. Whatever they were before doesn't matter.

Guard: You're no one now. Who are you? (to the first young person in line)

The boy gives a name and the guard clubs him to the ground. Next is Lily who keeps her eyes on the ground. When asked who she is, Lily says, "No one." This happens with another young person. The theme of identity is explicit here, even more so when the guard gets to Buffy.

Guard: Who are you?

Buffy (looks up and meets his eyes): I'm Buffy, the vampire slayer. And you are?

That's Buffy's more typical tone, a bit sarcastic. The guard tries to hit her. She gets the club and fights him, then leads the humans through the darkness towards that platform where she and Lily were brought in. It's a large, dark space and no one else seems to notice them. They gather under a wrought iron staircase. Buffy tells Lily they'll run into guards. She'll create a distraction. Lily needs to lead the others out.

Lily doesn't want Buffy to leave. But Buffy tells her she can do it, adding "because I said so." This is where Lily's identity story falters for me. It feels off that Buffy telling her she can do this answers her identity questions. But I'll talk about that at the end. Maybe there is a reason for it.

Buffy starts to run. An alarm goes off, but Lily pauses and says she's sorry she blamed Buffy. Buffy tells her this can wait.

Lily: In case we die.

I really like that Lily has this intrinsic kindness and caring about her. Though she's thinking she'll probably die and she can't do this, she wants Buffy to know that she's sorry she blamed her.

More Themes Happen On The Way To The Climax

The story is moving toward the Climax. Around 37 minutes, 40 seconds, Buffy runs, luring away some guards. She fights them as Lily gets other prisoners up the stairs. Buffy grabs a scythe from the guard. There is a great shot of her holding it in a fighting stance on a platform, looking fierce, spotlights crossing over her. (That shot remains in the series credits for quite a long time.) During the fighting, Ken appears a level above Buffy and stares down in shock at the chaos.

Ken: Humans don't fight back. That's how this works.

This could be seen as another theme, but the point isn't quite clear. Is the episode saying people just need to fight back in life, band together? Or does it relate to Ken's view of who humans are versus who we really are?

Ken catches Lily and drags her to the edge of the platform with a knife at her neck. He yells out that if any of them fight, they all die. This makes me wonder why the humans didn't fight before. They've seen that people work until they get old and they're thrown away. What is the incentive for them not to try to escape? There seem to be no other good alternatives, so why not take the chance?

That minor plot hole, for me, detracts from the story's power.

Ken taunts Buffy, telling her he'd like to slice her guts out. Because Ken doesn't see Lily as a real threat, he lets go of her as he and Buffy spar verbally. I see this, though subtle, as arising out of his character flaw of hubris. It's very believable that he never considers Lily as a potential threat. But as he goes on about the price of rebellion, Lily pushes him off the platform. That's the climax of Lily's story. It's a huge moment for her.

Buffy's demon fighting climax happens next. Ken plummets to the concrete floor below. Buffy slugs the nearest guard. She then climbs a heavy chain to the top of the platform. The humans run, but a heavy iron grate blocks their exit. Buffy manages to lift the grate, but she is struggling. At last, everyone squeezes under.

Ken follows them, and Buffy lets the grate drop. It spears both Ken's legs, trapping him face down. Pinning Ken is not the final confrontation between Buffy and the demon antagonist because she does need to neutralize him completely, which she'll do in a moment.

Buffy: Hey Ken, want to see my impression of Gandhi?
She clubs him on the head and kills him.
Lily: Gandhi?
Buffy: Well, you know, if he was really pissed.
This is more Buffy-like because she's quipping as she slays

the demon. The Gandhi joke all the same feels a bit off to me, though I can't articulate why. But I suspect it's purposeful because Buffy has gone on this journey, but is still not quite done.

Falling Action And Lily's Choice

In the Falling Action part of a story, the writers tie up loose ends, resolve subplots, and sometimes hint at the future. Here, Lily and Buffy help everyone up and out through that pool.

In the next scene, Buffy gives Lily a tour of Buffy's one-room apartment. The rent has been paid for three weeks and Buffy arranged for Lily to take over her waitressing job. Buffy assures Lily she'll check up on her. Lily says she's not great at taking care of herself. And Buffy tells her it gets easier. It takes practice. This can be seen as part of the self-reliance or the identity themes. Or it may be yet another theme about taking care of yourself.

Often Falling Action relates to theme because it's part of what the writers feel they need to resolve. So I question whether part of the point here is that Buffy was not taking care of herself. Clearly, she was doing so physically but not emotionally.

But the practice line, for Buffy, throws me. Because in the story, she starts dealing with her feelings less by practicing at it and more because her values are such that she can't refuse to help people. She needs to deal with her emotions so she can come back to herself and help Lily and the other humans. For that reason, the theme seems to be different for Buffy and Lily. That muddles the emotional resonance for me.

All the same, I love that the scene ends when Lily sees Buffy's name tag on the uniform and asks if she can be Anne. They both smile. That moment suggests you can grow and change and choose a new identity by modeling someone else.

And Lily choosing the identity shows a lot of growth. Yes, it is still a name and identity Buffy created. But Lily doesn't adopt it because she's following or joining Buffy. In the past, Lily was Sister Sunshine when she followed the preacher and Chanterelle when she joined the vampire-worshipping cult. Ricky chose the name Lily. Now, in contrast, Lily chooses a name herself and plans to go forward on her own.

And perhaps Buffy's change does parallel Lily's after all. Lily models deep love, connection, and caring even in the face of grief — the emotions Buffy's been avoiding. Now Buffy will take a huge step back toward love and connection.

At 43 minutes, 27 seconds, Joyce is working on her dishwasher. She hears a knock at the door, starts to hurry to answer, then sighs. We can see she's probably thinking she's being foolish. It's never been Buffy.

But as she nears the door, she moves faster. She opens it, sees Buffy, and they hug. This scene always makes me cry. It's all in the expressions of the two actresses, because they don't say anything but we know how they feel.

That's the end of the episode.

Protagonist Goals, Stakes, And Where The Demon Plot Falters

Buffy The Vampire Slayer works best for me when there's an emotional story and a strong plot about fighting evil and one informs the other. Much of *Anne*, though, feels less like its own story and more like a bridge from Season Two to Three. The episode gets Buffy back home and updates us on relationships among the friends and Joyce and Giles.

The emotional plot for Buffy has good momentum. Buffy starts in denial and distance and re-embraces or re-finds her own identity, which allows her to go back home. But the demon plot doesn't feel strong. It's slow to get going. When it finally does, everything happens at once and sometimes without a lot of effort on Buffy's part.

There also are some protagonist issues with *Anne*. Ideally, a protagonist actively pursues a goal throughout the story, is the main viewpoint character, and has the most at stake.

Buffy's first goal is to be left alone. She pursues it by deliberately isolating herself. She resists Lily's attempts to connect with her. But this negative goal—to not engage with people—contributes to the story's lack of momentum. In contrast, her friends are actively pursuing goals. Giles pursues the goal of finding Buffy. The others pursue the goal of improving their vampire slaying.

Buffy's the main viewpoint character in the Los Angeles scenes. Not many happen where she's not there. But the friends also get a lot of screentime.

Who has the most at stake is also challenging. In the demon story, both Ricky and Lily have more to lose than Buffy. Until well beyond the Midpoint of the story, Buffy could walk away with no harm to her at all. She'd basically be where she started out — detached, not helping people, and isolated. Even after Ken traps Buffy in the underworld, I'm not that worried for her. I feel sure she can get out. The key question is whether she can also get Lily and the others out.

On the other hand, Buffy's emotional stakes in the demon plot are high. If she didn't save Lily or the others, that would be a massive loss for her. But Lily could be trapped in the underworld, hopeless and lost forever. So she still has more at stake than Buffy.

If Buffy's need to find herself again is the main plot, though, Buffy has the most at stake emotionally. Because if she can't face her emotions, she risks withdrawing for the rest of her life.

The problem for me with that plot is that the episode doesn't address why Buffy chose to leave Sunnydale beyond being unable to cope with grief. In no way does she deal with her anger at her friends and at her mom in *Anne*. While she returns home at the end of the episode, which shows growth for her, how she'll handle all of that remains unresolved.

Spoilers And Foreshadowing

Pilots

Often the season pilot episodes in *Buffy* have a different tone from the rest of the series or the season. We'll see that again in Season Four when Buffy starts college. There, too, she is somewhat isolated from her friends. She is not feeling like herself.

The Season Five pilot, *Buffy vs. Dracula*, feels almost outside of the series. That's partly because it's something of an homage to the character of and lore about Dracula. Also, at the end, Dawn is inserted into the Buffyverse. I see it as a deliberate way to tell us the season will be different. Not because Dracula will be part of it, as he won't. But there will be someone new. Someone we did not expect to be in the world of *Buffy*.

Lily Becomes Anne, Foreshadowing Mr. Faithful

In *Angel* the series, Lily keeps the Anne identity and runs a shelter for homeless youth. *Anne* is a great set up for that. Lily's compassion and very engaging nature fit that very well. Also, the resourcefulness and determination she'll exhibit in *Angel* is foreshadowed when she pushes Ken off that platform.

Cordelia calls Xander "Mr. Faithful" and worries about him having met someone else. That's a hint that Xander will not be faithful to her and how devastating that will be. Also, Cordelia worries about him being drawn to someone supernatural. While Willow is human, she does have powers, and Xander kisses her while still involved with Cordelia.

Wish Fulfillment

Ken tells Buffy she tried so hard to disappear and got her wish, which signals a theme for the season. The episode *The Wish* is about wish fulfillment and how dangerous that is when Cordelia wishes Buffy never came to Sunnydale.

Buffy's strongest wish in *Anne* isn't to disappear but for Angel to return. Yet when he does, for so much of the season that brings her heartache. She lies to her friends and mom about him. They try to stay apart and can't, then try to stay together and don't.

And so much of Faith's story involves getting what you wished for but not the way you hoped.

Identity Themes For Season Three

The theme of choosing your identity runs through Season Three. Faith strives to figure out who she is as a Slayer. Buffy, too, struggles with her role as the Slayer as she sees how differently Faith approaches it. And how differently her friends and mother react to Faith. Both Slayers reflect, learn from, and envy one another.

The identity of the Watchers Council also comes into play. This season explores more of what the Council is and does and why as two new Watchers appear. And Giles and Buffy both quit working for the Council, changing their identities as Watcher and Slayer.

Angel And The Underworld

Buffy's experience of this demon underworld feels like deliberate foreshadowing of Angel's experience. When he returns, we find out he was in another dimension, a sort of hell. And Buffy learns that time did in fact move differently there. Angel spent decades there though he was gone from Buffy's world only for a summer.

Questions For Your Writing

- If you included exposition in your story in the form of (a) prose or (b) one character just giving information to another, can you revise so it's revealed through conflict?
- When does your main plot start? If it occurs later than 10% through, can you cut earlier scenes entirely or move them later in your story?
- Are you able to identify the major plot turns? If not, what changes might you make so that they stand out more and clearly spin your story?
- Does your plot touch on more than one theme? If so, what do you think the story overall says about each theme? Do you need more than one?
- At the start of the story, what wounds, weaknesses, or struggles is your protagonist already dealing with? How do they affect the range of choices your protagonist can make?
- What's your protagonist's goal at the beginning of your plot? Does it change? Is it a negative goal or an active one?

The next chapter talks about *Dead Man's Party*, where Buffy has a rocky reunion with her friends and zombies invade Sunnydale.

CHAPTER 2
DEAD MAN'S PARTY S3 E2

THIS CHAPTER TALKS about *Dead Man's Party*, Season Three, Episode Two, where Buffy's friends struggle with her return as zombies invade Sunnydale. Written by Marti Noxon and directed by James Whitmore Jr. Original air date: October 6, 1998.

Along with the episode breakdown, topics include:

- Powerful universal themes that resonate, but a slow-paced plot
- Showing character emotions through small acts
- The effect of inconsistent characterization
- What makes conflict false
- A Climax without enough emotional resolution

Okay, let's dive into the Hellmouth.

Opening Conflict And Story Sparks

In the opening scene, Buffy unpacks in her room. Then she walks into Joyce's room, startling her so much that Joyce puts a hole in the bedroom wall. She was hanging a Nigerian mask she brought home from her art gallery. Buffy tells her the mask is angry at the room. It wants the room to suffer.

I see Joyce hanging the mask as the Story Spark for the zombie plot. Usually, that spark occurs about 10% into the story. Here we're only about one minute in, so it's very early. But the mask triggers the awakening of the zombies later. If Joyce didn't hang it, there's no action plot. And later, around 10%, there'll be a spark for the emotional plot of Buffy returning home.

Joyce and Buffy have an awkward exchange that fills new audience members in through minor conflict. Buffy says she wants to go see what Willow and Xander are doing. Joyce offers to make her a snack, though she already made her a large dinner, or to drive her. Buffy finally says if Joyce doesn't want her to go, just say so. And Joyce tells her it's fine, she can go see Willow and Xander. She asks if Buffy will be slaying. Buffy jokes only if they give her lip.

Buffy heads to the Bronze. On the way, she hears odd noises in an alley. When she investigates, she startles someone in a dark coat who spins around. It's Xander. Both Xander and Buffy have stakes raised. Buffy asks didn't anyone warn him about pointy stakes. It's all fun and games until someone loses an eye. Xander starts to say something but a vampire bursts through the fence. The radio on Xander's belt crackles.

Cordelia: Come in, Nighthawk, you okay?
Buffy: Nighthawk?

Buffy fights the vampire, but Willow and Cordelia rush in and grab it away from her. They don't realize it's Buffy until the vampire kicks Oz and throws Cordelia into Buffy.

Cordelia: Hey Buffy.

At 3 minutes, 30 seconds, Buffy stakes the vampire. The others, on the ground, stare at her in shock.

Buffy (smiling): Hey guys.

And we go to credits.

On return, at 4 minutes, 46 seconds, the friends stand

outside Giles's door. Buffy says maybe it's too late at night to knock, or maybe he's mad. Xander says something to the effect of why would Giles be mad just because Buffy abandoned her post, her friends, her mom, and made Giles lie awake at night and worry. I see this exchange at a little past 10% as the Inciting Incident or Story Spark for the emotional plot of Buffy re-integrating into her life. It's the first time someone she loves is hostile to Buffy.

To me, the emotional plot feels like the main plot and the zombie plot is the subplot. That's because while the zombie story started first, it takes up much less space in the narrative.

As Buffy's still hesitating, Giles opens the door. He takes off his glasses when he sees her and he looks so relieved. Xander rambles on about look who they've brought.

Giles: Welcome home, Buffy.

That's all he says, and it's the first time we see Buffy truly smile.

Showing Emotion Through Action

Giles disappears to make tea. In the living room, Oz tells Buffy she's not wanted for murder anymore. It's a good quick way to deal with that open question from Season Two where the police thought Buffy killed Kendra. Xander asks Buffy where she was and if she went to Belgium.

As they joke, Giles, in his galley kitchen, takes off his glasses. He closes his eyes and squeezes them tightly shut, holding back tears. Then he swallows hard, nods to himself, and finishes preparing the tea. This moment, done so well by Anthony Stewart Head as Giles, shows how much emotion small actions can convey. We see how worried and frightened Giles was, his relief now that she's back, and how concerned he still is for Buffy.

At times, those small actions convey emotion with more

weight than when a character tells someone else their feelings or a story includes the character's inner thoughts. Those approaches work well, too. The audience often likes hearing a character's thoughts directly. But actions can be stronger because they allow the audience to infer the feelings. Television and movies are great for learning how to do this because, other than voiceover, they can't include a character's inner monologue.

Character Consistency

Giles brings out a tray with a teapot and cookies. Cordelia asks Buffy if she was living in a box or what. Buffy tells her it's kind of a long story. Xander asks more questions. Giles, perceptive as ever, says maybe Buffy could use some time to adjust before they grill her.

Buffy: What he said.

Xander tells her she can leave the slaying to them. Buffy though, wants to get back to her normal routine and asks what they're doing tomorrow. Xander and Cordelia are busy. Willow starts to say she is, too. But when Buffy presses she reluctantly agrees to change her plans.

This moment starts behavior from the friends that strikes me as inconsistent with what we know of them so far, or even what we saw last episode. They were so concerned about what Buffy was doing and so anxious about her. Now they want to ignore her. It's partly because they're angry. They feared for months that she was dead. So much so that Willow insisted that they not use the past tense to talk about her. Buffy didn't call or send a note to at least let them know she was alive.

If Buffy had taken off for no reason, I'd believe that their response when she returns is to resist dropping everything just because she decided to come back. But Buffy had a reason. While they don't know the details, they do know Angel never returned and the world didn't end, strongly suggesting she had to kill Angel. It seems odd that they don't recognize that she was traumatized. The passive aggressiveness of it feels off, too. Xander is typically quick to say what he thinks, Cordelia always says it, and Willow is usually upfront with Buffy.

Giles says Buffy needs to talk to Principal Snyder because she is still expelled from school. The scene cuts to Snyder.

Snyder: Absolutely not.

Joyce argues the principal can't keep Buffy out of school. Buffy was cleared of the murder charges. Snyder is truly awful, which fits his character. He says while Buffy may meet the "not a murderer" standard, she's a troublemaker. He feels great pleasure keeping her out of school and mentions that Hotdog On A Stick is hiring. Joyce tells him if she has to, she'll go all the way to the mayor.

Snyder (as Buffy and Joyce leave): Wouldn't that be interesting.

Joyce drops Buffy at an outdoor coffee shop where she is supposed to meet Willow and tells her maybe they can swing private school. This appalls Buffy.

Willow never shows up at the coffee shop. When Buffy gets home a friend of Joyce's (Pat), exits the Summers house. In an annoying, bright tone Pat, too, says all sorts of passive aggressive things. She tells Buffy she took it upon herself to look after Joyce while Buffy was "off and away" and refers to Buffy's "situation." She also tells Buffy Joyce was a wreck. Inside, Joyce tells Buffy Willow called but she didn't leave a message.

The One-Quarter Twist Of *Dead Man's Party*

Now we reach the One-Quarter Twist in the emotional story. This major plot turn should come from outside the protagonist and spin the story in a new direction. Here, Joyce decides to invite Giles, "Willow and everybody" for dinner. She tells Buffy to get the company plates. Buffy argues Willow and everybody aren't company plate people, they're normal plate people. Joyce's decision turns the plot about Buffy reconnecting with her friends.

When Buffy goes down to the basement to retrieve plates from a dusty shelf, a dead cat falls off the top shelf. The scene cuts to Joyce and Buffy burying the cat in the yard.

Buffy: Next time I get to pick the mother-daughter bonding activity.

The dead cat is part of the zombie story, but Buffy doesn't know it yet. Because simply finding it doesn't spin the story, I don't see that as a major plot turn in the zombie plot.

In the next scene, Buffy lies awake in bed and looks toward the window. I love this moment. If you started watching this season and didn't know the backstory, it still works because it shows how alone Buffy feels in her bedroom. At the same time, it evokes so much from Season Two for ongoing viewers because Angel often appeared at her window, including in the Season Two pilot.

Now we get to the One-Quarter Twist in the zombie story. The zombie cat's eyes glow, and the cat reanimates and crawls out of that grave. This comes from outside Buffy and spins the story in a new direction, as it should.

Storytelling Through Dreams

The scene cuts to Buffy walking into the school, which is eerily deserted. In the courtyard, in sunlight, Angel appears. He walks behind Buffy. It's unclear whether she knows he's there until she says she thought they'd be here, likely referring to her friends. Angel tells her they are waiting for her. Buffy says she's afraid.

Angel: You should be.

A school bell rings, but it's really Buffy's alarm.

This dream reminds fans about Angel (and provides a teaser for commercials) but otherwise doesn't move the story along. Buffy shares how she's feeling, but I think that's already clear. As a fan, I find the Angel cameo fun, but it's less interesting on rewatch because I already know what happens later in the season.

Unlike most stories that include dreams, the ones in *Buffy* almost always work for me because they do move the story. When a dream doesn't (as here), it often frustrates the audience by stopping the story. Or, worse, by fooling them if they thought it was real and then the writer pulls the rug out from under.

Conflict Between Joyce And Buffy

Joyce tells Buffy she talked to the superintendent of schools but got no answer yet. Just in case, she found out Miss Porter's accepts late admissions. Buffy's angry and frustrated. Not only can she not go back to school with her friends, Joyce wants to send her to an all girls school. Now Joyce gets angry. She tells Buffy she made some bad choices and she just might have to live with the consequences.

As with Buffy's friends, I'm not quite sure I buy this from Joyce. It feels more like what Joyce might say if she had no idea why Buffy left or that Buffy's the Slayer. But she does know, even if they haven't yet talked about it very much. Also, Joyce must remember the things she said to Buffy. And while later she'll say, basically, that Buffy needs to cut her some slack, I don't see Joyce totally ignoring the context of Buffy leaving.

It is, though, easier for me to buy Joyce's anger than that of the friends. I imagine hers comes out of her worry for Buffy plus her own guilt over whether she drove her daughter away. She also doesn't know that Buffy had to kill Angel.

Metaphors And Universal Themes

Joyce softens a bit, saying she wishes they didn't have to be so secretive. Can't they just tell the police and Snyder about her being the Slayer? They ought to make allowances for her special circumstances. She adds that you'd think they'd be happy to have a superhero to help out.

Joyce: Is that the right term? It's not offensive, is it?

Joyce's question fits the coming out metaphor from *Becoming Part Two* when Buffy told Joyce about her hidden Slayer identity. This metaphor is a large part of why many people relate on a deep emotional level to Buffy's story. There's an explicit parallel to children who are gay or bisexual and feel afraid to tell their parents. And to parents who find out and throw them out of the house.

It also resonates with other differences over values, such as religion, that damage the parent-child relationship. I related to Buffy in a personal way because while my mother never threw me out of the house, when I moved in with my boyfriend she barely spoke to me for almost two years. She was embarrassed over my choice because of what she felt her friends and family would see as her failing to raise her daughter right, and because she saw it as my rejecting her religion.

A child's fear, anger and sadness over a parent turning their back on them is a universal theme. Exploring that theme through a story helps the audience to deal with their feelings, making the narrative powerful.

Joyce begins to try to understand Buffy's point of view, but their discussion is cut off when Joyce opens the back door to take out the trash. The dead cat comes in.

At 16 minutes, 56 seconds, Giles brings a cage to the house and up to Joyce's bedroom. There's no logical reason Joyce and Buffy have the zombie cat in the bedroom, but from a story perspective it allows Giles to notice the mask. Joyce tells him it's

Nigerian and launches into its background. Buffy claims she loves boring art talk as much as the next person, but she and Giles need to get to the library. Giles hems and haws and finally tells her she's not allowed on school property.

At the library, Oz studies the cat in the cage.

Oz: Looks dead. Smells dead. Yet it's moving around. It's interesting.

Cordelia: Nice pet, Giles. Don't you like anything regular? Golf? *USA Today*?

Willow mentions the dinner at Buffy's. Oz asks if it's a gathering, a shindig, or a hootenanny and makes distinctions about the type of food and music. Xander favors a band because that avoids talking, which involves thanking Buffy for ruining their lives for the last few months. He says Buffy doesn't want to talk anyway, so why not dance?

Xander's words give another clue to why the friends are angry at Buffy. They feel they had to patrol and do something about the vampires. Despite that they had some fun with it, it ruined their summer, along with their fears about Buffy being dead. None of these reasons are stated, though. If they had been, I might have been more on board with the terrible things they say to Buffy later.

Giles, again the only one with some insight, is not sure a big party with a band is such a good idea. He suggests Buffy might be disoriented right now and they want her to feel at home. Willow argues a big welcome home party will do that.

Midpoint Reversals In *Dead Man's Party*

Buffy is expecting a more formal dinner party, as in the next scene she wears a pretty dress and has her hair up. The doorbell rings. It's Pat, which clearly does not thrill Buffy.

Pat: Oh, there you are. Not thinking about any more flights of fancy, I hope.

Buffy takes the empanadas Pat brought and yells for Joyce. We're about 21 and a half minutes in, right around the Midpoint of the episode. And soon there will be a Midpoint Reversal in the emotional plot. Joyce inviting Pat hints at it, as it suggests Joyce isn't ready to spend time with Buffy and her friends without reinforcements.

The doorbell rings again. It's the band. Buffy looks so confused and unhappy as they set up, more people arrive, and the party gets loud. This is a major reversal because despite not being ready to talk about her summer the first night she got home, she clearly wants to reconnect with her friends. The party shows they're not willing to do that.

In a loud voice so she can be heard, Buffy assures Willow the party is great but adds that she was hoping it could be just them. Willow pretends she can't hear. Buffy pulls her aside to a slightly quieter spot and asks if Willow's avoiding her. Willow denies it.

In Joyce's bedroom, the mask's eyes glow. The scene cuts to a car accident. A man is killed in the street. But then he opens his eyes and stands. This occurs a little past the Midpoint but serves as a reversal in the zombie plot because many zombies come to life. This plot, though, never feels very strong. There's no significant threat or conflict until the first human becomes a zombie, and we're already halfway through the story.

As Buffy walks past Xander and Cordelia, who are making out, Xander comments on how wonderful it is so many people are happy Buffy's back. Buffy says it seems like people she didn't even know are happy. She then asks if Giles said he'd be late. That last line tells us so much about how Buffy is feeling. While she cares about Giles, normally she's not hoping that he'll show up and hang out with them. But he is the only one who seems to understand her. Cordelia says it's great to have Buffy back, but Xander was kind of turning her on with his Boy Slayer look.

The mask's eyes glow again. At the hospital, an emergency team stops trying to revive a burn patient. After the doctor pronounces him dead, though, he gets up. There's screaming off screen.

Eavesdropping As A Plot Device

Buffy overhears a guy say the party is for some chick that just got out of rehab. In the kitchen, Joyce and Pat drink shots of schnapps. Pat asks Joyce how she's holding up. Joyce shares her feelings, and it strikes me as the most authentic thing any of our characters say, maybe because Joyce is more in touch with her emotions. She says when Buffy was gone, all she could think about was getting her home. She just knew if she could put her arms around Buffy and tell her she loved her, it would all be okay.

Unfortunately, Buffy doesn't hear that part. Instead, at 26 minutes, 17 seconds, Buffy pauses outside the kitchen and hears Joyce continue on that in some ways having Buffy home is almost worse.

Joyce's experience is one most people can identify with. I never had kids. I don't know what it would be like to have one of them run away. But I empathize with the feeling that everything will be okay if you can just get that person back. And how hard it is when they're back and everything isn't perfect. Her words also remind me of people with friends or family members who struggle with addiction. All the focus is on getting the person to quit and believing that will make everything good. But that doesn't fix everything. It can be hard to handle that.

I also believe Joyce as a character might say this to her friend whom she trusts but would never say it directly to Buffy, knowing it will upset her. That's part of why I don't love Buffy overhearing only the worst part. We know Joyce doesn't mean that it's truly worse having Buffy home, so it feels contrived. On the other hand, it's been pretty rough for Buffy, so I buy that it doesn't take much to push her over the edge. If it hadn't been Joyce's comment, it probably would have been something else. She goes to her room and starts packing, concluding everyone might be happier if she left.

Why The Zombie Plot Feels Slow

At 26 minutes, 56 seconds, there's more scary music and more glowing mask eyes. A group of zombies shuffles forward in the street. The repetition of the mask's eyes glowing, then an animal or human zombie coming to life or moving, is another reason the zombie story feels slow. We already understand the mask's connection to the zombies. And we're well past the episode's middle, but not much has happened to move that plot along.

In the dim library, Giles reads. (I have no idea why he doesn't turn some lights on.) After looking at a drawing, he says, "Oh, Lord," and tries to call Buffy. The same guy who made the comment about a chick in rehab answers. He thinks Giles is asking for Bunny and calls out that name. With all the noise, no one responds.

Guy: You've got the wrong house, Mr. Belvedere. (hangs up)

(Mr. Belvedere is from an old American TV show. The character was a British butler.)

False Conflict In An Emotional Three-Quarter Turn

At 28 minutes, 48 seconds, the Three-Quarter Turn in the emotional plot occurs. This last major plot turn should grow out of the Midpoint and take the story in another new direction. Here, it comes out of that reversal where Buffy realizes instead of reconnecting with her mom, friends, and Giles over a small dinner, she gets Pat and a noisy party full of people. It spins the story by prompting a major confrontation that starts when Willow discovers Buffy packing.

Willow: You're leaving again?
Buffy: It's not like anyone would care.
Willow: Don't forget to not write.
Buffy asks why they're attacking her. She's trying.
Willow: Wow, because it looks so much like giving up.

When Buffy says they were doing fine without her, Willow responds that they did the best they could, but it's not like they had a choice. The exchange shows Willow's anger focuses on Buffy not letting them know she's all right and that the friends had no choice about any of it. This fits Xander's first comment about worrying Giles, a way of telling Buffy he, too, felt angry over how much they all worried about her.

But Willow saying all this in a sarcastic, passive-aggressive way ("don't forget not to write") feels like false conflict. False conflict in a story means conflict that could be resolved if two characters simply talked openly to each other. But they don't, and there's no good character or plot-based reason they don't. Here, if Willow simply told Buffy how she felt at any time before this moment, the conflict wouldn't happen. Buffy would have sought Willow out to talk about how upset she felt about Joyce's words. Willow would have helped her deal with it.

The show had a great example of true conflict in *Phases* in Season Two. Willow tried to confront Oz and share her feelings about the slow pace of their relationship, but there was a good reason she didn't do it. He was on the verge of turning into a werewolf, which he'd realized only minutes before Willow arrived. He had no time to process it. Also, Oz is a man of few words who rarely expresses deep emotion and now is petrified. With all of that, I buy that they don't fit in a relationship talk before he turns.

It did feel authentic that Buffy on her first night home didn't feel ready yet to talk about her summer. She'd already taken a big step returning to Sunnydale and it might be all she could handle right then.

Now Buffy again holds back, saying Willow can't understand what Buffy went through. On first watch, I didn't quite buy that. But it worked better when I remembered that Buffy thinks Willow sent her a "kick his ass" comment about Angel at the end of Season Two. She may truly feel Willow won't understand. All the same, Buffy and Willow had a close friendship, and I'm not sure one comment undercuts all of that. Or that Buffy wouldn't just tell Willow how much that comment upset her.

Buffy points out that she can't talk to Willow when Willow is avoiding her. Willow then shares some feelings by telling Buffy it wasn't an easy summer for her. Buffy thinks that's because Willow missed her. But Willow says it wasn't only that. She's having serious dating with a werewolf, she's growing as a witch, and it's scary. And Buffy, her best friend, wasn't there. Buffy starts to cry. It seems like there's some connection there.

Zombie Plot Turn Or Not?

At 31 minutes, 6 seconds, Giles drives toward the Summers home, talking to himself.

Giles: Unbelievable. "Do you like my mask? Isn't it pretty? It raises the dead!" Americans.

Someone jumps in front of the car, and Giles hits that person. He gets out to see if the person is okay. It turns out to be a zombie that attacks Giles. The attack might be a Three-Quarter Turn in the zombie plot. But while it escalates the story (because now Giles, someone we care about, is at risk), it doesn't change the direction of the story.

The scene cuts to Buffy, who says she wanted to call

Willow every day. Willow tells her that doesn't make it okay. But there is a feeling that they've connected until Joyce walks in and demands to know what's going on. Willow tells Joyce Buffy's running away again, snapping right back to being angry despite that she and Buffy were sharing with each other. Joyce tells Buffy she can't just come and go as she pleases. This leaves me feeling Joyce didn't learn anything since the end of last season, which I'm also not sure is true to her character.

Buffy cries, asking them to stop it, and runs down the stairs. Joyce follows. The music stops as Joyce says they are going to have it out. This conflict with Joyce would feel more genuine if before this Buffy refused to talk with Joyce. Instead, we've seen her talk much more with Joyce than with her friends. As a result, Joyce comes off as tone deaf to anything Buffy's gone through. She says she doesn't care what Buffy's friends think because Buffy put her through the ringer. She goes on about the months of not knowing.

Buffy: You told me to go. You found out who I really was and you couldn't deal. Don't you remember?

I'm so glad Buffy says this because finally a character is open about what hurt her. Joyce argues that Buffy didn't give her time.

Joyce: Guess what? Mom's not perfect. I handled it badly.

She says, though, that her mistake didn't give Buffy the right to punish her by running away. While I believe Joyce's strong feelings and that she'd say this, the Joyce we've known so far also strikes me as a parent who might pause and ask what else Buffy went through. What happened to her. This Joyce, though, doesn't seem interested.

Buffy: I didn't do it to punish you.
Xander: Well, you did.
Buffy: Great. Anyone else want to weigh in on this? How about you by the dip?

The boy by the dip is Jonathan (whom we know from the previous season). He pauses with a chip halfway to his mouth.

Jonathan: No. Thanks. I'm good.

Xander tells Buffy she was selfish and stupid. Buffy says he has no idea what she went through. He asks if she tried talking to anyone and she says no one could help. She had to deal with it. Had we learned sooner that Buffy didn't try to talk to anyone because she didn't think they could help all this conflict would feel more genuine to me. But here it feels like more false conflict because Xander blames Buffy for not talking when they planned a whole party to avoid Buffy.

While the characters might have changed over the summer in ways that make them unwilling to talk directly with Buffy about their feelings, there's nothing that tells us that. As it is, Buffy's friends and Joyce don't feel consistent with who they were in Seasons One and Two. They seem to be written this way solely because if every character was just upfront with their feelings, there wouldn't be much story. Xander now tells Buffy she can't bury stuff. It'll come right back up to get her.

Xander's line transitions the episode to the zombie attacking Giles. His keys are on the street, so he hot wires his car and drives away.

The scene cuts here don't quite work. While the timing doesn't need to be perfect, cutting this Giles scene this way gives a sense that Giles struggled with the zombie in the street throughout all the dialogue in the previous Buffy scenes. That undercuts the danger the zombies pose because in all that time they didn't manage to overpower him.

Out Of Character Or In?

Buffy gets to the point at last. She tells Xander that it wasn't as if she could go to him when he made his feelings about Angel clear. Xander's next line, though, feels over the top even for him. He's had his petty jealousy and been possessive of Buffy before, but here he's mean.

Xander: I'm sorry your honey was a demon, but most girls don't hop a Greyhound over boy troubles.

I don't buy Xander being this insensitive. At the very least, he knows she fought Angelus and now he's gone. And he knows how hard it was for Buffy when Angel turned evil. Even with Xander's personality and emotional issues, calling all of that "boy troubles" doesn't feel like something he'd say. (Though perhaps I'm giving Xander too much credit.) Cordelia tries to defend Buffy, which fits. She was away all summer and less directly affected by Buffy's absence. She's also the least close to Buffy and so probably feels the least betrayed.

But her defense is to try to put herself in Buffy shoes.

Cordelia: I'm Buffy, freak of nature. Naturally, I pick a freak of nature for a boyfriend.

She goes on until Buffy tells her to get out of her shoes. Oz tries to intervene before a physical fight starts but Willow says talking isn't helping, might as well try violence. On that line, zombies burst in through the front window. Willow says she was being sarcastic.

Reconnecting Through Fighting Leads To The Climax

Buffy, her friends, and Joyce reconnect by fighting the zombies. It feels unsatisfying, though. It doesn't really resolve anything other than maybe with Joyce who finally gets a first-hand look at what Buffy's life as a Slayer is like. She asks if these are vampires. Buffy tells Joyce No and leads the fight. Everybody's coordinating just like they used to. Most of them, including Pat, Buffy, and Joyce, run upstairs and barricade themselves in Joyce's bedroom. Downstairs, Oz and Cordelia hide.

Pat gets knocked dead by a zombie, and the mask is knocked off the wall. Its eyes glow. Pat opens her eyes, reanimated, and we cut to a commercial. On return, the house is quieter. Cordelia and Oz encounter Giles. Cordelia asks how they know it's him and not Zombie Giles.

Giles: Cordelia, do stop being tiresome.
Cordelia: It's him.
Oz: The dead man's party moved upstairs.

Giles says they're after the mask. The zombie that puts it on becomes evil incarnate. In the bedroom, Pat stands. Joyce, relieved her friend is alive, tries to hug her. Pat flings her away and puts on the mask. Her eyes flash. Then a big flash of light fills the whole room. The zombies cower. Xander tells Joyce that when scary things get scared, it's not good.

Pat flashes her eyes at Willow, and Buffy knocks Pat out the window into the front yard. Downstairs, the others fight more zombies. Giles yells to Oz to go tell Buffy she has to get to the eyes to defeat the evil. Oz runs to the yard, but Pat's eyes are already flashing. There's white light everywhere. Buffy has a shovel.

Buffy: Hey, Pat. (Buffy thrusts shovel into Pat's eyes.) Made you look.

The light flashes again, and Pat and all the zombies disappear.

Oz: Never mind.

That was the Climax of the zombie plot. The Climax is where the opposing forces have their final confrontation and resolve the main plot conflict. Some of the strongest climaxes in *Buffy* occur when the monster plot parallels the emotional plot. Here, there's a little of that. Pat is one representation of the hostile, passive-aggressive way the others treated Buffy, and Buffy defeats her in a symbolic way by killing the big-time zombie she's become. She also was an obstacle between Buffy and her mom. If the episode's emotional conflict centered more on Joyce and Buffy, resolving the zombie plot would feel like an emotional catharsis as well.

But it doesn't relate to or resolve the key conflict between Buffy and her friends. They're all working as a team again, which is good to see. But it feels more like the zombie threat reminded them of their old roles as evil-fighting team members than that they resolved anything. For this reason, the Climax lacks power. While it resolved the less developed zombie plot, it barely touched on the emotional plot that took up so much more of the episode.

Falling Action

The Falling Action, where the writers tie up loose ends, starts around 40 minutes, 20 seconds. Joyce stumbles downstairs, runs to Buffy, hugs her, and asks if she's all right. Buffy says she is. I appreciate that moment because it seems Joyce is asking more than whether Buffy's all right from the zombie attack. She's conveying that she loves Buffy and is concerned about everything Buffy went through. Earlier she said she wanted to put her arms around Buffy, and she finally did.

Joyce: Was that a typical day at the office?

Buffy says it was nothing, only half joking. This exchange could explain in part why Joyce didn't show more compassion for Buffy earlier. She didn't understand what Buffy faces day after day. Though you'd think Giles might have filled her in over the summer.

The fighting, though, is nothing new for the friends, so it gives them no new insight into Buffy's life. All the same, they now act like everything's okay.

The scene switches to Giles in Snyder's office trying to get Buffy readmitted to school. Snyder says his view of Buffy is good riddance. Giles tries to reason with him, but Snyder scoffs and tells him he can go the city council if he wants, he'll get nowhere. Giles suggests the state supreme court, saying Snyder is powerful in local circles, but Giles can make life difficult for him professionally. Snyder is not convinced. Giles shoves him against the desk.

Giles: Would you like me to convince you?

In the last scene, Willow and Buffy sit at the outdoor coffee shop. They talk about Willow, summer, and witchcraft. Buffy asks if it scares Willow and Willow says it has. She tried to communicate with the spirit world. Buffy apologizes for not being there. Willow says she understands Buffy had to bail. She can forgive, and she needs to make allowances and be a grownup. She's partly serious and partly adopting a superior tone.

Buffy: You're really enjoying the whole moral superiority thing, aren't you?

Willow: It's like a drug.

Willow and Buffy trade insults, kind of playfully and a little bit seriously, until we cut to the credits. That's where the episode ends. In the foreshadowing section I'll talk about why some of these emotional issues are left unresolved.

Spoilers And Foreshadowing

Giles And Buffy

Giles is the only one who understands what Buffy's going through in this episode. This understanding drives the emotional side of the plot in *Faith, Hope & Trick* when Giles pushes Buffy in a very subtle way to talk about what happened with Angel. I suspect that's why, from a series planning perspective, Buffy doesn't tell her friends now about Angel regaining his soul. Buffy has to hold back so the next episode pays off emotionally. But without a good reason, her choice feels artificial. These unresolved emotional issues also affect Buffy's feelings and create conflict when Faith comes to town next week. That, too, provides strong moments I wouldn't want to miss.

It's unclear if the last scene with Giles and Snyder affects Buffy's return to school. Joyce will say the school board required it. But effective or not, it shows how protective Giles is of Buffy. It also illustrates that sometimes a scene works though it doesn't move the plot so long as the character driving the action does their best to achieve their goal.

Eavesdroppers

Later in the series, the writers will again use eavesdropping as a plot device. Dawn mistakenly lets vampires into the house, and Buffy rants about her, including saying she's an idiot. Dawn hears only that and misses the part about how Buffy's concerned for Dawn because she can't always be there to protect her. Dawn runs out of the house and gets captured. It feels contrived to me.

There is a worse example after Dawn finds out she's the key. She hears Buffy say she and Joyce aren't Dawn's real family and that Dawn isn't a person. Buffy later claims she was trying to express how Dawn must be feeling at the moment, but Dawn misses that part and (again) runs off.

That scene troubles me more because I don't buy Buffy saying what she does for any reason. And it's unlikely Dawn wouldn't stay to listen to everything that's said about her. It seems like most eavesdroppers would.

Questions For Your Writing

- **What gestures, movements, or actions in real life helped you infer how someone else felt about something?**

Buffy and the Art of Story Season Three Part 1

- Choose a character in your story, or create one, who feels intense emotion. What might that character do (not say or think) that signals their feelings?
- Do any of your characters act in ways that don't fit how you developed them? Can you create circumstances that make the actions feel authentic?
- Does your story include characters in conflict because they simply aren't talking? Why don't they talk to each other? If there's no strong reason, brainstorm four or five possibilities. Which is most believable?
- Does your story resolve the emotional issues it raises? If not, was that intentional? If your answer is No, how can you resolve the issues?
- Sketch out key points in your main plot. Does enough happen to keep your audience interested? If not, can you make it harder for your protagonist to prevail? What obstacles can you add?

The next chapter talks about *Faith Hope & Trick*, where a new Slayer and new villains come to town. Coincidence? Maybe not.

CHAPTER 3
FAITH, HOPE & TRICK S3 E3

THIS CHAPTER TALKS ABOUT *Faith, Hope & Trick*, Season Three, Episode Three, where a new Slayer and new villains come to Sunnydale. Written by David Greenwalt and directed by James A. Contner. Original air date: October 13, 1998.

Along with the episode breakdown, topics include:

- How late or missing major plot turns affect pacing
- An action plot that prompts Buffy to finally deal with her emotions over losing Angel
- Conflict and drama that keep the exposition and backstory engaging
- Dream sequence storytelling that affects plot and character
- How Faith's and Buffy's stories work together to create a compelling overall plot and a strong emotional arc for Buffy
- A highly effective game changer (not cliffhanger) at the end of the episode

Okay, let's dive into the Hellmouth.

Opening Conflict And Exposition

The opening shot shows feet standing on a concrete step on the edge of Sunnydale High's grounds. Willow's voice says she's giddy at the freedom now that they're seniors and allowed to go off campus for lunch. She waxes eloquent about savoring the moment. Xander and Oz, on either side of her, finally grab her arms and carry her over the school boundary. Willow panics. What if the rules changed? The others reassure her.

This small conflict draws viewers in and gives context for what happens next. As the friends cross the park, they hint at a major episode conflict. Cordelia and Xander are arm in arm, as are Willow and Oz. Willow says maybe they shouldn't be so couple-y since they're meeting Buffy. Then Cordelia provides some exposition in a quick, fun way.

Cordelia: Oh, you mean because the only guy who ever liked her turned out to be a vicious killer and had to be put down like a dog?

They agree to uncouple and let go of each other. Buffy's sitting on a picnic blanket in a pretty dress, surrounded by Tupperware containers of food. She's prepared a beautiful lunch. Xander provides more backstory:

Xander: Banned from campus, but not from our hearts. What's for lunch?

After they talk a bit, Willow tells Buffy that Scott Hope is at 11 o'clock. She tells the others Scott wanted to ask Buffy out last year, but she wasn't ready. Maybe now she is. Buffy's not sure. But when Scott walks by and says hello Buffy half smiles at him. Willow thinks it went well.

Cordelia: He didn't try to slit our throats or anything. It's progress.

Buffy says she's not trying to snare Scott Hope. She just wants her life back. She wants to date, shop, go to school and save the world from unspeakable demons.

Buffy: You know, I want to do girly stuff.

It's a little more exposition about what Buffy does for any audience member who doesn't already know. This also foreshadows the conflict for Buffy when Faith, the new Slayer, arrives. Buffy's trying to get her life back and she feels as if Faith is taking it from her.

At 2 minutes, 56 seconds, a limousine pulls up to a fast food burger place. Someone from the back of the limo orders a diet soda. He's a vampire, though not in vamp face now, and one of the few named characters of color on the show. We'll learn later his name is Mr. Trick. He comments on how Sunnydale is quaint and people call him Sir though admittedly he says it's not a haven for the brothers.

Mr. Trick: Strictly Caucasian persuasion here in the 'dale, but you got to salute that death rate.

He goes on that they could fit right in here.

When he calls out the whiteness of Sunnydale it feels like the writers' way of acknowledging this problem with the show. Now, looking back, the lack of diversity is striking. But from what I recall that was sadly typical of network shows at the time. *Buffy* might have had more diverse characters than most of them. (I'm thinking of *Friends,* among others.) It also seems realistic that a Black character in this town would notice that nearly everyone else is white.

Story Spark

Another large vampire who's very old is with Trick. Around 4 minutes, 32 seconds, that vampire growls and says they're here for one thing, to kill the Slayer. This is about 10% through the episode, right where we normally see the Story Spark or Inciting Incident that sets the main plot rolling. And this does set off part of the main plot.

The older vampire says he'll rip the spine from the Slayer's body and suck the marrow from her bones. That makes Mr. Trick hungry. He reaches through the window, grabs the employee at the takeout window, and hauls him into the limo, which squeals away.

Dream Scene Story Spark

Buffy dreams she's dancing with Angel at the Bronze. She says she missed him. The Claddagh ring Angel gave her falls off her finger onto the floor. And she has this quick flash of killing him as the vortex swirls behind him.

Buffy: I had to.

Angel closes his fist over his own ring. Blood oozes through his fingers.

Angel (glaring at Buffy): I loved you. (blood oozes through his shirt at his chest) Go to hell. (his face cracks as he laughs) I did.

I see this as the emotional Story Spark, though it also provides backstory and exposition. Like the dream in the last episode, it gives the audience a glimpse of Angel. But it moves the story, too, as it reinforces Buffy's fears, guilt, and sadness. These feelings drive her choices and actions later, including finally talking to Giles and how she reacts when Scott Hope gives her a similar ring. That's why this dream doesn't slow the story or frustrate me as a viewer.

What sounds like the school bell rings. But, as in the last episode, it's Buffy's alarm. At 7 minutes, 12 seconds, she wakes up and opens the drawer by her bedside. She looks at the ring Angel gave her. Joyce opens the door.

Joyce: Morning, Sunshine. Ready to face the Beast?

Buffy and Joyce meet with Principal Snyder in his office. Snyder tells Buffy the terms of her re-entry to school, take them or leave them. This scene uses conflict to inform the audience in an engaging way why Buffy gets to return to school. Also, some conditions Snyder includes set the stage for future episodes.

He tells her she needs (a) to pass a makeup test in each class where she got an incomplete; (b) a glowing recommendation from a faculty member who is not an English librarian; and (c) an interview with the school psychiatrist who must conclude her violent tendencies are gone. Buffy taps a nail file against her fingers as he talks, a great way to show her feelings. The tapping likely adds to Snyder's irritation, as he walks around his desk to take the nail file from her.

Joyce tells him she doesn't like his attitude and these conditions. The school board requires him to let Buffy back in. (I like to think Giles's talk with Snyder had some influence, but it's never mentioned.) Buffy adds that the board decision basically overruled Snyder.

Buffy: That's like having your whole ability to do this job called into question when you think about it.

Joyce: I think what my daughter is trying to say is NaNa-NaNaNaNa.

They both smile and leave. I love seeing Joyce back up Buffy. It shows a lot of growth from the events of *Dead Man's Party*. After they leave, his assistant tells Snyder the mayor is on the phone. This line adds a story question at the end of the scene, leaving the audience to wonder if the call relates to Buffy.

In the library, Buffy asks Willow if she thinks Giles is mad at her. Willow doesn't think so because he makes that funny cluck, cluck sound when he's mad but too English to say it. At that moment, Giles appears from behind the counter and pretends he didn't hear them. He says they need to do a binding spell for Acathla (the demon Buffy stopped by killing Angel) to make sure he doesn't emerge again.

Buffy: Giles, contain yourself. Yes, I'm back at school, but

you know how it embarrasses me when you gush. So let's just skip all that and get straight to work.

Giles says it's wonderful to have her back, which we can see in his face, and does she want him to say it? She does, so he does. But he quickly returns to the importance of keeping Acathla dormant and the dimensional portal closed. He asks Buffy what happened when she killed Angel.

Willow wants to help with the spell, but he tells her it's very difficult and sensitive.

A One-Quarter Twist And Giles's Concerns

Giles pushes Buffy to talk about Angel and Acathla about 10 minutes into the episode. I see the conversation as the first major plot turn for the emotional arc. It comes from Giles, so it's from outside the protagonist, as it should be. And it spins the story in a new direction, causing Buffy to grapple more directly with the trauma, though she resists.

Giles asks how long after Xander rescued him did Buffy kill Angel. She tells him about half an hour. Then he wants to know if the vortex was open and more about the fight. Buffy just says it was a big fight, Angel got the pointy end of the stick, and that's it. She rushes off for her first makeup exam.

Willow, who still wants to help, starts picking up magical ingredients and commenting on them. She says a smidge of one of them mixed with a virgin's saliva…. She switches gears when Giles gives her a look and finishes "does something I know nothing about." Giles tells her these are not forces to play around with and asks what she's been conjuring. Willow tells him she tried the spell to cure Angel and it didn't work. Then she talks about a few other things she tried.

This exchange, too, includes backstory and exposition. It stays interesting, though, because of the conflict. First, Buffy's reluctant to share what happened. Now Giles resists letting Willow help with the spell and worries about her doing things that could be dangerous. The scene ends with humor. Willow asks Giles if he's mad.

Giles: Of course not. If I were, I would be making a strange clucking sound with my tongue.

At 12 minutes, at the Bronze, a dark-haired young woman dances very close to a guy on the dance floor. Willow and Oz kiss. Buffy, very happy, sits down with some drinks. She passed her English exam, she's out with her friends.

Buffy: Hello, my life, how I've missed you.

This comment sets the stage for Faith to intrude on Buffy's life. It's one of many small moments I didn't notice on my first few watches but that all the same prepare the audience for Buffy's negative reaction to the new Slayer. At 12 minutes, 45 seconds, Scott Hope walks over.

Willow: Hi, Scott, uh, what are you doing here?

Scott: Well, you told me if I came after eight Buffy would be here.

Willow looks guilty, and Scott apologizes and says he's a bad liar. Buffy smiles but becomes flustered when he asks her to dance. She stutters and stumbles. Scott tells her there's no pressure, he'll be standing over there. If she changes her mind, she can mosey on over. No big deal if not.

Willow says Scott's normal and charming and doesn't Buffy want to get back to normal. Oz gives Scott points for use of the word mosey, but Buffy is just not ready. The episode is 14 minutes in and there's still no major turn in the story about Faith or the two new vampires, who only appeared once so far.

Cordelia and Xander join the others.

Cordelia: Checkout Sluttorama.

She's looking at the dark-haired young woman dancing. (I hope girls are not still saying this about other girls now.) Cordelia comments on the guy's outdated outfit, and Buffy realizes he's a vampire as the couple heads off the dance floor. Buffy hurries after them. Scott thinks she's coming to talk to him and steps toward her. Once again awkward, she tells him she wasn't heading toward him to dance. She has to go do something.

Outside the Bronze, Buffy and friends hear noises in an alley. Buffy tries to help but the young woman turns and tells her she's got it.

Faith (as she's fighting the vampire): You're Buffy, right? I'm Faith.

Oz: I'm going to go out on a limb and say there's a new Slayer in town.

Faith borrows Buffy's stake and kills the vampire.

Faith: Thanks, B, couldn't have done it without you.

And we cut to a commercial.

Faith And The One-Quarter Twist

The Faith scene ends nearly 16 minutes into the episode, quite a bit past the one-quarter mark. And while sometimes with TV that first major turn comes closer to a third of the way through, it's rarely that late in *Buffy*. The placement contributes to the plot feeling a bit off.

It doesn't lack momentum the way the zombie story did in *Dead Man's Party*, as there's much more to the Faith story. But at this point in the episode the pieces of the various plots feel disconnected. The old vampire talked about killing the Slayer, but over a third of the way in hasn't appeared on screen again. Now there's a new Slayer, but we don't know if those two storylines connect. There's Scott Hope, too. And no story seems related to Giles's questions about Acathla. All of it will come together. But on first watch in particular I felt a bit lost and frustrated.

In the Bronze, Faith tells stories about slaying, including one about sleeping in the nude when vampires attacked a church bus. It ends with a preacher hugging her while she's nude and the police arresting them both. Xander's fascinated. Cordelia sits, arms crossed, clearly not thrilled — another example of strong body language.

Faith: Isn't it crazy how slaying just always makes you hungry and horny?

The others stare at Buffy.

Buffy: Well, sometimes I — I crave a non-fat yogurt afterwards.

Cordelia says she gets it. Not the horny part, why there are two Slayers.

Cordelia: Oh. Buffy died. And we got Kendra and then Kendra died and we got Faith.

This is more exposition for the audience, sandwiched into the minor conflict caused by Cordelia's irritation that Xander's enthralled with Faith.

Faith explains she showed up now because her Watcher is on a retreat in the Cotswolds, so she came to meet the infamous Buff. She asks if Buffy really used a rocket launcher, but Xander interrupts Buffy's answer. He wants more Faith stories, especially if they involve being nude. Cordelia tells him to find a new theme.

The writers could have made Faith try to push Buffy aside. Instead, they made a far more interesting choice. Here, Faith tries to share the floor with Buffy, but Xander shifts the spotlight to her again. Which makes some sense because Faith is new, and her friends already know Buffy's stories. (Also, he's Xander.) After Faith's next story, she tries again to bring Buffy into the conversation by asking what her toughest kill was.

But Buffy flashes to killing Angel, which she definitely doesn't want to talk about. She awkwardly starts to say they're all difficult when Oz cuts in to ask Faith's position on werewolves. That's understandable, too, as it could involve his survival. When Faith finds out he's a werewolf she says she's okay with it so long as he doesn't hump her leg.

She then talks about how much fun she and Buffy will have being Watcherless and free. Buffy looks surprised and Faith asks didn't her Watcher go on the retreat.

Everyone Loves Faith

The scene cuts to Giles going on about how lovely the retreat is. It's a great honor to be asked to attend. Clearly, he's a little put out by not being invited.

Faith: Oh, it's boring. It's too stuffy for someone like you.
Buffy, shocked, asks if Faith's met Giles.
Faith: Yeah, I see him. If I knew that they came that young and cute I'd have requested a transfer.
Giles is flattered. Buffy is grossed out. Giles says it's fortuitous Faith's there because two people disappeared from the Sunset Ridge area. This might relate to the new vampires in town, but we don't know for sure.

Willow and Xander prompt Buffy to invite Faith to dinner. Faith accepts, eager to "meet the Fam." Buffy's tone as she says that's great and that later they can patrol together conveys she's less than thrilled with all this togetherness. Willow reminds Buffy she has another makeup exam. As Buffy starts to say she can use some coaching, Willow interrupts to offer, along with Xander, to keep Faith company while Buffy's busy. After they leave, Giles says Faith has a lot of zest. Then he asks Buffy about the physical locations of Acathla, Buffy, and Angel. She gives him a cursory explanation and heads for the door.

Buffy: Next time I kill Angel, I'll video it.
As Willow and Xander show Faith around they narrate in a joking way all the horrific things that happened in the school. Faith enjoys the tour and says if she'd had friends like them in high school, well, probably she would have still dropped out, but she would have felt sad about it. She then asks about Buffy,

who seems wound really tight. She says Buffy needs to find the fun, like them.

Faith runs into Scott Hope at the drinking fountain. As they chat away, Buffy happily bounces down the stairs and says she is two for two on tests. Then she sees Faith and Scott. Willow says maybe Faith and Scott could hit it off if Buffy's done with Scott.

Midpoint Reversal In *Faith, Hope & Trick*

We're near the Midpoint at 22 minutes, 30 seconds. Usually here we see a major reversal for the protagonist, a major commitment, or both. Seeing Scott with Faith, Buffy tells Willow she hadn't said No for all time to Scott, but you can't enter into these things lightly. Now she suffers something of a reversal because Willow, her best friend, criticizes her.

Willow: You really do need to find the fun, B — Buffy.

I feel for Buffy. Finally, after last week's difficulties with her friends, they seem to be on the same page. They're excited to have her back. And now there is this new Slayer in town.

The scene shifts to Mr. Trick in a warehouse with the old vampire. The old vamp is quite large and has a scarred face and hooves for feet. He interrupts as Trick explains all the amazing things technology can do. All he cares about is the Slayer. Trick tells him the news is mixed. Sunnydale has two Slayers because the town already had one. This tells the audience the old vampire is after Faith, not Buffy. The old vamp says he doesn't care how many there are, he'll kill a hundred of them. He also says the Slayer's going to pay for what she did and motions to his scar.

That occurs at 22 minutes, 48 seconds and could serve as a reversal for Buffy in the monster plot — if it changed anything. But the vamp got to town with a plan to kill a Slayer. Whether he learned about Buffy ahead of time or not, it's likely he'd try to kill her, too, if she's with Faith. Because of that, I don't see any reversal in the monster side of this plot, which adds to the episode as a whole feeling uneven.

The sense of menace grows a bit when someone knocks on the door, though. Trick says the food's there and opens the door. It's a pizza delivery guy, and Trick grabs him, not the pizza.

Real Conflict Between Faith And Buffy

At a little over 24 minutes, Joyce dishes out food at the dinner table, ignoring Buffy when she asks for potatoes. Joyce focuses on Faith, who loves slaying. Joyce says Buffy never talks that way and asks Faith why she loves it. Faith tells her the whole world goes away when she's fighting and she knows she'll win and they'll lose. And it's the best feeling.

Buffy: Well, sure. It beats that dead feeling when they win and you lose.

Faith, though, says she doesn't let that kind of negative thinking get to her, which Joyce thinks is great. She comments that Buffy can be awfully negative.

Joyce: Honey, you've got to fight that.
Buffy: Working on it.

Buffy follows Joyce into the kitchen, semi-complaining about Faith. Joyce tells her it's probably a good thing that she's an only child.

Buffy: I'm just getting my life back. I'm not looking to go halfsies on it.

But Joyce points out it's safer with two of them, so she's happy Faith is there. Then she suggests Faith could take over when Buffy goes to college next year. Buffy explains no one can really take over. You only get a new Slayer if the current one dies.

Joyce: You never told me you died. I hate your life....I

know you didn't choose this. I know it chose you. I've tried to march in the Slayer Pride parade. But I don't want you to die.

These lines make the metaphor to being gay from the last episode more explicit.

While the "I hate your life" comment might not be ideal parenting, it fits Joyce's very real worries. And it shows some growth from how she related to Buffy in the finale of Season Two because she immediately makes clear it's because she's afraid to lose Buffy. Buffy hugs Joyce and reassures her she's not going to die. She knows how to do her job. And now she has help.

Later that night, Buffy and Faith patrol. Faith questions why go back to an area they've been to before. Buffy a little sarcastically says something like the funny thing about vamps is they just come back even if you've already patrolled there. Faith says Buffy has all the experience, but suggests Buffy needs to loosen up. Maybe she's been doing this too long. And she asks if it's the Angel thing. Buffy is not happy Faith brought up Angel and asks what she knows about it.

Faith tells her just what Buffy's friends say. Big love, big loss, Buffy needs to deal and move on, but she's not. Buffy gets really angry and tells Faith to shut up about Angel.

Right then, vampires attack. Buffy kills a few as Faith wails on only one. She clearly could stake him, but she's too angry and riled up. (And, we'll later find out, afraid.) She punches and punches, reminding me of the episode *Ted* where Buffy beat up the vampire and Giles kept saying she could stake him now.

Faith's preoccupation is more problematic, though, because Buffy's outnumbered and could use Faith's help. One vampire tells Buffy he lives for Kakistos. Buffy kills him and the other vampire attacking her, then pulls Faith off the last one and kills it. She asks what Faith's problem is. Faith tells her if she has trouble with violence against vampires, she's in the wrong profession. Buffy points out that Faith should have staked the vamp and come to help Buffy.

Faith: I thought you could handle yourself.

At 28 minutes, 47 seconds, in the hallway Giles tells Buffy she and Faith have very different temperaments.

Buffy: Yeah, and mine's the sane one. The girl's not playing with a full deck, Giles. She has almost no deck. She has a three.

Giles asks more about the vampires that attacked.

Buffy: No tats. Crappy dressers. And, uh, oh, the one that nearly bit me mentioned something about kissing toast. He lived for kissing toast.

Giles: Do you mean Kakistos?

Buffy: Maybe it was taquitos. Maybe he lived for taquitos. What?

Giles: Kakistos.

Buffy: Is that bad?

Giles races for the library. After some quick research, he tells her the vampire is so old that its hands and feet are cloven. Buffy's sure this must be connected to Faith. Giles plans to try to reach Faith's Watcher and Buffy heads off to look for Faith.

Scott Hope steps in her way. Buffy says she has to be somewhere. Scott says he understands, he just wants to give it one last try. He realizes anything beyond that will qualify as stalking. So Buffy stops, and he tells her he's thought a lot about how to get to know her. He invites her to a Buster Keaton film festival that weekend. Finally, Buffy says yes and seems happy about it.

A Three-Quarter Ring And A Vampire Turn

We're about 33 minutes in, a little over three quarters through the episode. This is usually where we see another major plot turn, the one I call the Three-Quarter Turn. It should grow out of the Midpoint and spin the story in yet another new direction. Sometimes it also raises the stakes.

Here, there was no Midpoint Commitment. Buffy did suffer something of a reversal emotionally, though. While it didn't involve Scott, her issues cause her reaction to Scott that spins the emotional plot in a new direction

Scott gives Buffy a box. He says the guy in the retro shop said it represents friendship, which he'd like to have with her. But in the box is a Claddagh ring just like the one Angel gave her that fell off in the dream. Buffy stammers that she can't do this and drops the ring. Scott backs off.

Giles followed Buffy and sees this. He asks if she's okay. She's wiping away tears but says she is. She asks about Faith's Watcher. Now there's a Three-Quarter Turn in the plot about Faith and the old vampire. We didn't really see a Midpoint Commitment or Midpoint Reversal there. But there's a strong shift now when Giles tells Buffy that Faith's Watcher is dead.

At the motel where Faith is staying, she tells the owner's son she'll have money tomorrow for the room, flirting with him. He's not fooled but does let it go for the night. Buffy appears and tells her Kakistos is in town. Faith looks petrified and immediately starts packing. Buffy says she can help. Faith says she can handle it. And Buffy comments that, yeah, Faith's great at running away. This plot turn parallels the Three-Quarter Turn in *Dead Man's Party*, where Buffy packed her bags to run away from her problems.

Buffy's angry at Faith for leaving her to deal with Kakistos, but she wants to help Faith, too. And Faith, echoing how Buffy felt in the last episode, feels Buffy can't understand.

Faith: You don't know me. You don't know what I've been through. I'll take care of this.

Buffy: Like you took care of your Watcher?

Faith freezes. There's no more bravado. No more claiming

she can deal with it. She says there's no word for what Kakistos did to her Watcher.

There's a knock on the door. Faith looks through the keyhole and sees the owner's son, asks what he wants, and opens the door. But it's Kakistos. The owner's son is dead, and Kakistos held his face to the door. Buffy slams the door, but the vamps break through as she and Faith get out through the window.

It's not clear how the scene fits with the rules on vampires not being able to enter unless invited. Was Faith's offhand question to the owner's son enough? Is there something different about hotel rooms?

Buffy urges Faith on as they run. They reach a warehouse where they think they're safe, at least temporarily. Faith tells Buffy that she couldn't stop Kakistos from killing her Watcher. And then she ran. She's clearly having trouble dealing with that. Buffy tells her she did the right thing by running.

Buffy: The first rule of slaying: don't die....There are two of us now, and one of him. Do the math.

As Buffy tells her that, Faith recognizes things in the warehouse as belonging to Kakistos.

Vamp Plot Climax

The Climax for the vampire subplot, where the opposing forces engage in their final confrontation, begins when the vampires burst in. Kakistos goes for Faith. Buffy throws her what looks like a crowbar.

Buffy: Faith. Don't die.

Buffy fights the other vampires. Kakistos keeps hitting Faith hard. She screams, and Buffy jumps into the fight. Mr. Trick sees how this is going and tells another vampire that the Master could get killed. Then he gives a very Spike-like sort of shrug.

Mr. Trick (to another vampire as they leave the ware-

house): Well, our prayers are with him. There's a reason these vengeance crusades are out of style. Modern vampires see the big picture.

Kakistos throws Buffy down, laughs, and says he guesses she needs a bigger stake. Faith gets to her feet, grabs a giant piece of wood, and sticks it through his heart.

At 38 minutes, 47 seconds, it's a little early for the episode to reach the Falling Action section and start tying up loose ends, though the vampire plot resolved when Faith (and Buffy) prevailed. But we get a quick moment of Falling Action for Faith and Buffy before the Climax of Buffy's emotional plot.

Buffy: You hungry?
Faith: Starved.

The scene cuts to the library. Giles tells Willow and Buffy the Council approved his request. Faith will stay in Sunnydale and Giles will look after both Faith and Buffy until a new Watcher is sent. Buffy thinks that's good. Faith had a lot to deal with, but she really came through in the end.

Buffy's Emotional Plot Climax

Now we get the Climax for Buffy's emotional arc. If we view that arc as a subplot, these last moments are part of the overall Falling Action. Writers resolve subplots in that section if they haven't already resolved. If we see Buffy's arc as the main plot, this scene is the Climax of the episode overall, and the vampire plot was a key subplot.

Buffy, right after what she said about Faith, takes a deep breath. She tells Willow and Giles that Angel was cured, surprising both of them. She says Willow's spell worked at the last minute. He was Angel again and didn't remember what happened. But the vortex was open. So Buffy says she told him she loved him, kissed him, and killed him. She turns to Giles.

Buffy: I don't know if that'll help with the spell or not.

Giles: It will.

Willow feels for Buffy, but Buffy says it's okay. She held onto this for a long time and it was good to get it out. The Buffy and Angel theme music plays as Buffy leaves the library.

Willow tells Giles she knows he wants her to be careful, but she really can help with this spell.

Giles: There is no spell.

How Giles handles all of this shows so much about him. He knew Buffy needed to talk about killing Angel but it was hard for her, and asking directly didn't work. So he pushed in a different way, in a context that might make it easier for her. As part of a spell, answering becomes a Slayer duty, opening more space for her to talk about it.

Now the Scott Hope subplot resolves. Buffy waits for him outside his class. He doesn't seem thrilled to see her. She goes into a long, rambly explanation, telling him there was someone before. It was difficult and it's over, but she was having a hard time with it and the ring confused her. And she says one of my favorite Buffy lines ever.

Buffy: Wow. If I'd known I was going to go on this long, I probably would have brought some water.

Scott needs to think about it when she says she hopes he'll give her another chance. He starts to walk away, but immediately turns around and says, okay, he thought about it. He still wants to go out with her. Buffy says she has just one thing to take care of and she's free for the weekend.

The Game Changer

At 42 minutes, 19 seconds, Buffy goes to the mansion where she killed Angel. The Buffy and Angel music plays as Buffy takes off the ring Angel gave her, sets it on the floor, and quietly says good-bye to him. She walks out. That moment could have been the end of the episode. But now there's a game changer.

As I talked about in earlier *Buffy and the Art of Story* books and podcast episodes, a cliffhanger is where the main plot doesn't finish. Typically, something dire happens and the audience must come back to the next episode, movie, or book to find out how it resolves. (And sometimes, if the protagonist survives.) Here, in contrast, the main plot and key subplots resolved. Faith won the fight with Kakistos and worked out her issues. Buffy dealt with her feelings about killing Angel, told Giles and Willow what happened, connected with Scott, and said goodbye to Angel. Nothing's left hanging.

But a game changer is an event that changes the world of the story going forward after the main plot resolves. That's what occurs here. The camera zooms in on the ring. For a moment all fades to black. Then the ring glows and vibrates. The vibration becomes what sounds like thunder. A white light flashes, and Angel, naked, falls to the concrete floor. He's not in vamp face. He looks human and confused. And we cut to credits.

That is the game changer of all game changers. I loved it on first watch and still do. It was hard when *Buffy* first aired to wait to see what was going to happen. And, of course, as is typical in the Buffyverse, it happens after Buffy finally came to terms with the loss of Angel, let go, and started a relationship with someone new.

Comparison To *Dead Man's Party*

The plot threads in *Faith, Hope & Trick* were much better connected than in *Dead Man's Party*. There, the friends moved through a completely separate story from Buffy's. Also, Buffy's emotional arc wasn't quite clear. She struggled, her friends and mom were angry at her and a little mean, they fought together, and that was it. Buffy didn't necessarily resolve her issues.

Here, though, Buffy's journey is clearer. She's nearly in the same place when *Faith, Hope & Trick* starts as she was at the beginning of *Dead Man's Party*, though her friends are kinder. But she ends *Faith, Hope & Trick* in a far better place emotionally and closer to her friends because she tells them what happened. (Xander doesn't hear directly what happened with Angel, but it's likely Willow (or Buffy) tells him.) Her friends can now understand why Buffy left and her struggles when she returned.

And the different storylines connect because Faith's story reflects Buffy's, and Buffy helps Faith deal with her issues. Faith's appearance at first angers Buffy, but it puts her more in touch with her life. And helping Faith causes Buffy to recognize her own issues and denial. That, in turn, allows her to connect with Scott. So the threads, which seemed unrelated at first, all weave together.

Plot And Characters In Faith, Hope & Trick

The only issue for me with this episode, and the reason it's not a favorite, is the pacing. It feels slow because the monster plot lacks strong plot turns, and the key shifts in the emotional plot don't quite keep the momentum of the overall story going. All the same, a plot with major turns at each quarter point isn't the only way to construct a story. And a new Slayer who is very different from Buffy or from Season Two's Kendra is intriguing. Also, the emotional plot is extremely moving. So much so that as integrated as the storylines are, I often remember Buffy's breakthrough at the end separately, forgetting it's in the same episode as Faith's introduction.

Buffy grows significantly in the episode, too, and the story deepens the bond between her and Giles. Finally, the episode foreshadows quite a bit for the rest of the season and series.

Spoilers And Foreshadowing

Unanswered Story Question

Story questions keep the audience returning to get an answer. This episode raises one the series never definitively answers: what brought Angel back. The glowing ring suggests that Buffy saying goodbye and putting the ring in the mansion triggers Angel's return. Yet in *Amends* The First Evil will take credit for Angel's return. It's never clear if that's true or if it tells Angel that to manipulate him. In the series *Angel,* entities called the Powers That Be send visions to Angel through other people. That always left me thinking they brought Angel back, though the events of Season Two call that into question, too. In a lot of ways, that unanswered question drives *Angel* the series.

Snyder's Conditions

Because Snyder requires it, in *Homecoming*, Buffy will try to get a recommendation from the teacher of her favorite class. But the teacher doesn't remember Buffy, which is part of what prompts her to run for Homecoming Queen against Cordelia. Snyder's conditions for Buffy's return to school also include seeing the school psychiatrist. In the next episode, he'll start to help Buffy. He'll also get killed, and Buffy will fear that Angel did it.

Faith Foreshadowing

Faith's eagerness about slaying contributes to her killing a human later in the season. That's subtly foreshadowed here because what Joyce reads as a *joie de vivre* and a lack of negativity has some dark roots in Faith's fear of Kakistos and inability to handle her emotional issues.

This episode, too, foreshadows the body switching arc in Season Four. There, Faith's catchphrase, five by five (which she says for the first time in *Faith, Hope & Trick*), cues the audience that she's in Buffy's body. Seeing Joyce and Buffy together here likely begins her envy of Buffy's life. Though she takes Joyce hostage, it's easy for the audience to see her vulnerability over never having had the type of mom Buffy has.

Joyce tells Buffy it's good she's an only child. That comment, and Buffy's reaction to Faith, foreshadows how Buffy feels at first about her new sister Dawn in Season Five. Buffy also refers to Faith as her "bestest little sister," though Faith is older — more foreshadowing.

Giles's Roles, The Council, And Communication

Giles acts as Buffy's Watcher when guiding her to deal with her emotional issues. But he's also acting as a parental figure as their bond grows. Their closeness foreshadows *Helpless*, where the Council fires Giles from being her Watcher because he has too much of a father's love for Buffy.

The way Giles and Willow interact foreshadows Giles's role as mentor for Willow, as well as his later concerns about how she uses magic. You could easily miss that here because, as Willow discovers, there was no spell. But when Giles asks what she's been conjuring and warns her about danger, Willow backpedals. In Season Six, Giles will confront Willow over what he sees as her recklessness in bringing Buffy back from the dead, and it causes a rift between them. The seeds of their conflict, and of Willow's going too far with magic, are sewn throughout the end of Season Two and here.

As to his role as Watcher, Giles expresses wistfulness about not being invited to the retreat. It's played for humor, but it foreshadows, or suggests there already exists, conflict between Giles and the Council. If Giles didn't know when the retreat was, it also foreshadows lack of communication that causes major consequences in *Revelations*, when a "new Watcher,"

Gwendolyn Post, comes to train Faith. The Council claims there was a memo about Post being kicked out for dealing too much in the dark arts, but Giles never saw it. In addition, the Council's failure to invite Giles to the retreat foreshadows his vulnerability to manipulation when Post plays on his insecurities.

Questions For Your Writing

- Do major plot turns occur at or near the one-quarter, one-half, and three-quarter points? If not, and you revise so that they do, does your story still work? Does it move more quickly?
- Does the main plot of your story prompt an emotional breakthrough for a key character? Could it?
- If you use a dream sequence, does it change anything for the character who has the dream? Does it influence their actions or choices? If not, does the dream move the plot?
- Have you considered adding a game changer at the end of a chapter, at a key plot turn, or at the end of your novel or screenplay if it's an installment of a series? If so, did you resolve your main plot first?

The next chapter talks about *Beauty And The Beasts*, when Angel returns and there's a dramatic storyline for Oz and Willow.

CHAPTER 4
BEAUTY AND THE BEASTS
S3 E4

THIS CHAPTER TALKS about *Beauty and the Beasts*, Season Three, Episode Four, where Angel returns and everyone fears werewolf Oz is killing people. Written by Marti Noxon and directed by James Whitmore Jr. Original air date: October 20, 1998.

Along with the episode breakdown, topics include:

- Intertwining multiple storylines
- Challenges with the metaphor to abusive relationships
- Playing fair and point of view
- When a character gets what they want but wishes they hadn't
- Using a framing device to bookend the story

Okay, let's dive into the Hellmouth.

Opening Conflict And Voiceover

In voiceover, Buffy reads aloud from Jack London's *The Call Of The Wild*. On screen is a forest. The point of view is that of someone or something breathing hard and running — a slight opening conflict. The voiceover also sets a tone and suggests the danger here will come from an animal or the wilderness. While that's not literally true, the episode speaks to the nature of humans and beasts or monsters.

Buffy's voice fades into Willow reading the same passage to Oz in the library. He's locked in the book cage in his werewolf state. There's another minor conflict when Willow says "rabbit" as part of the text. Oz the werewolf lunges and hits the front of the cage. Xander walks in, yawning, to report for duty. Willow tells him she's reading *The Call Of The Wild* aloud to help soothe Oz, and it'll help Xander stay awake.

Xander: Aren't we reading the CliffsNotes version of that for English?

Willow: Some of us are.

Willow put towels on the front of the cage for privacy. She's not ready for Oz full monty, she's just getting used to half monty. Willow refuses to tell Xander which half. Though she gives Xander a tranquilizer gun just in case, she tells him Oz is more manageable tonight than he will be tomorrow night when there'll be a full moon. Immediately after she leaves, Xander lies down on a table with the book as a pillow.

This scene conveys a lot of information through mild conflict and humor. The audience learns (or is reminded) that Willow and Oz are dating, he's a werewolf, someone needs to watch him on his wolf nights, and there are three of those.

The Chase, A Theme, And The Story Spark

We cut to Buffy and Faith patrolling in the graveyard. Faith asks about her and Scott. Buffy says things haven't gone far, but she really likes him. But the best thing is he's not any sort of hell beast. Faith tells her all men are beasts.

Buffy: I was hoping not to get that cynical until I was at least forty.

Faith: It's not cynical, I mean, it's realistic. Every guy, from Manimal right down to Mr. I-Loved-The-English-Patient, has beast in him. And I don't care how sensitive they act; they're all still just in it for the chase.

This exchange sets up an episode theme about the beast within. That theme relates to the key story question about what beast is killing people in Sunnydale. It also transitions to the next scene. When Faith says "chase," the scene shifts to a young guy running through the forest. Something or someone's chasing him, and we see it all from the beast's point of view.

While usually the Story Spark or Inciting Incident sets off the main plot around 10% through an episode, here it's a bit early at 3 minutes, 49 seconds. (Most episodes are 43 or 44 minutes long.) The creature chasing this guy growls. The guy screams as he's dragged towards the camera. And we cut to the credits.

After the credits, Willow, Oz, and Buffy talk outside the Sunnydale High campus. Willow says she doesn't think all men are in it for the chase. Scott Hope calls out to Buffy. He's with two friends, Pete and Debbie. Debbie asks Oz whether he'll be in jazz band this year. He jokes that it's too much pressure. Not the music, but the marching, because jazz is improvisational and everyone goes off in all directions. The others look slightly puzzled.

Willow: He's just being Oz.
Oz: Pretty much full time.

Debbie holds flowers Pete got her. When Buffy admires them, Pete says he bets Scott gives Buffy flowers all the time. Scott looks awkward and says they're not up to flowers yet. Then he turns to Buffy and asks if he missed flowers. She assures him they are pre-posey. This is a nice way to tell viewers

Buffy and Scott are early in their relationship and to show them having a bit of fun with each other. Buffy seems happy and relaxed, especially compared to the previous three episodes.

She has to leave, though. She needs to convince the guidance counselor, Mr. Platt, that she's Little Miss Stable so she can stay in school. This is one of Principal Snyder's conditions from the last episode.

Debbie sees Platt, too. She says she doesn't want to, but she's flunking senior bio and the teacher thinks she has success issues. Oz tells her he aced senior bio and is happy to give her his notes. The dialogue felt on first watch like it was there simply to introduce new characters. But all of it plays into the mystery Buffy must solve later about the beast.

At the library at about 8 minutes, 15 seconds, Giles tells Xander they need to check all the exits and make sure there was no way out. Willow and Oz enter.

Giles: It's good to see you. Um, no need to panic.

Oz: Just a thought: Poker? Not your game.

Giles tells them a student, Jeff Walken, was found dead in the woods. He was mauled. Oz knew Jeff.

Giles: Much as I hate to say it, it could be the work of a —

Oz: Me.

Willow: Wolf you. Not you you.

Xander insists it's neither. The book cage was locked and the window was — he walks into the cage, looks up, and says, "Open." But then he tells them not to worry. He rested his eyes now and then but that's all, and he never heard Oz leave. Oz was right there when he—

Giles (yelling): Woke up?

Willow tries to comfort Oz, who looks shaken.

Guidance And Themes

Buffy walks into the guidance counselor's office. His high-backed chair faces her so she can't see him, just his arms sticking out as he holds a burning cigarette. I don't know if they really allowed cigarette smoking in high school at the time. (My college did in the late eighties.)

Whether it did or not, we haven't seen other teachers who smoke. It hints that this counselor is unorthodox. Before he speaks or spins around Buffy tells him she'll look at his ink blots, she'll do whatever she has to, but she doesn't want to talk about her childhood and she doesn't want to be friends.

He spins around and tells her they're not going to be friends. She's a little surprised, but he says she has friends, he hopes, which is good. Friends tell you what you want to hear. What he's offering is a trained, not too crazy professional, who'll always give his honest opinion.

Buffy: Not too crazy. That's your credential?

Platt tells her any person who claims to be totally sane is lying or not very bright. Everyone has demons.

Buffy (very quiet): Gotta say I'm with you on that.

Though Buffy seemed light and happy with Scott and his friends earlier, her demeanor shifts here. She's more serious and her tone is a bit muted. Platt tells her demons can be fought and people can change. Buffy can change. He asks why she ran away. She shares an abbreviated and somewhat metaphorical version. She was dating someone. It ended badly. She and her mom were fighting. She freaked out and ran. Platt wants to hear more about this bad ending guy.

Buffy: He was my first — I loved him. And then he —
Platt: Changed?
Buffy: Yeah.
Platt: He got mean.
Buffy: Yeah.

Platt: And you didn't stop loving him.

Buffy doesn't respond. She just looks at him.

This covers another theme of the episode, one that fits with the first one. What happens when you love someone who changes or becomes dangerous, or you realize that person is dangerous? Platt tells Buffy there's no shame in losing yourself in love. But sooner or later, you need to get back to yourself.

Buffy: And if you can't?

Platt: If you can't, then love becomes your master and you are just its dog.

Buffy's question "if you can't?" tells us so much about where she is. She likes Scott. But she's afraid she can't let go of Angel.

This episode illustrates the writers' skill in creating stories that work for first-time viewers but add layers for return viewers. The longtime viewer knows something vital that a new viewer does not, which is that Angel is back, that Buffy's talking about Angel, and that she had to kill him but has no idea he's been returned to earth. For that reason, the episode has more emotional impact for viewers who watch the episodes in order. That's not unusual now for television. But before *Buffy* most shows could be watched in any order.

Buffy enters the library. Oz and Willow sit on the steps, looking sad. Cordelia tells Buffy Oz ate someone the night before. Willow protests. Xander makes it worse by saying Oz didn't eat anyone, he just had werewolf fun with them. Oz suggests there could be another werewolf roaming the woods. Giles agrees that's possible. He tells Buffy to patrol and the others to check out the morgue. He'll ask Faith to watch Oz tonight.

Oz: Oh, you're having a Slayer watch me. Good we're not overreacting.

This is one of the few times we see Oz rattled. He was rattled as soon as he heard someone was killed and he might've done it, and he's more so now. It's striking because normally he doesn't get upset over things. He has great perspective. Now he tells Willow he needs to bail, though he knows it's kind of dramatic. Willow's supportive except that it's almost sunset.

Oz sighs and gets in the cage. She tries to reassure him, but he tells her, raising his voice, to get away. For another character, his words and actions still might feel low key. But because of the way Oz's character has been developed, the audience knows how disturbed he is. It's a great example of tailoring your character's words and actions to suit who they are.

A Later But Powerful One-Quarter Twist

We're a little bit past 25% through the episode, where we often see the first major plot turn. It should come from outside the protagonist and spin the story in a new direction. It also sometimes raises the stakes.

It does all of that here. At about 13 minutes, 16 seconds, Buffy patrols the woods. A creature runs at her from the side and knocks her over. It's Angel. He's not in vamp face, but his lips are bloody and he's breathing hard. And we cut to a commercial.

This moment turns the story, which is now about not only who is killing people but whether Buffy will need to stop or kill Angel again. The two fight. His punches are wild and flailing. Buffy knocks him out.

At the morgue, Cordelia, Willow, and Xander check out the mauled body. Cordelia and Xander are grossed out, but Willow is very thorough and calm as she gets samples from under the nails. She can't say yet if Oz is cleared. Anything could have done this.

Cordelia: Anything with big sharp teeth and vicious —
Xander: Can you go back to the car and wait?

Willow, still appearing calm, says she just needs to get a

couple hairs that might have come from the perpetrator. The second she's done, she passes out.

Xander comments that it doesn't look good for Oz. The guy was ripped apart by a wild animal.

The scene cuts to Buffy opening a trunk after sweeping a bunch of dolls off of it. The dolls are a nod to Drusilla who kept them there. Buffy gets out handcuffs and a long chain which she uses to restrain Angel. He struggles, breathing hard. After he's chained, Angel lunges for Buffy. She cringes. He makes guttural sounds, almost growling.

The scene cuts to a werewolf growling in the cage. Faith dances to music on her Walkman. Because her ears are covered, she doesn't hear Buffy come up behind her. Buffy taps Faith's shoulder. Faith swings around and punches Buffy, then apologizes. Buffy rubs her chin and says it's okay. She came to give Faith the night off. As soon as Faith is gone, Buffy pulls out a card catalog drawer.

The next morning, Oz sleeps in the cage. Giles comes in and unlocks it. He sees Buffy asleep in a chair, holding books, with more books around her. Though she, too, fell asleep, he doesn't yell at her the way he did Xander. Maybe the assumption is that as the Slayer Buffy would have woken up if she heard something. But even on first watch I found that distracting, as I got sidetracked thinking it was unfair to Xander.

Giles comments on the books, which include some on exploring demon dimensions and Acathla. Buffy tells Giles she had a dream Angel came back and it brought up some questions. He sympathizes because after Jenny was killed, he dreamed he saved Jenny.

Buffy asks if Angel could return. Giles tells her there's no record of anyone returning from that demon dimension. If Angel did get back Giles can't say what he would be like. He also tells her it's a dimension of brutal torment. Time moves quite differently there. And Buffy says she remembers.

This exchange reminds viewers about Jenny, who was killed by Angel, and that Buffy was in a demon dimension. It's a good example of how to throw in quick reminders about past events without giving everything away if you write a series. Those same moments might spark new audience members to seek out earlier books or episodes.

Giles confirms that if Angel had come back, it would be after hundreds of years of torture. He says it would take someone of extraordinary will and character to retain any semblance of self. More likely he'd be a monster. Buffy says he'd be a lost cause, but Giles tells her there are two types of monsters. The type that can be and wants to be redeemed. And the type that's devoid of humanity and can't respond to reason or love.

Two Possible Midpoints

That scene ended at around 21 minutes. It's a little early for the episode Midpoint. But Giles's last line could be a Midpoint Reversal. At a strong Midpoint you will see the protagonist committing in full to the quest, suffering a major reversal, or both. Here, this idea of a monster that cannot be redeemed, which we see in Buffy's face devastates her, could be a reversal, especially given how Angel behaved earlier.

If this is a Midpoint, it raises the question of which story is the main plot. Buffy dealing with Angel's return or the beast terrorizing Sunnydale? Both possible Midpoints suggest the main plot is the former, though the two are related. But the plot about the beast focuses more on Oz and Willow.

Willow now comes into the library with donuts. She talks rapidly about how she watched them make the donuts at 4:00 AM.

Willow (to Buffy): How come you're the wakey girl? I

mean, this time it's not your boyfriend who's the cold blooded —

Buffy nods as Oz walks in. Willow spins around and holds out the donuts.

Willow: Jelly donut?

Buffy keeps asking Willow what she found. Was the killer a vampire or werewolf? Willow says it's not conclusive, and Buffy, upset, keeps pushing her.

The scene cuts to the lunchroom. Scott sees what's on Buffy's tray and says he can't back her on that lunch. She tells him her stomach doesn't want hard food, but there's fruit in the Jello. He tells her those are marshmallows. He's sitting with Debbie and Pete. When Buffy says she didn't sleep well, Debbie advises her not to tell Mr. Platt. He'll make her start a dream journal. Debbie's surprised when Buffy says she kind of liked Platt. Debbie agrees he's funny, but she doesn't like some of the things he says.

Buffy: He definitely marches to the beat of his own drummer. Actually, I think he makes his own drums.

Scott is supportive about therapy and tells her she looks amazing, especially considering she's not feeling well. In a sort of disconnected rambling way, Buffy tells him that's sweet and she wishes she didn't have to, but she does. And she gets up and leaves.

At 23 and a half minutes in, this is a possible Midpoint Commitment. It's subtle, but Buffy commits to going to see Angel rather than staying with Scott, who right now appears to offer the sort of normal life she wanted. On the other hand, you can see it as less of a commitment and more of a reaction to Angel's return. Given their history, and the recent killing, it's hard to see Buffy doing anything else. After Buffy leaves, Pete comments about Scott liking the manic-depressive chick.

This scene weaves in a lot of clues to the mystery that don't appear significant at first. When Debbie comments about Platt and the dream journal, Pete makes fun, joking about whether it's like a Barbie Dreamhouse type of thing. Because of the jokes and Pete's comment about Buffy, it's easy to overlook that he doesn't like Debbie seeing Platt. But later when Platt is killed and Buffy considers both Pete and Debbie as suspects, the audience doesn't feel blindsided. The scene also weaves in subtle clues that there may be problems in the Pete and Debbie relationship, such as Debbie's trouble sleeping.

Nearly 24 minutes in, Buffy finds Angel still in chains at the mansion. She asks if he understands her, and he doesn't respond. When she tentatively touches his shoulder, he lunges at her, growling. She runs out.

Misleads And Cheats

At school in the courtyard, Pete pulls Debbie toward a door. She keeps saying she can't, she'll be late for class, but he tells her she'll be late but happy. He kisses her. The point of view is unclear. It's a little like what we saw in the early scene where the guy was attacked. There's a narrow frame to the shot and the camera shivers a bit, giving the impression we're seeing Debbie and Pete through a particular person's point of view, not an objective camera.

Because we've only had an objective camera viewpoint or the beast's viewpoint so far, this point of view makes me question whether the episode plays fair with the audience. It's broad daylight, so the POV can't be Angel's or a werewolf's. Pete and Debbie become suspects later, but it can't be either of them because we're viewing them. It could be Oz's point of view since we'll see later that he comes to the courtyard to meet Debbie. But that's quite a bit later, and it seems unlikely he's standing there watching now.

This POV framing misleads the audience, suggesting the beast can't be Pete. It's fine to do that if there's an alternate story explanation for the misleading technique or moment. But if there's not, it leaves the audience feeling that you as the author cheated.

The door leads into what appears to be a very large janitorial closet or shop. It's where Pete makes and stores a formula he drinks. It adds to the sense that most adults in Sunnydale pay no attention to what's going on, as he doesn't seem worried that anyone else will find it. Debbie tries to distract Pete, but he notices an empty jar with neon green residue in the bottom. Frightened and angry, he demands to know whether she drank it.

Buffy's Commitment And Reversal With Platt

The scene cuts to Buffy in Platt's office. He has the chair turned around and his back to her. One hand is extended and holding a cigarette. She tells him not to turn around. She just needs to tell him something, and it will probably convince him she's loony bin material, but she can't talk to anyone else.

Because she's so distraught, I believe that she doesn't find it odd that Platt stays silent and still. And I find it true to her character that it's easier for her to talk if he doesn't look at her. Buffy says she can't tell Willow or Giles or anyone because they'd freak out on her or do something, presumably something to Angel.

Though it comes much beyond the Midpoint, Buffy spilling all this out feels like her real commitment. She's telling this counselor the truth when she has no idea how he'll react or what he'll do. That tells us the deep stress she feels. She tells Platt she needs help and needs to talk to someone. She goes on that she's scared, and starts to tell him this guy — and she moves closer and sees Platt's cigarette burned down to ash.

Buffy (whispering): He's come back.

The camera pans around so we can see Platt sitting in his chair, face mauled, one eye gone. And there's all this blood.

This part feels like a Midpoint Reversal, though it's late in the overall episode for it. The person killed is the one person Buffy went to for help. This calls back to when Angelus killed and tormented people Buffy loved. While Angel has no way of knowing about Platt, I can understand why Buffy might not think that through in the moment.

A small bit of reality distracts from the moment. As he was being mauled, it's impossible that Platt held onto his cigarette. That it's there, burned to ash, suggests he was posed. That fits the Angelus of old. But not the feral Angel we just saw. And not Pete, who we later find out becomes crazed and kills people.

Pete becomes angry when Debbie admits she threw out that formula. She wanted to help him and doesn't like what it does to him. She tells him he knows how he gets when he drinks it. He claims he does it for her. To be the man she wants. But now he doesn't need the formula for that.

He breaks all the beakers and tells her she can pour out everything and it won't help. He punches her and tells her all it takes is her stupid, grating voice. Pete jerks his head around and turns into a sort of beast. It's still him, but his face distorts. There's an obvious Jekyll and Hyde reference. He accuses Debbie of flirting with other guys and asks if her shrink taught her that. And then he says even Platt's not going to listen to her pathetic ramblings anymore.

Pete: I'm all you've got now.

Debbie, on the floor, cowers. She's crying. Seeing what he's done, Pete turns back into himself, but of course still blames her. He tells her she shouldn't make him mad. She holds and comforts him. The parallels to non-supernatural abusive relationships are clear.

Three-Quarter Turn And Cold-Blooded Jelly Donuts

At about 30 minutes, Giles tells the others in the library that the creature is especially brutal, but the coroner confirmed Platt was killed during the day. Willow raises her arm and says, "Yes!" Then she lowers it and says more quietly that it's horrible. Buffy tells her it's okay, they're all glad Oz is off the hook.

I see all this as the Three-Quarter Turn, that last major plot turn that spins the story yet again. When Giles reveals Platt was killed during the day that shifts the story. We know it's not Angel or Oz. That changes Buffy's focus for the killing plot and eases her mind a bit about Angel.

The next scene turns the story of the beast (Pete), shifting his focus to Oz.

Giles asks where Oz is. The scene cuts to the courtyard where Oz waits for Debbie, one eye on the nearly setting sun. He's about to leave when Debbie runs out of that side room. She apologizes for being late. Oz gives her his notes and notices her black eye, covered partly by her hair. He asks if she's okay. He touches her shoulder or arm lightly.

**Debbie: What? Oh yeah, I'm, I'm such a klutz. I, uh —
Oz: Fell down?**

Debbie claims it was a door knob. Oz starts to say if she wants to talk, but she thanks him for the notes and leaves. We get that distant point of view again. But it's Pete this time because the camera shifts and we see him watching Oz head toward the library.

Giles says the killer is a depraved, sadistic animal. Oz walks in.

Oz: Present. Hey, I may be a coldblooded jelly donut, but my timing's impeccable.

Willow rushes to him to assure him that he's not. It's a kill-in-the-day monster. Now the gang talks over what the two victims have in common. Oz says Debbie and Jeff were in jazz band together and they used to horse around.

Faith: They were screwing?

Oz: I don't think so, but he hid her music comp book once.

Buffy points out that Debbie was seeing Platt and clearly had no love for him. Oz mentions that black eye. They talk about whether Debbie might have gotten it when Platt fought back. But Buffy says Platt was dead in an instant, he didn't even drop his cigarette. (Despite that the non-dropped cigarette is a clue, I still don't buy that Platt could have held onto it.) Buffy suggests maybe it's boyfriend Pete doling out the punishment. Oz locks himself in the cage. The others split into teams to track leads.

At 33 minutes in Buffy and Willow find Debbie in the girls' locker room. Debbie is putting makeup over her black eye.

Buffy: You know what works for that? Don't get hit.

Buffy then asks her what's going on because she bets Debbie knows. Debbie claims she doesn't. And Buffy says normally if she wants to keep a secret that's fine but people are dying. Debbie tells them it's not Pete's fault, it's hers. Pete's not himself. He does what he does because he loves her too much. Willow points out that Platt and Jeff were killed by an animal.

Buffy (to Debbie): Pete's not like other guys, is he, Debbie?

The scene cuts to Angel, who's also not like other guys. He struggles with his chains, which are hooked to the ceiling. A link breaks. He still wears the handcuffs with a chain attached between them. He runs.

Back in the locker room, Buffy asks Debbie where Pete is. When Debbie claims not to know Buffy tells her she's lying.

Debbie: What if I am? What are you going to do about it?
Willow: Wrong question.

Buffy grabs Debbie and pulls her over in front of the mirror.

In the mirror, they all see Debbie's black eye clearly. Buffy tells her anyone who really loved her couldn't do this to her. Using the mirror makes it clear, if we didn't get it already, that Buffy's also talking to herself. This refers to the past when Angelus killed people and Buffy couldn't bring herself to kill him. Buffy's also likely troubled by keeping Angel's return a secret, as she told Debbie keeping a secret's not okay when people are dying, but she told Platt she couldn't talk to her friends because she's afraid of what they'll do.

Now Debbie echoes Buffy's fears by asking if they'll take Pete away someplace. She could never do that to him. She's everything to him.

Buffy: While you two live out your Grimm fairy tale, two people are dead. Who's going to be next?

Pete goes to the library to confront Oz, who's in the cage. Pete accuses him of putting the moves on Debbie.

Oz: We talked, yeah, but it was move free.

He starts to warn Pete about the danger he poses when the sun sets.

Pete: You won't be alive to see it.

Oz: I'm serious. Something's going to happen that you probably won't believe. (Pete begins changing.) Or you might.

And we cut to a commercial. On return, Pete yanks Oz out of the cage and throws him on the floor. In the locker room, Debbie sits on a bench.

Debbie (chanting): He does love me. He does love me.

Buffy says it's useless, she has to go find Pete.

Willow: I think we broke her.

Buffy: I think she was broken before this.

Back at the library, Pete beats up Oz, but now the sun is down and the moon has risen.

Oz: Time's up. Rules change.

Which leads into the Climax.

Troubling Metaphor And Theme

The exchange at the mirror between Debbie and Buffy shows the challenge metaphors can pose. Buffy almost seems to blame Debbie for Pete's behavior, or at least for allowing it to continue, which is close to the way Pete blames her. It's different in that Buffy's trying to get information about where Pete is to stop him. But on first watch especially, it felt more like pointing a finger at Debbie. Willow's line ("Wrong question.") suggests Buffy might use violence against Debbie, the victim of violence, which adds to that impression.

Buffy doesn't, and the comment was probably there to add suspense. But because Pete abuses Debbie, anything hinting Buffy might be violent with her feels far outside both Buffy's character and the tone of the show.

Buffy's lack of empathy when she says Debbie was already broken is striking, too. In previous episodes, Buffy's power often was not only her physical strength but her ability to understand and empathize as another human being. That's missing here, probably because Buffy is being hard on herself over her continued love for Angel. But it adds to the challenge of the metaphor.

When I was in law school, we talked about how at the time there was a "battered woman syndrome" but not a "battering man syndrome," identifying the problem as a woman "allowing" herself to be battered. This episode evokes that same idea. It may be that this framing was so ingrained in the public's mind that it crept into the story without the writers realizing it. Or they were so intent on the parallels to Buffy and Angel in particular that they didn't pause to consider that both stories seem to say that what needs to be fixed is women or any victim of abuse rather than the anger issues and actions of batterers.

The Climax

The Climax of this episode is fairly long. There's a lot that needs to play out. Remember, in the Climax, the opposing forces engage in their final confrontation. Because of that, you could see the Climax here as starting later, as I'll note in a moment. But because the Oz as a werewolf plot and the beast plot are intertwined and both feel important to the audience, I think the Climax covers the resolution of both. Which means it starts at 36 minutes, 50 seconds, when Oz changes into the werewolf and he and Pete fight.

Buffy hears it and runs for the library. The others run there as well, including Debbie. When Buffy grabs the tranquilizer gun and shoots, Debbie pushes her and the shot goes into Giles.

Giles: Bloody priceless.

Giles falls on the floor. Buffy gives Faith the gun and tells her to chase Oz, who's run off. Buffy chases Pete. He escapes and, still as a beast, goes to that hidden room. Debbie's there, too, and she runs to him and hugs him, asking if he's all right. She points out that she stopped Buffy from shooting him and tells him he has to leave because Buffy knows. Pete asks how she found out. Did Debbie run her mouth and tell her? Debbie insists Buffy just knew, but Pete blames her. He tells her she's a waste of space and punches her.

At about 39 minutes, Buffy finds the room and Debbie's dead body on the floor. Pete attacks her from behind. That moment could be seen as the start of the Climax because now Buffy and Pete confront each other. Oz fighting Pete likely weakened Pete, though, and Oz is an ally of Buffy's, another reason to see this scene as part of resolving the main plot.

The scene cuts to Oz. As a werewolf, he chases Willow, who yells for Faith to get the gun. Faith does and shoots the werewolf. He falls to the floor.

As Pete and Buffy fight he yells at her, saying things like, "You're all the same." He throws her on the floor. She's about to get up when Angel bursts in. He vamps out as he and Pete fight. We see them face-to-face, both faces distorted. Finally, from behind, Angel throws that chain that's still between his handcuffs around Pete's neck and chokes him to death. Pete falls to the ground.

Normally it wouldn't be satisfying for someone other than Buffy to win the fight for her. But it works here. First, because it starts to resolve the plot about Angel's return. But it means, too, that (as in previous seasons) Buffy does not kill a human being. She probably would have tried to incapacitate Pete, but Angel kills him. Before that, Oz fought him as the werewolf. Oz's and Angel's roles meant Buffy spent relatively little time fighting someone who is human, though enhanced.

Falling Action Ending With Voiceover

Now we shift to the Falling Action to tie up loose ends and resolve subplots. This next scene, though, can be seen as part of the Climax if Buffy's struggle over what to do about Angel's return is the main plot.

At 40 minutes, 36 seconds, Angel, still in vamp face, inches toward Buffy. For a moment it looks like he might attack. But as he gazes at her his face changes back to human. He says her name, falls to his knees, wraps his arm around her legs, and presses his face against them. Buffy's mouth drops open when he says her name, and her eyes are wide. We know she can't believe he recognizes her. As he clings to her and repeats her name, one tear runs down her face.

The scene changes to our friends walking through the courtyard in the sun the next day. They talk about rumors about Pete, including that he had eight iced mochas and lost it or that he took all his mother's birth control pills and went crazy.

I'm sure it is no accident that in this episode about this guy deliberately turning himself into a monster, someone's theory is that it was too much estrogen. That suggests the writers didn't buy into the battered woman rather than battering man syndrome viewpoint. Instead, perhaps they were trying to make a point with the overall story that didn't come through to me. Or they unintentionally ended with mixed messages.

Willow shares the true story. "Mr. Science" did a Jekyll and Hyde to try and become super macho because he was afraid Debbie might leave him. Eventually he didn't need the formula to become a beast.

Cordelia: So it was a real killing. He wasn't under the influence of anything?
Buffy. Just himself.

One loose end not tied up is who the police think killed Pete. When Buffy found Kendra, they assumed she was the murderer. Now if they know she found Debbie and Pete, they'd likely suspect her, but there's no hint of that. It seems obvious Debbie didn't strangle Pete. Because the story hits so many emotions, though, I don't think I noticed any of that until I rewatched the episode for the podcast.

Buffy joins Scott, who is sitting alone. He tells her he was friends with Pete and Debbie since before they all started school. He says he guesses you never really know what's going on inside somebody else. Buffy just looks sad. While we don't know what will happen with Buffy and Scott, this exchange suggests there might not be a bright future.

The scene fades to the woods. In voiceover, Buffy again reads from *The Call Of The Wild* as the scene shifts to Angel sleeping on the floor. He's twitching and flinching in his sleep. Buffy sits in the moonlight watching him as the voiceover continues.

Buffy: And the strain of the primitive remained alive and active....He retained his wildness and wiliness. And from the depths of the forest, the call still sounded.

We end with a closeup on Buffy's face.

Buffy's voice reading the same book but now showing Angel rather than the POV of an unknown beast bookends the episode. The audience returns to the themes of wilderness and the nature of humans and monsters. Buffy's expression shows us how troubled she is that Angel won't be able to return to himself. And his primitive or wild nature will always remain and pose a danger.

Using bookends can help emphasize a theme, deepen emotional impact, and bring the story to a close in a way that satisfies the audience. Here, it does all three.

The Cost When Characters Get What They Want

This episode shows the power of giving a character (here, Buffy) what she wants most, but at the worst possible time or in a terrible way, something we'll see again in *Homecoming*. It also happened in *Becoming Part Two*. Angel regained his soul, but only after Buffy resigned herself to losing him for good. She got what she had longed for, and it made it far harder for Buffy to kill him.

Here, Buffy gets Angel back when she's finally ready to let go. And his return itself feels awful because he's feral and violent.

There is some hope in that the answer to what kind of monster Angel is appears to be that he's the type that can be redeemed. Though still wild and dangerous, he protected Buffy, he didn't harm her, and he became more like himself again. But along with the abuse parallels, his actions raise concerns about Buffy for the season. In that sense, the episode does a great job of resolving all the storylines while leaving key story questions open.

Spoilers And Foreshadowing

Love And Loss, Faith And Buffy

The line about love becoming your master and you're its dog could be a theme for all of Season Three. In the next episodes, because she loves him, Buffy hides from her friends and Giles that Angel's alive, causing great strife. She later tries to kill Faith to save Angel. Faith loves the Mayor as a father figure, which factors into so many choices she makes that are self-destructive.

Buffy confiding in Platt that she can't tell her friends about Angel because she's afraid of what they'll do foreshadows the way this fear drives her behavior through the next few episodes. Her choice to hide the truth about Angel because of it reverberates through her relationships, especially with Giles and Faith.

Before rewatching the episode for the podcast, I forgot how well Faith and Buffy clicked early in the season. When they're patrolling, Buffy shares how she feels about Scott. When Scott breaks up with her Faith will be outraged for Buffy. This building closeness sets up why it matters so much to Buffy to keep trying to get through to Faith. And it sets up Faith's hurt and anger when Buffy doesn't tell her about Angel.

When Scott says you never know what's going on inside someone, it's ironic because he has no idea what's going on in Buffy's mind at that moment. But his comment foreshadows Buffy's cluelessness about his thoughts and feelings. In *Homecoming*, he'll blindside her by breaking up with her.

Oz's Inner Wolf

One of the podcast patrons shared that this episode was the first *Buffy* episode he watched, and he thought the whole series was about Willow and Oz. That makes sense. There's a lot of screen time here for the couple. And the episode raises many story questions about Oz and Willow and seeds future events.

The way Oz withdraws from Willow when he thinks he might be a killer foreshadows Season Four, when Oz realizes he can't control the wolf. He doesn't tell Willow what's happening and he decides to leave without talking to her until his mind is made up. On first watch, I was shocked when Oz did that. But on rewatch I saw how *Beauty And The Beasts* sets that up. Oz deals with almost everything so well, but the wolf is the exception. It's as if he needs to push Willow away to manage his feelings and make a decision.

Questions For Your Writing

- If your novel includes multiple storylines, is it clear which one is the main plot?
- Have you used metaphors, intentionally or unintentionally? If so, are you happy with how those metaphors play out?
- Is the point of view for each of your scenes clear? If you chose to leave a scene ambiguous, does that choice make sense once you reach the end of the story?
- What does your protagonist want most? How could getting that make their life harder or cause emotional pain? Ask the same question about your antagonist or any other key character.

- Have you considered using bookends? What character moment, scene, action, or narration might work? How could it enhance the effect of your story?

The next chapter talks about *Homecoming,* where Buffy runs for Homecoming Queen against Cordelia and Mr. Trick hosts Slayerfest '98.

CHAPTER 5
HOMECOMING S3 E5

THIS CHAPTER TALKS ABOUT *HOMECOMING*, Season Three, Episode Five, where Buffy and Cordelia, both running for Homecoming Queen, become unwilling contestants in Slayerfest '98. Written and directed by David Greenwalt. Original air date: November 3, 1998.

Along with the episode breakdown, topics include:

- Ratcheting up tension through unspoken conflicts
- What makes a strong antagonist: comparing Mr. Trick, Spike, and The Master
- Giving a character what they want most at the worst possible moment
- Propelling a story with interweaving plots and subplots
- Story questions that keep viewers coming back
- The pluses of bringing back a side character

Okay, let's dive into the Hellmouth.

Opening And Unspoken Conflicts

In the opening conflict, which is there to quickly draw viewers into the story, Buffy sits at a table at the Bronze with Willow, Xander, Cordelia, and Oz. Xander suggests taking a bus to the Homecoming dance instead of a limo. Oz offers his van if cost is an issue. Cordelia, though, rejects that idea because the Homecoming Queen doesn't go to the dance in a van. Xander points out she's not elected yet, but quickly adds that she definitely will be.

The underlying economic differences add tension to this scene. We saw these differences when Cordelia talked about her luxury family vacations at the beginning of Season Two while Xander and Willow wandered through the graveyard playing word games for summer fun. Now Xander doesn't say he doesn't have money for a limo, but he tries to persuade everyone to go in a less expensive way. Oz is sensitive to that. Cordelia's oblivious. This exchange is a great example of creating characters with different circumstances they never directly state, but that increase conflict.

Now there's a second conflict. Willow likes the idea of a limo and says if they all split it, the cost won't be too bad. Buffy admits she's not sure she's going. Willow asks why she wouldn't since she has tickets. Unless she doesn't have a — and she changes "date" to "day" as Scott joins them. Willow then says they should take a day or two to think about it.

Cordelia dives right in to ask what's going on. Did Scott not ask Buffy to the dance? Buffy thanks her, saying humiliation is really her color. Scott awkwardly tells Buffy he assumed she'd think it was corny, but if she wants to go, he's in. Buffy's in if he wants to. He responds in kind, and Oz helpfully cuts off the awkward conversation.

Oz: The judges will accept that as a yes.

The interplay with Cordelia is another great example of a

character whose nature forces conflict into the open. Because Cordelia observes what's going on and says what she thinks, she pushes other characters to deal with their issues. This type of character is ideal to include if your other characters tend to keep their feelings to themselves or avoid conflict. A Cordelia-like character can also say things you want your audience to hear but that other characters are too polite to put on the table.

Scott offers to get Buffy another drink. She declines. She's a little tired and is calling it a night. But she kisses him and says she's looking forward to the dance.

The next scene escalates the tension further. Angel paces in front of a roaring fire. He's breathing hard and appears distressed. He hears someone coming and yanks the curtains over the doorway apart, seeming ready to attack. It's Buffy. He backs off.

Buffy brought him a paper bag with a container of blood. The way he holds it and inhales the scent as he turns away from her tells us how much he needs to drink it, though he doesn't say so. He sets the bag aside. When Buffy asks how he is, he says he's in pain, but it's less. His tone isn't convincing.

Buffy tells him she hasn't told Giles or anyone that he's back.

Angel: Giles.

His expression and tone tell us he's thinking about the last time he saw Giles and tortured him. Buffy goes on to explain that she's not telling anyone because they won't understand that he's better. She'll keep helping him get better, but everything's different now. She's a senior. She's thinking about college, and she's involved with someone. Angel draws in a quick breath, spins around, but holds himself steady.

Buffy says the guy she's seeing is a nice, solid guy who makes her happy and that's what she needs. Someone she can count on.

Of course, because this is how the Buffyverse works, we cut

to Scott breaking up with Buffy the next day at school. Buffy asks if she missed something. Scott says before they started seeing each other Buffy seemed full of life, like a force of nature. Now she just seems distracted. Buffy tells him she knows, but she's getting better. He'll see a "drastic distraction reduction" from now on, and she jokes about trying to say that ten times fast. But Scott doesn't want to keep trying.

A Story Spark From Scott

Scott walks off, leaving Buffy standing alone at nearly 10% through the episode. That's where most stories include a Story Spark that sets the main plot rolling. For Buffy's emotional arc, Scott breaking up with her is it. That drives her throughout this episode.

While when I first watched Season Three, I felt as blindsided as Buffy, when I rewatched I saw more of what Scott is saying. Buffy gave mixed messages when he asked her out, but she was always on her way somewhere, presumably about to do something exciting and important. Then after Angel comes back, Buffy doesn't talk much with Scott and tells him she's either not feeling well or tired. Those clues don't make me feel Scott's a good guy. If you're seeing someone and they seem unhappy or upset, rather than break up you might ask if you can help.

But the writers did a great job of weaving in hints that Scott might not think things were going so well, but not so many that it ruins the shock of the break up.

At 4 minutes, 51 seconds, a little past the 10% mark in the episode, there's a Story Spark in the action plot. We see a view of Buffy, alone, from a distance through binoculars. The scene switches to a parked van. Two somewhat ominous looking guys, twins, who look a little bit like young Arnold Schwartzeneggers, watch TV monitors showing Buffy. Their equipment is linked to Mr. Trick's lair. There, an older man in a wheelchair oversees all of it. He's never named, so I'll call him the Commander because he runs the show with these two guys. Mr. Trick sees Buffy on screen and says she's the target. And we cut to credits.

A Layered Villain

On return, a thin, nervous-looking guy, Allan Finch, goes into the mayor's office at City Hall. He's sorry to bother the mayor, but he shows him photos of those twins. They're wanted for capital murder and terrorism and were spotted in town. The mayor, though, is a bit distracted by smelling the paper. He tells Allan to hold out his hands, which Allan very tentatively does, as if he thinks the mayor is going to chop them off. Mayor Wilkins tells Allan he needs to clean under his fingernails. That's where the germs live.

(In an interview, one of the writers commented on having fun creating a villain who is super powerful, but fears germs.)

The mayor tells Allan to put the twins under surveillance, and he wants to know if any other colorful characters come into town.

At school, yearbook photos are being taken. Cordelia checks the competition for Homecoming Queen, cataloguing each girl's faults. Buffy is missing out on the photo shoot. Cordelia volunteers to go remind her.

Buffy's in the library training with Faith. Buffy punches hard, and Faith tells her guys should break up with her more often. She also tells her Scott was a jerk and suggests since Buffy already has the tickets, they can go to the dance together. They'll pick up some studs, use them, and discard them. Buffy agrees, except maybe on the using the studs part, though she says that might be fun.

The One-Quarter Twist

The episode is nearing 25%, where we often see the first major plot turn. It should come from outside the protagonist and spin the story in a new direction, and a few moments here fit the bill.

At about 10 minutes, 15 seconds, Cordelia, distracted by trying to get more votes, veers away from the library to talk to some students. This spins the story because Buffy then misses the photos. Her feelings about missing them set off a chain that eventually leads to her and Cordelia in the cross hairs of vampires and demons.

In the next scene, in the school's courtyard Buffy asks the teacher of her favorite class —the class that changed her life — for a recommendation. (I love the title of the class, which I have to think the writers made up as their dream class: Contemporary American Heroes From Amelia Earhart To Maya Angelou.) But the teacher doesn't remember Buffy, no matter how much Buffy tries to spark her memory, and finally asks if she was absent a lot.

At lunch, while Cordelia campaigns, Buffy tells her friends about the teacher and says she feels like a non-person. At her old school, she was the prom princess and a cheerleader, and "the yearbook was like the story of me." Now she'll just be one tiny photo. Xander tells her she won't even be that. The photos were taken yesterday — didn't Cordelia tell her?

At about 12 minutes, Buffy confronts Cordelia, who genuinely doesn't see why it's a big deal. Buffy tips over the edge and says Cordelia could have thought of someone else just once. Cordelia says Buffy knows nothing about Cordelia's life or how to campaign for Homecoming Queen.

Cordelia: Just because you were Guacamole Queen when you were three...

Cordelia goes on to say campaigning involves being part of

the school and having actual friends. She says she'd like to see Buffy try to win. Buffy tells her she has no idea who she's dealing with.

Buffy: I'm not talking about the Slayer. I'm talking about Buffy. You've awakened the Prom Queen within. And that crown is going to be mine.

Buffy's choice also turns the story. But it's more of a reaction to her feelings about being forgotten. So Cordelia failing to tell her about the photos is the first major turn. The scene cuts to Mr. Trick instructing a group of demons and vampires.

Mr. Trick: Competition. Competition is a beautiful thing. It makes us strive. It... makes us accomplish. Occasionally, it makes us kill. We all have the desire to win. Whether we're human...vampire...and whatever the hell you are, my brother. You got them spiny-looking head things. I ain't never seen that before.

Trick's words link the two storylines. Buffy will be competing with Cordelia, which brings Cordelia into the competition between the vampires and demons.

The vampire team is Lyle Gorch and his wife. Lyle is from *Bad Eggs* in Season One. Buffy killed his brother. Using a side character from earlier in the series makes it easier for long-time viewers to remember who's who. And easier for the writers because it's one less character they need to create from scratch.

Mr. Trick, as we saw in *Faith, Hope & Trick*, is the big picture guy, very enterprising. He's running this competition for the money, though I'm sure he wants to kill the Slayers. He tells the competitors the first target is Buffy, whom they know a lot about. Faith is more elusive, but both will be together and ready for the killing at one particular time.

Mr. Trick: Ladies, gentlemen, spiny-headed looking creatures[1], welcome to SlayerFest '98!

Trick says this line at 14 minutes in. But while a bit late, this could also be the One-Quarter Twist. It sets in motion the actual competition, turning the story to whether Buffy and Faith will survive.

Spike, Trick, And On Being An Antagonist

Mr. Trick, as I talked about in an earlier chapter, is similar to Spike from Seasons One and Two. But Trick doesn't engage me the way Spike did. Though Trick runs the show, he does it from behind the scenes. He doesn't confront Buffy directly. Spike, on the other hand, has a love of the battle. And he admires Buffy for her fighting and strategy skills. When he couldn't fight because he was injured and in a wheelchair, Spike longed to be on the front lines, to dive into the action.

The Master in Season One acted behind the scenes, too, much like Trick does. But The Master's whole goal was to get out and take over the world. And he fought Buffy directly more than once in her real life as well as in her dreams. Here, we don't know Mr. Trick's main goal beyond earning a profit. If we did, I'd find him more intriguing.

Giving Willow What She Most Wants

In her bedroom, Willow tries on different outfits behind a room dividing screen. She wants Xander to tell her which one looks most likely to drive Oz wild. Xander struggles to tie the tie for his borrowed tux, which he looks great in, as they talk.

Xander tells Willow the first couple dresses are nice, but he doesn't seem wowed. She helps him with his tie. They reminisce about their eighth-grade cotillion and joke that when they're old, they'll be in neighboring rest home rooms. It's a quick, fun way to show their history to new viewers and remind ongoing viewers about it. Xander sort of jokingly asks how far Willow and Oz have gone. She says it's none of his business and, while she's behind the screen changing again, asks about Cordelia.

Willow emerges wearing a beautiful black formal dress that flatters her as Xander says that a gentlemen never tells.

Willow: Oh yeah. Since when did you become a — (gets a good look at him with his tux and tie on) — gentleman. (looks down at her dress) Ah, I know, nice.

Xander: I was going to go with gorgeous.

They walk toward each other. Xander tells her Oz is a lucky guy. She says Cordelia's lucky "in a girl way." Willow suddenly worries she can't dance in this dress, likely because the skirt is somewhat narrow and long. Xander suggests they dance now for practice. Which is a bad idea, or a very good one. As they dance, there's tons of chemistry. They move closer and closer and kiss for a few minutes. Then they panic and break apart.

Xander: That didn't just happen.

Willow: No. I mean, it did, but it didn't.

Xander: Because I respect you. And Oz. And I would never —

Willow: I would never, either! It — it must be the clothes. It — it's a fluke.

Xander: It's a clothes fluke, that's what it is. And there'll be no more fluking.

Willow: Not ever.

Xander: We gotta get out of these clothes.

Willow: Right now. Oh, I didn't mean...

Xander: I didn't...me, either!

Willow waves her hands, like she's grossed out and they both bolt away from each other.

This subplot is another example of the series giving a character what she wants, but at the worst possible time. Willow pined after Xander forever, but he never saw her in a romantic light. Now he's attracted to her, but it's when she's with Oz. And, more specifically, when she's happy with Oz.

The shift is believable because we see how grown up both of them look in their formal clothes and how surprised they each are by the other. And there is some foreshadowing of this change. Xander's not only protective of Willow, he jokingly expresses some jealousy of Oz at times. Seeing Xander in the best light, perhaps Oz appreciating how attractive Willow is made Xander see it, too. In the worst light, now that Xander believes he can't have Willow, he wants her.

Most likely both those things are true, which is part of why *Buffy* characters are so fascinating.

Midpoint Reversal, Commitment, And Montage

Buffy stands in the library in front of a whiteboard with photos of her competition. Willow, Oz, and Xander listen as she talks about strategy and how a campaign is like war. She thinks they'll get the fringe musicians, who normally don't vote, because of Oz. Willow can help her with a database. Buffy concedes this is different from all the popularity contests she won in the past because she's not actually popular.

At about 19 minutes, Cordelia walks in. Buffy gives a sort of apology but says there's no reason they can't be friends. Cordelia agrees and turns to ask Willow how the database is coming. Then she looks at Xander, who says he's got her flyers.

Xander (to Buffy on the way out): She's my girlfriend.
Willow: It's just that she needs it so much more than you.
Oz: As Willow goes, so goes my nation.

After they leave, Giles joins Buffy and says it seems like a lot of stress for a little title. Buffy tells him it's just for fun, but she squeezes the glass bottle she's holding so tight it breaks.

The story is nearing the Midpoint, where we usually see a strong commitment by the protagonist, who throws caution to the wind, or a major reversal. Or both. The previous scene, though a bit early, is a major reversal. Buffy's closest friends let her down.

Now Buffy commits all out to winning, shown in a fun montage of her campaigning. The scenes cut between her and the competitors training to kill the Slayers. Montages, like dreams, can be tricky for storytelling. This one works well because it advances the plot and illustrates more about the characters. The spiny creature flips his arms and spiny weapons come out that he shoots across the room. The Gorches make out on the couch. Buffy, at school, covers a Cordelia poster with one of her own. There are many shots showing how hard everyone is working.

In the next scene, at about 21 minutes, Buffy pretends to drop her notebook, and Scott Hope picks it up. He tells her he respects her for doing this and she has his vote. She starts to tell him he doesn't have to vote for her but then thanks him. After he leaves, she opens her little notebook and checks off his name. Another guy walks by and she once again drops the book. Buffy also gives out cupcakes, but Cordelia takes them away and hands people baskets of treats instead.

Integrated Action-Based And Emotional Plots

In earlier episodes, including *Faith, Hope & Trick*, I struggled a bit with the action plot not having strong plot turns. Here, too, that's the case. The Midpoint revolves around the queen competition, though there are moments showing Slayerfest training. But those aren't a reversal or a turn for Buffy, partly because the foes already looked formidable. Too, none of them interact with Buffy directly until later in the episode. All the same, the two plotlines, one action and one about Buffy's school experience and emotions, work well here because they're interdependent.

Also, compared to previous episodes, it's clearer that the

main story really is Buffy and Cordelia. That plot reflects Buffy's internal struggle with having lost her identity as the popular girl and prom queen (and now her new boyfriend, too). For that reason, when the emotional plot collides with the Slayerfest plot, it fits, as Buffy's Slayer identity drives her emotional turmoil. Plus, the subplot about Willow and Xander is compelling and well integrated, as we'll see that it affects Buffy directly. At 22 minutes, Buffy approaches Willow and guilts her into letting Buffy look at Cordelia's database.

In another example of intertwining plots, the twins listen and watch through their binoculars. Buffy walks with Jonathan (another recurring side character), who eats a cupcake. She tells him she's always felt they have a special bond. He cuts her off to tell her that Cordelia gave him $6, which can buy a whole lot of cupcakes (which I guess it could in the late nineties, even the giant kind Buffy gave him).

Buffy confronts Cordelia about literally buying votes. Cordelia asks if it's any more tacky than Buffy's faux "I'm shy, but deep" campaign. Buffy says it is, and Cordelia tells her this whole "trying to be like me thing" isn't funny anymore.

Buffy: I was never trying to be like you. And when was it funny?

Their feud escalates. Cordelia disparages Buffy's past, making clear she doesn't believe Buffy was ever popular. Buffy calls Cordelia shallow and mean. Cordelia says at least she has two parents, unlike some people. Xander tries to stop them before they say anything they'll regret. But Cordelia calls Buffy a crazy freak, and Buffy calls her a vapid whore. Xander pulls Cordelia away. Willow looks stricken.

Willow (to Buffy): This is just —

Willow (in new scene to Xander): — the worst thing that's ever happened. Ever. We have to do something.

Xander and Willow sit side-by-side on the edge of Willow's bed. Xander agrees, but says when he looks at her now, it's like he's seeing her for the first time. Willow tells him she means Buffy and Cordelia. Xander switches gears and agrees. Except he's not clear how that's his and Willow's fault.

Willow says they both felt so guilty about the fluke that they overcompensated. Xander understands what she's saying, but he is in hell. He thought being a senior and having a girlfriend at last would be a good thing. But Willow's distracted and comments on the way his mouth moves when he's upset, and she asks what they're going to do.

Xander: We just have to get the two of them communicating.
Willow: I'm talking about us.

In the next scene, the friends attempt to get Buffy and Cordelia communicating. At 26 minutes, 49 seconds, Buffy gets into the limo and finds Cordelia, not Faith, in the back seat. Cordelia hands her a note from their friends telling them to work out their issues because friendship is more important than who wins. And I love the PS.

Note: The limo was not cheap, work it out.

Cordelia already took the orchid corsage, and she and Buffy bicker about that. That minor conflict highlights a clue for later, as it will turn out the friends didn't buy corsages.

Slayerfest Three-Quarter Turn

At 27 minutes, the driver pulls over and runs away in the woods. Buffy and Cordelia get out and find a TV and a VCR with a note to watch. This next moment serves as the Three-Quarter Turn, the major plot turn that grows from the Midpoint, takes the story in yet another new direction, and sometimes raises the stakes. It's a bit early, as often it occurs right at 75% through, especially in a novel.

On the TV screen, Mr. Trick says this is Slayerfest '98, and they have thirty seconds to run for their lives. He ends by telling Buffy and Faith to have a nice day.

Cordelia: Hello, how stupid are you people? She's a Slayer. I'm a Homecoming Queen.

At 28 minutes, there's an explosion. Buffy and Cordelia run, and we cut to a commercial.

On return, Oz's band plays at the dance. Willow and Xander watch the crowd, their shoulders slumping. Faith asks what they're so mopey about. Xander denies being mopey. They're enjoying Oz's band. He adds that Oz is a great guy. Willow, staring at the floor, says Oz wrote this song for her.

In the woods, Cordelia helps Buffy avoid a trap. Buffy turns and throws the trap at a guy with an assault weapon. She threatens him into telling them who all the competitors are. He shares that the twins are tracking everyone electronically. Cordelia wants the guy to do her an eensy favor, but before she can ask him to explain to the others that she's not a Slayer, someone else shoots at them. Buffy and Cordelia run again.

Back at the dance, Faith sees Scott slow dancing with another girl. She cuts in to tell him "Good news, honey," she went to the doctor and the itching and burning should clear up soon. But they have to keep using the ointment. Then she says a cheery Hi to the girl, who is not happy. (Yay, Faith.) At 30 minutes, Giles tells Willow and Xander they did a fine thing helping Buffy and Cordelia work things out. He's heading to the library. Willow and Xander sit together, but facing opposite directions and slumping again.

Willow (looking at the floor): We did one fine thing.

Cordelia and Buffy shelter in a cabin. Buffy tells Cordelia to find a weapon. Cordelia's panicking like we've never seen her panic except maybe when she was trapped in the basement and the worm monster was upstairs. She says she's going to die, and she'll never be Homecoming Queen or finish high school, or know if it's real between her and Xander or temporary insanity that made her think she loves him. And now she'll never get a chance to tell him.

Xander Getting What He Wants

Buffy tells her they will get out. They'll go to the library for weapons and take out all the competitors one by one. All in time for Cordelia to congratulate her on her sweeping victory as Homecoming Queen. Cordelia says she knows what Buffy's doing. Trying to get her angry so she won't be so scared. And it's working. As she hunts for a weapon, Buffy asks if she really loves Xander.

Cordelia: Well, he kind of grows on you. Like a Chia Pet.

This is another example of giving a character what he wants. Xander did that love spell in Season Two because he wanted Cordelia to love him. Granted, it was with bad motives, but he did want that. And as he said before, he wanted a girlfriend. Now he has Cordelia, a beautiful, popular girl who tells Buffy she thinks she loves him. And though she doesn't know it, Xander betrayed her. So this will only make everything harder for her and for him.

Cordelia finds a spatula, which doesn't impress Buffy with its potential as a weapon. Cordelia says that's all she found other than a telephone.

Buffy: You didn't think a telephone would be helpful?

They call Giles and get the answering machine because he hasn't made it to the library yet. As Buffy talks, the line goes dead. She realizes the competitors must be tracking her and Cordelia. In the woods, the spiny headed guy offers to help the guy in the trap by cutting his leg off.

At about 33 minutes, 12 seconds, the plot turns in another new direction for Buffy and Cordelia. This could also be that Three-Quarter Turn, as it grows from the Midpoint where Buffy committed to winning and beating Cordelia. Cordelia asks why it always ends in violence and terror when she's with Buffy.

Buffy: Welcome to my life.

Cordelia says all she wanted was to be Homecoming Queen, not be in Buffy's life. And she doesn't get why Buffy cares about Homecoming Queen when she is so strong and can fight demons. Cordelia was a little vulnerable when sharing her feelings earlier. Now Buffy is vulnerable with Cordelia, and Cordelia listens. Buffy says because this is all her life is. She wanted to pick up a yearbook down the road and say she was there. She had friends.

Buffy: And for one moment, I got to live in the world and there'd be proof. Proof that I was chosen for something other than this. (She cocks her gun.) Besides, I look cute in a tiara.

The spiny guy breaks in. All three fight as the twins approach outside. Cordelia throws the gun to Buffy. It's a good throw, but the twins' grenade lands inside. Buffy and Cordelia dive out a window just in time. The spiny looking guy tries to do the same but doesn't make it and gets blown up.

At the library, Lyle Gorch's wife wants to kill Buffy as a wedding present to make up for Lyle's brother — a fun direct reference to *Bad Eggs*. He tells her the Slayer will be there as soon as she gets rid of some of their competition. After all, they've got her Watcher. Poor Giles is lying on the floor, knocked out again.

The Commander and Mr. Trick, in the lair, are surprised Buffy and the girl they think is Faith have gotten away so far.

Mr. Trick: Give it up for the Slayers. They've got character.

He answers a knock on the door. It's two cops, who drag him away.

Buffy and Cordelia reach the library and see the Gorches. Buffy kills the wife with a stake Cordelia throws her. But the wife manages to throw a punch before she dusts and it knocks

Buffy out. Lyle charges at Cordelia, sputtering about what he's going to do to her. Cordelia straightens up, acting completely unaffected.

Cordelia: You'll what? Rip out my innards, play with my entrails....I took out four of your cronies, not to mention your girlfriend.

Lyle: Wife.

Cordelia: Whatever.

She tells him in the end, Buffy is just the runner up. Cordelia's the queen, and what does he think she's going to do to him? Reminiscent of *Bad Eggs*, Lyle says, "Later," tips his hat, and runs away. This resolution shows the value of using a minor side character again, as his actions fit him perfectly. At 38 minutes, Buffy wakes up.

Buffy: That should teach them to mistake you for a Slayer.

Giles feels bad because he encouraged the limousine switch. But Buffy says it's all right. She and Cordelia spent some quality death time and got corsages. Giles says no one mentioned corsages, and they realize that's how they are being tracked. Buffy asks for some wet toilet paper.

In some ways, the scene served as a climax for the Buffy and Cordelia relationship subplot. They not only set aside their hostility, Cordelia showed her value as a faux Slayer, which leads Buffy to respect her more.

The Climax

At 38 minutes, 40 seconds, the Climax for the main plot begins. This is the final confrontation between our opposing forces — Buffy and the Slayerfest competitors. (Or Mr. Trick, since he's running the show.) This Climax has always felt a bit anti-climactic, maybe because the Buffy and Cordelia part of the story is more compelling. We care about those two characters and don't care about the competitors. Or Mr. Trick.

Also, the last competitors are disposed of pretty quickly. The twins break into the school. They're being fed electronic data on the locations of the two Slayers. Guns out, they separate and search. Buffy hides in a crucial spot. At a key moment she throws a wad of wet toilet paper with an electronic bug on it onto one of the twin's backs. Though we don't see it, either Cordelia or Giles does the same to the other twin. The twins, based on the data location, fire through a wall at each other. They kill one another. The Commander at the lair thinks his team won because both Slayers' blips go out.

Falling Action And Story Questions

In the Falling Action, with an ongoing series, writers often not only tie up loose ends but raise story questions to keep the audience coming back. Here, at 40 minutes, 54 seconds, Mr. Trick is in the mayor's office. Mayor Wilkins says Trick's suit is an exciting color. Trick responds that the clothes make the man, but the mayor notes that Trick is not a man.

He tells Mr. Trick he's been mayor for a long time here. He wants things to run smoothly. This is an important year. Mr. Trick guesses it's an election year, and the mayor tells him it's something like that. Trick is not impressed. He says if the mayor's about to tell him that's why his kind isn't welcome in this nice little town, that got old long before he became a vampire.

But that's not what the mayor is saying. In fact, he can use some help dealing with certain rebellious elements. He heard about Slayerfest and thinks it was enterprising. That's what he needs on his team. Trick says what if he doesn't want to be on the team.

Mayor (borderline threatening): Oh, no, that won't be an issue.

It was hinted before that the mayor was on the side of evil. Now that's clearer, and we learn something big is happening for him this year.

The scene to some extent undercuts Mr. Trick as a threat. Until now, I thought he was the season's Big Bad (what the writers call the villain of the season). But now it appears he'll merely — maybe — be part of a team, though Trick doesn't seem that enthused. Overall, though, the scene raises story questions about both Trick and the mayor that leave the audience wondering and wanting more.

At the dance, Willow worries Buffy and Cordelia will miss the Homecoming Queen election results. But they rush in, dresses torn, bare arms dirty and scratched. Willow asks where they were.

Oz: I'm going to go with mud wrestling.

Buffy: Tell you one thing. You don't want to mess with Cordelia.

Xander gulps and agrees. As the announcement begins, Cordelia says to Buffy something like after all they've been through, this whole queen thing seems —

Buffy: Pretty damn important.

Cordelia: Oh, yeah.

It's a first for Sunnydale High. There's a tie. But the two other competitors won. Buffy and Cordelia leave, together, in disgust, ending the episode.

Spoilers And Foreshadowing

This whole episode is an excellent example of how to hint at what's to come without slowing the action.

Angel And Giles

When Angel says "Giles," clearly remembering that he tortured Giles, this foreshadows how sharp Giles is with Buffy, and how disappointed he is in her, when he learns Angel is back. Giles tells her she doesn't respect him or his role as her Watcher. He's angry that he has to remind her that Angel tortured him. That same moment also foreshadows the scene where Angel goes to Giles for help in *Amends*. Visions are haunting Angel and he fears losing his mind. Giles gets a crossbow before letting him in and expresses satisfaction that the visions torment Angel.

Jonathan

To try to get his vote, Buffy tells Jonathan she's always felt a special bond between them. They do have a bond later in this season and the next. She keeps him from killing himself or hurting anyone else when he climbs into the clock tower in *Earshot*. And in Season Four, when Jonathan remakes the world through a spell, being friends with Buffy is part of what he wants. After it all, she still talks to him and offers some advice, and he gives her advice about Riley. In Season Six, Jonathan becomes part of the trio that tries to be Buffy's nemesis. But he is the one of the three who feels the most guilt and regret over it, partly due to Buffy having been there for him.

The Mayor

Finally, the brief exchange about the big year for the mayor hints at his plan to become a demon.

Questions For Your Writing

- Is there a compelling side character you could bring back in a later installment or later in your current story rather than introducing a new character for a walk on or bit part?
- Are there significant differences in backgrounds and experiences that exist between your allied characters that they might not talk about? If not, can you create some? If so, how might those differences cause minor conflicts?
- Are there moments in your story that undermine the strength or power of your antagonist? Was that intentional?
- What is the worst possible moment for one of your characters to have their deepest desire fulfilled?
- Do your subplots affect and propel your main plot and vice versa? Are there key emotional moments from one plot that prompt a character to act differently in an unrelated storyline?
- What story questions can you raise early in your narrative to keep the audience hooked throughout? Can you end many of your chapters (or sections of your screenplay) with a story question?

The next chapter talks about **Band Candy**, one of my favorite episodes. The adults, including Principal Snyder, regress to their teenage years, setting the stage for a demon tribute and allowing Joyce and Giles to spend some quality time together.

CHAPTER 6
BAND CANDY S3 E6

THIS CHAPTER TALKS about *Band Candy*, Season Three, Episode Six, where the adults in Sunnydale become their teenage selves and Buffy must thwart a demon. Written by Jane Espenson and directed by Michael Lange. Original air date: November 10, 1998.

Along with the episode breakdown, topics include:

- **Commenting on social issues in subtle ways**
- **Scene transitions that move viewers through the story**
- **Universal themes about adulthood**
- **Conveying exposition elegantly by using a new character (here, Oz)**
- **Conflict between good characters who care deeply about each other**
- **Double duty dialogue that's fun for fun's sake and advances the plot**

Okay, let's dive into the Hellmouth.

Opening Conflict Commentary, Theme, And Foreshadowing

Here, the opening conflict both draws viewers in and relates to the main plot. In the graveyard, Giles reads to Buffy in a serious tone about a tragic day in history, but then recites multiple choice answers A and B. Before he can read C, Buffy chooses B because they haven't had B in forever. Giles sighs.

Giles: This is the SATs, Buffy, not connect the dots.

He urges her to concentrate, as it's important for getting into college. This exchange is the first of several points about the SATs that lead me to believe that the writers are engaging in subtle commentary, or weaving in a minor theme, because one argument against standardized testing is that what students learn in expensive prep classes gives them an unfair advantage. And some tips include things like Buffy's "we haven't had B in forever" point.

Buffy spots a vampire behind Giles, warns him, then leaps over a tombstone and stakes the vampire. She then says she broke her Number Two pencil so they'll have to stop.

Giles (hands her a pencil): C. All systems tend toward chaos.

Buffy: I just know that us and the undead are the only people working this late.

The chaos line foreshadows the episode. The back-and-forth about the SATs begins a theme of the season about Buffy's impending graduation, adulthood, and what she'll do about college. And all of it is done in such a quick, fun way.

On the undead line the scene cuts to city hall, where at least one undead character, Mr. Trick, is working late. Trick tells the mayor not to worry, he knows a beast who knows a guy who can help with the urgent, delicate matter they're discussing. The mayor questions whether subcontracting is the way to go, but Trick reassures him the guy has worked this town before.

The mayor stresses that he's made deals to get where he is, and this demon requires its tribute. The mayor is quite proud that what separates him from other politicians is that he keeps his campaign promises. As he speaks he opens an antique armoire in his office. He takes a shrunken head from a row of creepy objects and wonders aloud where he put his Scotch.

And we cut to the credits.

At 3 minutes, 16 seconds, Buffy walks with her friends on the school grounds, talking about a dream where she's chased by an improperly filled in answer bubble that says, "None of the Above."

Willow hopes it wasn't a prophecy dream. She also proudly notes that Oz is the highest scoring person on the SAT ever to fail to graduate high school. Xander comments that he hates standardized tests, they discriminate against the uninformed. But Cordelia's looking forward to it because she does well on standardized tests. They all look at her.

Cordelia: What? I can't have layers?

This scene touches on the socioeconomic differences I mentioned in *Homecoming*. While it isn't stated that Cordelia's family sent her to prep classes, we know her family has money and Xander's does not. It's one reason he's uninformed compared to her, though I don't know that the writers purposely wove that in. If they did, though, it's a great example of including a minor theme you feel is important without hammering the audience over the head.

Willow offers to help Buffy study, but Buffy can't tonight. She says she needs to spend some quality Mom time. Both she and Giles have been supervising Buffy 24/7, and Buffy says it's like being in the *Real World* house.

Story Sparks

For Buffy's subplot about her relationship with her mother, her last comment could serve as the Story Spark. It comes about 10% through the episode and sets off a conflict between Buffy, who wants more freedom, and Joyce, who wants to keep an eye on her.

The demon plot, though, begins with a Story Spark or Inciting Incident that's very clear. Inside the school, Principal Snyder hands boxes of candy bars to each student. Xander thanks him, but it's not a gift, it's to sell the candy to pay for band uniforms. That happens at 4 minutes, 41 seconds into a roughly 44-minute episode, so exactly at 10%. Buffy says she loves going all Willy Loman, but they're not in the band.

Snyder: And if I'd handed you a trombone, that would be a problem. It's candy, sell it.

The next scene is in Buffy's kitchen.

Joyce: But you're not in the band.

Buffy: And yet.

Buffy angles for Joyce to buy forty bars. Joyce buys twenty.

Strong Scene Transitions

The scene-to-scene transitions are fantastic. The line about the undead working late transitioned to a scene showing exactly that. Now right after Buffy tells Snyder they're not in the band, Buffy's mother makes that same point.

Transitions like that work well in any type of writing, fiction or non-fiction, as they help draw readers from one scene, chapter, or paragraph to the next. You can pick up a word or phrase and use it again to help the reader follow you easily. In fiction, it helps connect disparate parts of a story early on if the connections aren't yet clear. It also helps readers feel, though they may not realize why, like they are part of a connected, believable universe.

Buffy now pushes her luck. After getting Joyce to buy twenty bars, she wants to know when she can drive. She took all the courses and watched the film strip with the death and destruction. Joyce points out that Buffy failed the written exam and wasn't even allowed to take the road test. Buffy protests that was a year ago. All of which, through minor conflict, fills the audience in on Buffy's backstory around driving.

Joyce says she spends enough time not knowing where Buffy is. She doesn't want Buffy driving off to Chicago. Buffy reminds her mom that she could just take the bus. Joyce gets angry. She wants Buffy there. It's clear how distressed she is. Logically, she knows Buffy can leave any time without driving. But it's just a little too much for Joyce.

Buffy: I'm here. See me here. (Pauses.) I've got to go.

Joyce is not happy. Buffy blames Giles, saying it's a slay and study double feature. Joyce complains that Giles monopolizes her time.

Buffy: And does he ever say he's sorry?

This line serves as another transition. In the next scene, Buffy complains as Giles ties a blindfold around her eyes and he says, "Sorry." He hands her a basketball and tells her being blindfolded is to help her use her other senses so opponents can't sneak up on her.

Buffy's now met her candy bar quota, as Giles bought the twenty candy bars that Joyce didn't. This detail adds another building block in the idea of Giles as Buffy's substitute father.

Giles tells Buffy he'll move away. She needs to count to five then try to hit him with the basketball. She turns in the wrong direction and throws the basketball at the wall opposite Giles. Just as he tells her it's not that simple, the basketball bounces off the wall and hits him on the side of the head. The scene ends with Buffy running out, claiming she can't patrol because her mother wants her home. Giles looks a little suspicious. The two endings nicely bookend the two scenes — one about Buffy's actual parent and one about her substitute parent. Both of whom will join forces shortly.

Internal Conflict For Buffy Over Angel

At the mansion, it's nighttime. Angel practices Tai Chi (of course, with his shirt off) in the dimly-lit courtyard. Buffy's impressed. He tells her he's feeling better, but he stumbles as she helps him inside. Angel asks how she got away so late. She tells him it was easy. She started a fire in the prison laundry and got out in a garbage truck. Angel seems to take this seriously for a second and she tells him she was kidding. She jokes he can smell her —no garbage smell. But that makes her aware they're standing too close. She backs off and sits a few feet away. He asks how Scott is.

    Buffy: Oh, um, boyfriend Scott, actually, he's not, oh, he's fine.
    Angel: You're being careful, right?
    Buffy: With Scott?
    Angel: With slaying.

    Angel tells her he worries about her. She says she worries about him too. He reassures her that he's getting stronger and it'll be better when he doesn't need her. Buffy blinks and agrees, and we can see that this idea disturbs her. Her words and actions show real conflict within Buffy. She doesn't tell him about Scott breaking up with her, suggesting she wants to keep that barrier between her and Angel. But it upsets her when he talks about things being better when he doesn't need her.

The One-Quarter Twist And Conflict With And Without Evil

One reason I love this episode is that of all the Season Three episodes, the plot and subplot are the most interwoven. It keeps the story moving well.

Buffy comes home late and apologizes to Joyce, still claiming Giles, who's "all slay all the time," kept her. But Giles steps out from the living room. He talked to Willow and learned Buffy also lied to her. As Buffy stumbles through an answer, Joyce hands Giles a candy bar. Buffy lets them think she was at the Bronze and tells them they're both treating her like a child. She can't live like this and doesn't need that much supervision. Joyce argues that the last time Buffy made a decision on her own Buffy "split." And she doesn't buy Buffy's argument that she took care of herself all summer. Giles steps in and says, "Let's not freak out."

Buffy: Freak out?

This scene is a great example of a conflict where no one is evil and everyone means well. Joyce isn't trying to punish Buffy for running away. She's afraid of Buffy taking off again, and afraid that once again she doesn't know what's going on in Buffy's life. Giles is likewise concerned.

All these characters care about each other, but are at odds. There's also added external conflict here the audience doesn't grasp yet. As Joyce and Giles eat the candy, they change gradually. Their language — "split" and "freak out" — shows it first.

Buffy goes upstairs. Joyce tells Giles Buffy is driving her crazy. She wants to protect Buffy. And she says at least most parents have some idea what to protect their children from. The two eat more candy and agree they need to be careful about Buffy.

I see the effect of the candy as the One-Quarter Twist. It comes from outside Buffy. It changes the entire direction of the demon tribute story, because this will be what gets all the adults out of the way so the mayor's henchman can act. And it raises the stakes.

The next scene makes the danger from the candy explicit. At 12 minutes, 41 seconds, an assembly line of people pack boxes in a warehouse. Giles's old friend Ethan Rayne, who we saw in *Halloween* and *The Dark Age,* supervises. So he's the outside contractor who worked this town before. A worker starts to eat some candy. Ethan puts a hand on his shoulder and tells him he doesn't want to eat it in a serious voice. This signals the audience the candy matters and it's dangerous.

In the science lab, Cordelia tells Buffy, who sits next to her, she heard there's a secret rule that if a teacher is ten minutes late, the students can leave. Buffy responds that Giles has study hall today, and he's never late. Cordelia goes on about Giles being wound so tight he made her pay a year's late fine on a philosophy book she didn't want to return because it was great for starting conversations with college boys. She says that was pre-Xander.

This exposition stresses Giles's usual character, contrasting how he'll act later. And it makes the next moment more intense because Xander and Willow sit next to each other behind Buffy and Cordelia. They joke about selling candy and their legs and feet, under the table, press together. Cordelia swings around suddenly and says she can't believe this.

Willow and Xander jerk apart, shaking the table. But Cordelia is talking about Giles not showing up. She's bored and wants Giles there to give her credit for it. Buffy looks worried.

Out in the hall, Snyder eats a candy bar and tells a gray-haired teacher, Ms. Barton, that the pinhead librarian didn't show up so she has to cover study hall. Snyder walks off complaining that everyone expects him to do everything just because he's the principal, and it's not fair. Snyder's character is so much fun in this episode. We get a glimpse of who Snyder would like to be, which is so different from this principal who enforces all these rules and expresses no sympathy for anybody. Ms. Barton tells the students that they're all stuck there, but they should pretend to read until old Commandant Snyder is far enough away. Then they'll all leave.

Xander: Does anyone else want to marry Ms. Barton?
Cordelia: Get in line.

At 15 and a half minutes, Buffy cautiously pushes open the door to Giles's apartment, which is unlocked. Giles is there looking through his record albums with Joyce. They tell Buffy they're having a summit meeting of sorts to coordinate a schedule for her. Buffy, not too thrilled about that, says it sounds nice and structured. Joyce tells her there's more work to do, gives her the keys, and suggests she take the car. Giles will drive Joyce home. Buffy's confused. Joyce repeats that Buffy should take the car.

Buffy: You don't have to tell me twice. Well, actually you did. Bye.

She grabs the keys and runs out.

Joyce: Do you think she noticed anything?

Giles lights a cigarette, and Joyce takes out a bottle of whiskey.

In the next scene, Buffy drives Joyce's SUV, taking turns very fast. The tires squeal. Willow, who is riding with her, looks nervous.

Willow: Do you know that you have the parking brake on?

Buffy claims she does, but takes it off. Willow questions whether they should really go to the Bronze with the SATs tomorrow. Buffy says they can study at the Bronze.

Joyce sits cross-legged on the floor. Giles lies on his back on his rug. They share cigarettes. She wants to know how come they call him Ripper.

Giles: Wouldn't you like to know?

Buffy and the Art of Story Season Three Part 1

A sixties song, ***Tales Of Brave Ulysses*** by Cream, plays. They decide to go out for some fun. Giles wears jeans and a white T-shirt and he makes his hair spikier before they leave. Joyce suggests going to the Bronze.

The Adults Change At The Midpoint

Oz's band plays at the Bronze. It is nearly all adults dancing, chugging beers, and yelling out to the musicians. Buffy and Willow are shocked by the scene. Ms. Barton jokes about Willow's name being a tree and asks "Little Tree" if there are any nachos. Snyder puts one arm around Willow and the other around Buffy and tells them to call him Snyder. Just the last name, "like Barbarino," a reference to a student in the seventies TV show ***Welcome Back, Kotter***. The principal in that show was pretty awful to the students in Kotter's class, so it's a fun note that Snyder references it.

We're at the Midpoint of the episode, where typically we see either a major commitment by the protagonist or the protagonist suffers a serious reversal or both. At about 21 minutes, 13 seconds, we start with a reversal, which is more of a doubling down on the chaos. Willow worries the adults will have heart attacks. Buffy says there might be a doctor there. At that moment, a somewhat heavy guy with his shirt off dives off the stage. Willow says that is her doctor, though usually he's a little less shirtless.

Buffy: They're acting like a bunch of us.
Willow: We don't act like this.

Willow has a point in that the behavior is exaggerated for the comedy of it, which can be seen as the effect of the spell. But the scene starts some character growth for Buffy by forcing her to see through her mother's and Giles's eyes the concerns about people acting irresponsible at any age.

The whole scene is a Midpoint Reversal because whatever

danger the candy poses now has a serious effect on adults. This is far beyond Giles and Joyce changing how they express themselves. The doctor dove off the stage, and a fight is about to break out. At the warehouse, Mr. Trick tells Ethan he loves this country.

Mr. Trick: You make a good product and the people will come to you. Of course, a lot of them are going to die. That's the other reason I love this country.

Trick snaps a worker's neck for eating some of the candy. Ethan asks how he knew the guy ate it. Mr. Trick didn't know, but now no one else will. Both agree it's almost feeding time. Back at the Bronze Buffy says something's changing the adults into teenagers.

Oz: Teenagers. That's a sobering mirror to look into.

Snyder tells Oz he has great hair. A bunch of middle-aged guys start singing acapella on the stage.

At 22 minutes, 49 seconds, Buffy doesn't quite make a major commitment, but she commits to uncovering what's going on because this has "Hellmouth fingerprints" all over it. Buffy and friends head outside. Snyder tags along, saying he hopes they aren't trying to ditch him.

Exposition And The New Character

On a Sunnydale street, two middle-aged men in cars next to each other rev their engines, about to drag race. It's a two-lane road, so one car is going the wrong way. In the SUV with Buffy, Oz thinks they ought to find Giles. He'll know what to do. He assumes even if Giles is sixteen, he's probably a pretty together guy.

Willow: Yeah, well...

Oz: What?

Buffy: Giles at sixteen. Less "together guy," more "bad magic, hates the world, ticking time bomb" guy.

This is a great example of using a newer character to add exposition in a natural way. Oz didn't know everyone when the events of **The Dark Age**, where Giles's past came back to haunt him, happened. Buffy needs to explain to him, and to new viewers, why Giles is so different when he reverts to his teenage self. And because the writers are so good at dialogue and conflict, it's all encapsulated in a few quick and funny lines. Oz now thinks Buffy's mother, who is with Giles, might be in a lot of trouble.

Universal Themes

Oz's thought provides another great transition to a scene that shows the opposite, as Joyce looks quite happy strolling with Giles. His arm is around her shoulders. Joyce wears a short skirt and looks a little hippy-like with her long coat. Giles has the whole bad boy look. Joyce tells him it's like she's just waking up. As if getting married and having a kid was just a dream and now things are how they're supposed to be.

This is one of those times when Buffy hits a universal theme. Whether people get married or have kids or not, most adults at some point feel as Joyce does in this moment and wonder how they got where they are. Because life is not smooth. Quite often, we're doing something very different than what we imagined, life is less enjoyable, or we have had to take on responsibilities that make us feel like different people than we thought we'd become. Joyce gets all of that into a couple lines.

Now Joyce sees a coat she likes in a clothing store window. Giles asks if she fancies it. When she says yes (it's "very Juice Newton" — a singer/songwriter popular in the eighties), he puts out his cigarette, breaks the window, and gives her the coat. He takes a hat for himself. Joyce giggles that he was so brave. A Sunnydale cop appears and immediately pulls a gun.

Snyder, in the back of the SUV, wants Buffy to do donuts in the football field. Buffy, though, is on a collision course with one of the drag racers. There's a crash and we cut to commercial.

On return, Giles taunts the cop.

Giles: Ooh, copper's got a gun.

He easily disarms the cop. Joyce says he's so cool, like Burt Reynolds. Giles grabs her and, after she takes out her gum, they kiss on the hood of the Sunnydale patrol car.

The scene fades to Buffy. After that crash, the driver gets out and runs away. It's chaos everywhere, and Buffy comments there are no grownups. No one's protecting the houses. But there are also no vampires.

Buffy: Soup's on, but no one's grabbing a spoon.

They all realize that, in Oz's words, something is happening somewhere that's else. This conflict further forces Buffy to think about the role of grownups. It is a complete flip from when her greatest desire was that Joyce and Giles would pay no attention to what she was doing. Snyder complains about a guy who stole his candy, causing Buffy to connect the adults' behavior to the candy, saying it must be cursed. Snyder looks genuinely shocked and worried, which tells us he wasn't in on the scheme. Buffy demands that he tell her where the candy came from. He says it was through the school board, a rough crowd. But he knows the warehouse where the source is.

Buffy sends Willow and Oz to research and goes to the warehouse with Snyder. Workers throw boxes of candy directly to a crowd. Buffy marches toward the warehouse, but freezes when she sees Giles there making out with Joyce. Now the role reversal becomes explicit. Buffy pulls them apart and asks what's going on. Then she demands to know where Joyce got the coat. Joyce wants more candy. Buffy tells her she doesn't need any more.

Joyce says Buffy gets to slay and Joyce can't stop her, so Joyce wants candy and to get off her back. Giles takes Joyce by the hand to get more candy. Trying to shock them out of it, Buffy points out the giant dent in Joyce's SUV.

Joyce: Oh my God. What was I thinking when I bought the geek machine?

Giles laughs. Buffy stamps out his cigarette. When he tells her to sod off, she fights her way into the warehouse. Giles and Joyce follow, as does Snyder. Buffy sees Ethan from behind. He's talking on the phone. Buffy says his name. He turns around and says into the phone, "You might want to hurry." Then he runs. Buffy and Giles chase him through the warehouse, leaping over a conveyor belt.

At the library, Cordelia says at first it was kind of fun. Her parents were in good moods, not like parents. But then her mom started borrowing her clothes, and she says there should be an age limit on Lycra pants. Xander touches Willow's hand. There's so much chemistry he backs away and goes to the second level of the library with Oz.

Cordelia (to Willow): You want to swap?
Willow: What?

Cordelia doesn't mean boyfriends, she means books. Hers is really hard to read.

At 31 minutes, Giles is breathing hard from chasing Ethan and Buffy tells him that's what smoking will do to you, sounding more and more like a grownup. Then she tells him to be quiet and she listens. She hears Ethan in a large cabinet. So she's using some of those skills that Giles was emphasizing in training. Buffy pulls Ethan out. In the meantime, Joyce and Snyder sit near the entrance eating candy. He leans close and asks if she and Giles are going steady. Joyce rolls her eyes.

The Three-Quarter Turn

The next major plot turn, the Three-Quarter Turn, spins the plot in yet another direction and grows from the Midpoint rather than from an outside force. Here, Buffy asks Ethan what's going on. Giles keeps interrupting to tell her to hit Ethan. Ethan tells Buffy about subcontracting for Mr. Trick. Ethan claims he doesn't remember what demon the tribute is for. Buffy punches him, which makes Giles happy, and he gives the demon's name. He explains, too, that the candy is not just a diversion. The tribute is so big that people would never let the vampires take it, so the adults needed to be so out of it that afterwards they would blame themselves. Buffy wants to know what the tribute is. The scene cuts to the hospital. Vampires grab the newborns.

All of this grew from the Midpoint Reversal where the candy took effect and the adults started drinking, goofing around, and drag racing.

Ethan does not know what the tribute is. Buffy gets on the phone with Willow. As they talk, Ethan grabs a tire iron to sneak up on Buffy. Giles pulls the gun on him. Buffy turns around, stops all of it, and makes Giles reluctantly hand over gun. Willow, on the phone, tells Buffy that the tribute is every thirty years. It's a ritual feeding, and it's babies.

Buffy needs to tie up Ethan so they can go to the hospital. Joyce sheepishly brings out a pair of handcuffs.

Buffy: Never tell me.

At the hospital, the babies are gone. The adults are confused. Giles remembers a poem about Lurconis the demon, something about filth beneath the city. They figure out the tribute is taking place in the sewer. Snyder doesn't want to go, and Giles, when he's not busy making out with Joyce, taunts him about being afraid of a little demon. Buffy tells them all to stop it. She needs them to be grownups. Children are going to die — echoing Joyce's fears about Buffy dying. (Joyce talked about those fears in a previous episode and alluded to it *Band Candy* when she talked with Giles.)

The Climax And Multi-Purpose Dialogue

In the sewers, vampires in robes chant in Latin by torchlight. The babies are lined up in a cart and they're crying. Mr. Trick is impatient.

Mr. Trick: Come on, Big Guy. They're not getting any fresher.

The mayor stands to one side making calls to the public works committee because he noticed the sewers need maintenance and repair. He's concerned about exposed pipes and ventilation. His calls add to the mayor's character, showing that whatever his other agenda is, he cares about keeping the city running well. He leaves, though, as soon as Buffy enters the sewer. It's not clear if she saw him or knows who he is. She fights the vampires, and Giles and Joyce wheel the babies away.

At 39 minutes, 30 seconds, the Climax begins. That's the scene where the opposing forces have their final clash and resolve the main conflict. Amidst a roaring sound the demon approaches through a side tunnel. It's another giant snake demon, somewhat like the one in *Reptile Boy*.

The demon grabs the nearest vampire and withdraws. Trick tells Buffy that usually he likes others to do his fighting for him (another way he's different from Spike), but he's got to see what she's got. Buffy says to tell her when it hurts, but before she and Trick can fight, Giles leaps in. Trick fairly easily throws him aside. He lands in the demon's path and barely scrambles away in time.

As the demon emerges, Buffy grabs a gas pipe. She lights it with a torch and uses it to set the demon on fire. I love this because the mayor's phone call looked like just some quick humor and a way to develop the mayor's character. But it set the stage for what Buffy does here because she relies on the leaking gas line. Using dialogue like that for multiple purposes is part of what makes this episode move so quickly. Nothing is wasted. It makes it feel very intense and tightly structured. It's fun, too.

Falling Action In *Band Candy*

The antagonist here is the mayor, as he's the one pushing against Buffy throughout despite that they never come face to face. By defeating the demon, she's defeated him for now. That confrontation over, the episode moves into the Falling Action, where the writers tie up loose ends.

Mr. Trick (before running off): You and me, Girl, there's hard times ahead.

Buffy: They never just leave. Always gotta say something.

Joyce wants to go home.

Buffy: Yeah, we can go home. I've got the SATs tomorrow.

Joyce: Oh, blow them off. I'll write you a note.

Buffy declines, saying she'll take the test, which confirms Buffy's growth here from the beginning where Giles chided her for not taking the SATs seriously.

The scene shifts to the mayor to tie up more loose ends. Mr. Trick sits in front of the mayor's desk. The mayor almost looms over him and asks about Trick's friend. Trick paid him. He did his job.

Mayor: This didn't turn out the way I had planned.

Mr. Trick: Where's the down side? You just got yourself one less demon you have to pay tribute to. The way I see it, I did you a favor.

Mayor (smiles): I guess you did. (leans in close with hand on Trick's shoulder) In the future, I'd be very careful how many favors you do for me.

The next day at school Xander calls Principal Snyder "Snyder." Snyder snaps at him for it. He then tells Willow, Xander, and Cordelia that it looks like they have too much time on their hands. Someone painted KISS ROCKS across the lockers. They are just the volunteers he needs to clean that up.

Willow: Kiss rocks? Why would anyone want to — oh, wait, I get it.

This is another bookend for the episode, as Snyder forced them to volunteer to sell band candy in the beginning of the episode. Later, Buffy and Giles walk out of the school building.

Buffy: It was just too much to deal with. It was like nothing made sense anymore. The things that I thought I understood were gone. I just felt so alone.

Giles: Was that the math or the verbal?

Buffy: Mostly the math.

Giles: Well, if you scored low then you can always take them again.

Buffy: More SATs? Is there really a point? I could die before I even apply to college.

Giles: And then you very possibly might not.

Buffy: Well, let's just keep hope alive.

I see this as the last bit of commentary on the SAT. Buffy is so skilled at slaying, and she manages it along with school. But her future in terms of college depends on filling in test bubbles correctly.

Joyce is waiting to drive Buffy home. She says hello to Giles, who looks at the car rather than her. Then they have my favorite exchange between them ever:

Giles: I say, your car seems to have had an adventure, doesn't it?

Joyce: Buffy assures me that it happened battling evil, so I'm letting her pay for it on the installment plan.

Buffy: Hey, the way things were going, be glad that's the worst that happened. At least I got to the two of you before you actually did something.

Joyce: Right.
Giles: Indeed.
Joyce: Yes.
And we go to credits.

Moving The Season Arc

Often, I'm not a huge fan of one-off episodes because they don't move the season story arc much. **Band Candy**, though, is so much fun, and it advances the season arc and develops character relationships in subtle ways. For one thing, it resolves much of the Joyce and Buffy conflict. It adds to and builds on this idea of Giles as a substitute father, not only because he buys the candy bars but because Joyce comments on Buffy playing them against each other. Plus, Giles and Joyce get together in this episode.

Here, too, the mayor is revealed as a major force of evil in the town with some sort of grand plan for the year. But we learn that Snyder, awful as he can be, isn't a part of the mayor's plans.

Spoilers And Foreshadowing

The Council

When Giles blindfolds Buffy for training it foreshadows the Watchers' tests of Buffy in Season Five's *Checkpoint*. And Giles acting more like a father figure for Buffy foreshadows this season's *Helpless*, where Giles gets fired after he violates Council rules to try to help Buffy. The Council thinks he's come to love Buffy as a daughter rather seeing her as a Slayer.

Joyce And Giles

The scene where Giles and Joyce drink, smoke, and listen to music in his apartment is echoed in Season Five. After Joyce's funeral, Giles sits alone with a glass of whiskey and listens to *Tales Of Brave Ulysses.* It is such a quick moment that you can easily miss it, but it says so much about his grief.

Comedic moments also are foreshadowed. Later in Season Three, in *Earshot*, Buffy's able to hear thoughts and learns Giles and Joyce slept together. Giles literally walks into a tree when Buffy confronts him on it. And in Season Four, Buffy, trapped in Faith's body, will use her knowledge of the fling to prove to Giles that she is, in fact, Buffy.

Buffy And Cars

I always feel Joyce is unfair to Buffy in making her pay for the damage to the car, as it was caused by the drag racers. But Buffy isn't an attentive driver in this episode. And it foreshadows that Buffy never learns to drive in the series. In Season Four she tells Riley she and driving don't mix, which is presumably a reference to *Band Candy*.

Questions For Your Writing

- Do you include dialogue lines that are there solely for humor? If so, is there a way they can also weave in a bit of foreshadowing or set the stage for a later event?
- Are there social issues your characters or your prose comments upon? Do they fit the plot well? Do they work whether or not your audience agrees with you?

- Look at your scene or chapter endings. Is there a way you can use a similar dialogue line, setting, or action to end one and start the next? What other ways can you transition your audience from one moment to the next?
- Are there universal themes your plot or subplot touches upon? What are they?
- Is there a new character in your fictional world? If you need to, how might you use that character to get information across to your readers?
- What opposing goals might characters who are otherwise on the same side have that bring them into conflict? Can you create other conflicts between characters who mean well and care about each other?

The next chapter talks about *Revelations*, where a new Watcher visits Sunnydale and fools everyone, including Faith.

CHAPTER 7
REVELATIONS S3 E7

THIS CHAPTER TALKS ABOUT *REVELATIONS*, Season Three, Episode Seven, where Gwendolyn Post, who claims to be a new Watcher, trains Faith and carries out her own evil agenda. Written by Douglas Petrie and directed by James A. Contner. Original air date: November 17, 1998.

Along with the episode breakdown, topics include:

- Plot manipulations and out-of-character actions that undermine the story
- Strong themes of guilt, vulnerability, and isolation that drive the plot and link multiple storylines
- Dialogue that quickly builds a new character (Gwendolyn Post)
- Unanswered questions that throw off the narrative

Okay, let's dive into the Hellmouth.

Three Opening Conflicts

The opening scene of *Revelations* escalates the conflicts from earlier episodes, drawing viewers quickly in. Cordelia, Xander, and Willow sit at the Bronze watching Oz's band play. He joins them during a break, and Xander moves his seat very close to Cordelia. She comments on him being all over her.

Willow: I think it's great when two people like two people and want to be close to them and not anyone else.

This is the first of many awkward lines Willow says because she feels guilty about kissing Xander in *Homecoming*. Oz squeezes into a seat, pushing Willow and Xander together. They jerk apart and their hands bang into their glasses, which crash to the floor. Cordelia asks what's wrong with them. Rather than answer, Willow asks a question that adds another conflict to the opening.

Willow: Speaking of people and things they do that aren't like usual, has anyone noticed how different Buffy has been acting?

Xander hasn't. He says she's slaying and fighting like usual, but Willow comments that Buffy's been off alone a lot. These two lines add some exposition about Buffy through minor conflict. There's more when the group speculates that she might have a new boyfriend. Cordelia explains exactly why Buffy might hide that.

Cordelia: Excuse me? When your last steady killed half the class, and then your rebound guy sends you a dump-o-gram? It makes a girl shy.

Xander: But we're the best of Buffy's bestest buds. She'd tell us.

Buffy appears and tells them she's not dating anyone, but she is going out with someone tonight. Faith joins them, puts her arm around Buffy, and asks if she's ready to go.

The scene changes to the graveyard and there's a third conflict. This one relates to the main plot about a new Watcher and the demon she's hunting. Faith and Buffy fight two vampires in a coordinated way. They seem to have fun, but

Giles looks a bit bored. He reads while they fight. They kill both the vampires at the same time and high five.

Buffy: Synchronized slaying.

Faith: New Olympic category.

Buffy asks Giles what he thinks. But a British woman (whom we'll learn is Gwendolyn Post) walks onto the scene. She wears a pencil skirt, heels, and pearls, and has her hair in a bun. Her first line sets her tone.

Post: Sloppy. You telegraph punches, leave blind sides open, and for a school night slaying, take entirely too much time. Which one of you is Faith?

Faith says it depends. Who the hell is she?

Post: Your new Watcher.

And we go to credits.

Three Story Sparks

On return from the commercial, the episode quickly moves to the Story Spark or Inciting Incident, that first plot point that sets the main plot rolling. We saw three quick opening conflicts. *Revelations* also has what can be seen as three sparks. The first one, before the credits, is simply Gwendolyn Post's arrival. That gets the story of a new Watcher in Sunnydale rolling. But a few later interactions go to the more specific plot about Post.

The second occurs in the library. Post asks Giles where he keeps the rest of his books. The "actual library." The question comes at 4 minutes, 35 seconds in, right about 10%, where the Story Spark occurs in most books, films, and television episodes. Giles assures her his collection is the finest occult collection — but Post cuts him off. She's sure it's the best on this side of the Atlantic, but she asks for two obscure sounding books.

Giles doesn't have one, and he mumbles that the other's on order. Post asks for another, which he's eager to say he has.

Post: Of course you do.

This exchange builds Post's character line by line. On first watch, I thought that's all it was. On rewatch I saw how expertly she manipulated Giles, purposely setting him off balance and making him feel inferior, which she continues to do. She says she was sent because Faith needs a new Watcher. Faith tells Post, no offense, but she doesn't need a new Watcher. She has a problem with authority figures in that they tend to end up dead.

But Giles tells Faith if the Council thinks she needs a Watcher of her own, they'll follow the Council's dictates. Now we get the last moment that could be a Story Spark. At about 5 minutes, 23 seconds, Post says the Council wishes her to report on the entire situation, including Giles.

Buffy: Hmm. Academic probation not so funny today, huh Giles?

So Post doubled down on undermining Giles. Now he's worried about being scrutinized and he's not questioning her. Though it's not mentioned, in his mind Giles may link this review of him to the lack of an invitation to the Watchers retreat in *Faith, Hope & Trick*. Post follows up by saying the thinking at the Council is that Giles has become too American.

Giles: Me?
Buffy: Him?

The Demon Plot And A Universal Theme

Now there's a moment that could appear to be a late Story Spark on first watch because Post tells them a demon, Lagos, is in Sunnydale. It appears the action plot will be about finding the demon. Much later, though, the characters learn Post is fooling them all, and that turns out to be the real main plot. For that reason, the story starts with Post setting Giles off balance so as to carry out her scheme.

Now she asks Giles for an illustration of Lagos. Poor Giles starts to look.

Post (immediately sighing): Maybe later.

She tells them Lagos is seeking the Glove of Myhnegon. It's a highly dangerous glove, and the demon must be stopped.

Giles: What do you propose?

Post: Well, if it's not too radical a suggestion, I thought we might kill him.

Once again, the series covers a universal theme — here, the awful boss or supervisor. Post reminds me of every person I worked with who treated people like an idiot when they asked a question or tried to clarify something. I doubt Giles would stand for this if he didn't already feel vulnerable after being excluded from that retreat and being told by Post that he's under review.

She tells him Lagos can be found in cemeteries. She isn't thrilled to learn there are twelve within Sunnydale city limits. Post says she'd appreciate anything in Giles's books that might help pinpoint the exact location of the tomb, "but then we cannot ask for miracles." Giles, sitting at the library table, suppresses whatever he was about to say. We barely hear that stifled noise, then he turns his head to one side and sighs — a wonderful way to show how he's feeling. Everyone agrees they'll start the hunt tomorrow at sunset. Post takes Faith with her.

Giles (to Buffy): That was bracing.

Buffy: Interesting lady. Can I kill her?

Giles tells her the Council might frown on that and asks how she feels about training. Another smooth transition occurs here. After Giles's line about training, the scene cuts to Angel and Buffy training together by doing Tai Chi in the courtyard of the mansion at night.

Plot Questions, Guilt, And Angel

On rewatch, this scene with Buffy and Angel prompted me to notice a plot hole or at least a question. A dangerous demon might be lurking in one of twelve cemeteries. There's no clear reason why everyone didn't start searching tonight. The practical answer is likely that the writers wanted this Buffy and Angel scene here in the story rather than before Post arrived. But that doesn't fit the plot. And though minor, this and similar plot questions contribute to the feeling that the episode is just a bit off.

Buffy and Angel gradually move closer. Eventually they almost kiss. Buffy pulls away and says she better go before anyone figures out what they're doing.

Angel: What are we doing?
Buffy: Training. And almost kissing.
Buffy calls it an old habit. A bad habit they need to quit.
Buffy: You think they make a patch for this?

Buffy shows so much vulnerability here. Despite knowing the consequences when she and Angel had sex, it's so hard for her to set aside her love for and attraction to him. And there's guilt, which will be a theme in this episode, because she hasn't told anybody about him. Now she tells Angel she's hunting for Lagos. He recognizes the demon's name.

In the library, Giles is frustrated that he, Willow, and Xander are getting nowhere finding Lagos (which links the last scene and this one together). Raising his voice, he says it's intolerable that they can't find anything in the books. There's no time for this. He tells Xander to learn all he can. Most importantly, why the demon wants the glove.

The intense researching might answer my plot question. Apparently, they don't want to go after the demon without knowing more. A line earlier to make that clear would help the plot feel more consistent.

Giles's anger shows more of his vulnerability because normally he is calm and measured. It's particularly rare that he would yell at Xander and Willow. Xander makes a good point in response.

Xander: Hey, you're not the Watcher of me.

But Giles tells him if he's going to stay, he should work. Xander goes up onto the second level and joins Willow, who says she's tired and it's late. They sit on the floor together against the stacks. Willow's rubbing her temples and says her eyes are blurry. Xander reaches around to rub her temples for her.

Willow: Stop.

Xander: Right. Stop means No. And No means No. So I'm stopping.

He withdraws. Willow turns and kisses him. As they kiss, Giles comes up the stairs and calls their names. They split apart. He tells them he found what he needs, the probable location of the glove in the Restfield Cemetery. It's unclear if he noticed them kissing, but he probably doesn't care if he did.

More Guilt At The One-Quarter Twist

Now we're getting to the One-Quarter Twist, as I call the first major plot turn. Here, as it should, it comes from outside the protagonist, spins the story, and raises the stakes. At 11 minutes, 42 seconds (a little over a quarter way through the episode), Xander offers to go check out the crypt because Giles doesn't know where Buffy is.

This turn serves a double purpose. It will truly spin the story because it leads to Xander learning Angel is alive. That's key to the main Gwendolyn Post plot and to a subplot about everyone learning Angel is alive. And it's a turn in the catch-the-demon plot, as eventually it leads to finding Lagos.

Plot Manipulation?

I question Giles letting Xander go alone at night to the cemetery. Xander explains his motives for volunteering when he talks to himself later. Clearly very nervous, he muses aloud about how dumb it was to volunteer because he was feeling so guilty about the kiss. I can also see Xander as trying to change the subject in case Giles did see them kissing. But there's no world in which I see Giles sending Xander alone. At the very least if he couldn't find Faith or Buffy, he'd go with Xander himself. This development feels like it's there so Xander can be alone when he sees Angel.

In a perfect world, when writers need a character to do something for the plot, they find a way to make it fit the story and characterization. But it's easy as a writer to be so intent on your plot (especially if you love plotting, as I do) that you don't realize you're manufacturing a bit, stretching a character out of shape, or at least failing to make the character's motives clear enough to the audience.

With television writing, particularly in twenty-plus episode seasons, writers have a limited time to finish a script. I'm guessing sometimes they just need to move the story along. And in *Buffy* in particular, because the emotional storytelling is so strong, most viewers will forgive a little plot manipulation to get there.

Faith and Buffy patrol in downtown Sunnydale. Faith catalogues her boyfriends.

Faith: Ronnie, deadbeat. Steve, klepto. Kenny — drummer. Eventually I just had to face up to my destiny as a loser magnet.

Now her view is get some and get gone. She asks about Buffy, who says there's not much to tell.

Faith: I've had my share of losers, but you boinked the undead. What was that like?

Buffy: Life with Angel is complicated —was complicated. And it's hard to talk about.
Faith: Well, try.

Buffy doesn't want to. Faith suggests they call it a night. They found nothing in six cemeteries. She'll swing through the next six by herself. This suggestion tells us Faith feels rejected when Buffy won't open up about Angel. Faith talked about her past and shared her feelings and Buffy didn't reciprocate.

On the one hand, her sense of rejection feels believable. On the other, it seems like Faith might see why it's different. She shared about a series of guys that didn't work out. But she knows Buffy slept with Angel, her first love, he lost his soul and killed people, then regained it just before she had to kill him, and that might be harder to talk about. Especially because Buffy hasn't exactly been oversharing with her long-time friends about it.

But this exchange does start building a theme of isolation that continues through the episode for Faith. And it may be part of her character that she's sensitive to feeling rejected.

When she gets to the cemetery, Faith runs into Lagos. He easily throws her aside, but she keeps coming back. She's not able to stop him entirely, but he leaves without finding what he wanted.

At about 14 minutes, Xander breathes hard as he walks through the Restfield cemetery. This is where he talks to himself about alleviating his guilt by getting himself "really, really killed." Then he sees Angel, who doesn't notice Xander. Angel carries something wrapped up in one arm. Xander follows from a distance. I can't decide if this is stupid or brave on Xander's part since Xander doesn't know if Angel is evil again or not.

The scene switches to Angel and Buffy inside the mansion, embracing and kissing. Xander sees them through the window. The two break apart and talk about how they can't do this.

Angel shows her the glove. It has all these prongs or tines around the base. Buffy moves to touch it but Angel stops her. Once you put the glove on, you can never take it off.

Buffy: No touching. Kind of like us.

She tells him she'll tell Giles, who will at least be happy.

Timing Question

The moment when Angel shows Buffy the glove makes me question the timing. Xander saw Angel carry the glove through the cemetery. He seems to follow Angel from a distance. Yet before Xander reaches the mansion, Angel has already put the glove aside because he later needs to take it out to show to Buffy.

Buffy's time of arrival also isn't clear. If she was there when he got back, he would have showed her the glove right away. Instead, it seems Angel puts the glove away and sometime later Buffy arrives, all before Xander gets to the mansion. Buffy and Angel start kissing, Xander reaches the mansion and sees them, then Angel shows her the glove. It's also unclear whether Xander sees Angel show Buffy the glove. The timing question isn't necessarily a plot hole. But it, too, undercuts the storytelling because it creates confusion or at least an unconscious feel for the viewer that something isn't quite right.

When Buffy says Giles will be happy about the glove, the scenes shifts to Giles with an illustration of the glove at his apartment. He shows Gwendolyn Post, who's there with him. She dismisses it as woodcarving known to be unreliable.

Post: The pictures are fun to look at, Mr. Giles, but one really ought to read the nice words as well.

Then she tells Giles that when you let little things slip, it all goes to hell, using Buffy as an example. Giles assures her he's in complete control of his Slayer. At that moment, Xander bursts in.

Xander: We have a big problem. It's Buffy.

This terrible timing for Giles likely adds to his anger at Buffy over not telling him about Angel.

An Intervention That Fits The Characters

At 18 minutes, 20 seconds, Buffy, seeming quite happy, strolls into the library. She says Lagos is out of luck. She's got the glove. Her friends sit around the table. Giles stands nearby. Everyone looks serious.

Buffy: What's with all the tragedy?

Unlike my questions about earlier scenes, here, everyone acts in character. Giles tells Buffy to take a seat. Xander half stands, moves his chair sideways toward Buffy with his back to her, then drops the chair and steps away. These movements convey how hostile Xander feels toward Buffy. After Buffy sits facing everyone, Giles tells her they know Angel's alive and she's been hiding him. Xander saw her. Buffy protests it's not what they think. Xander thinks she's harboring a vicious killer.

Willow: This isn't about attacking Buffy. Remember, "I" statements only: "I feel angry." "I feel worried."

Cordelia: Fine. Here's one. I feel worried. About me. Last time around Angel barely laid a hand on Buffy. He was way more interested in killing her friends.

As she often does, Cordelia states her concern clearly. And I believe this is the main issue for her because I doubt Cordelia would feel as personally betrayed as the others do that Buffy didn't share with her.

Buffy tries to tell them Angel is better and she doesn't need an intervention. But Giles thinks she does. She must've known it was wrong to see Angel because she hid it. Xander asks if she was waiting for Angel to go psycho again the next time she gives him a happy. Buffy claims they're not together like that.

Oz: But you were kissing.

This is so Oz. A simple declarative statement in an even tone.

Buffy (to Xander): You were spying on me? What gives you the right?

Buffy tries to say it was an accident. Xander asks what happened — she tripped and fell on Angel's lips? Buffy tells them she knows it was wrong. It can't happen again. And she would never put them in danger. If she thought Angel would hurt anyone —

Xander: You would stop him? Like you did last time with Miss Calendar?

This reference to Jenny must add to Giles's pain, not that he wouldn't be thinking about it already. Buffy insists Angel is good again. He found the glove. Xander scoffs at the idea of the scary guy with this dangerous glove. Buffy accuses Xander of jealousy, which he denies. I think most fans agree that some concerns Xander raises are valid, but Buffy's right, too. His anger has a lot to do with him feeling he can tell her who she can be involved with because she had the nerve to not be interested in him.

Giles ends it all, saying Buffy heard their concerns and her actions, though ill-advised, can be understood. He reminds them the priority is to retrieve the glove and tells them to go back to class. It appears Giles is trying to see it from Buffy's point of view, and he does protect her. But at the Midpoint Buffy finds out how he really feels.

Midpoint Reversal And A Human Giles

Typically, at a story's Midpoint there is a serious reversal of fortune for the protagonist or a major commitment. Here, at 21 minutes, 41 seconds, we get one of the most heartbreaking Giles and Buffy scenes. Post's critiques of Giles, his vulnerability, his fear of losing his job as Buffy's Watcher, and Xander's reminder about Jenny all play into it. Buffy pauses in his office doorway.

Buffy: Thanks for the bail in there. I know it's a lot to absorb —

Giles: I won't remind you that the fate of the world often lies with the Slayer for what would be the point? Nor shall I remind you that you've jeopardized the lives of all that you hold dear by harboring a known murderer. But sadly, I must remind you that Angel tortured me. For hours. For pleasure. You should've told me he was alive. You didn't. You have no respect for me or the job I perform.

Giles's words leave open a question of whether he feels that Angel, not Angelus, is personally responsible. I think not, as later he doesn't appear worried when he tells Post Angel has the glove. But he's angry because if Buffy told him, he might have listened to her and understood, but she didn't trust him. And she embarrassed him terribly and undermined him in front of Post.

In a way, it's good to see Giles as human, as someone who can feel vulnerable and react in a less than ideal way. If you're writing a character who is a mentor or generally the most stable, insightful person, it's good to remember that they will also have their moments. That when angry and hurt or fearful they, too, will lash out.

Faith answers a knock at her door with a stake raised, no doubt remembering Kakistos. Post tells her vampires rarely knock (showing she doesn't know Sunnydale very well). She calls Faith's room Spartan and tells her the Spartans focused on the battle and needed nothing else. She also tells Faith she'll be hard on her and Faith may come to hate her.

Faith: You think?

But Post promises to make Faith a better Slayer and keep her alive.

Post: You have to trust that I am right.

Faith seems very blue before she opens the door, perhaps a holdover from when Buffy didn't share with her about Angel, though that doesn't feel quite like a strong enough reason to me. But her mood definitely makes her more vulnerable to Post's manipulations, which are expert.

Post says she doesn't understand Giles's methods. When Faith tries to defend him, Post says he can have his games and secret meetings with Buffy and her friends. Faith, unhappy, guesses "Buffy's friends" doesn't include her. It's not clear if Post deliberately plays on Faith being excluded. But purposely or not, it has the desired effect. Faith buys quickly into Post when normally she's suspicious of everyone.

Plot Question: Faith's Exclusion

Another plot and character issue is why Giles didn't include Faith in the Buffy intervention. If the group is really concerned Angel might be evil, it seems he'd want the other Slayer in town to know Angelus might be back.

Omitting Faith may further show Giles doesn't worry that Angel is evil. He also may be concerned Faith will race off to kill Angel, which ought to help him understand Buffy's fears. Or he may think Faith already has too much allegiance to Gwendolyn Post, and he doesn't want Post to know any of this. So much happens in the episode that there probably wasn't time to add dialogue showing Giles's reasoning. Without it, though, Faith's exclusion feels a bit artificial. And it matters. Feeling left out drives Faith to follow Post somewhat blindly, which shapes much of the rest of the story.

Now Post asks Faith if she wants to train.

Faith: Punching, hitting, stabbing. I'm your girl.

Bonding And Secrets

Willow's secret about her and Xander makes her more sympathetic toward Buffy, though we'll see it doesn't affect Xander that way. At Willow's locker, Willow tells Buffy she's not mad at her. She understands Buffy was scared and kept a secret. Willow adds that secrets must be good. There's a reason people keep them. Buffy says she's going to try to kill Lagos as a peace offering to Giles. She figures Lagos must still be hunting for the glove, not knowing Angel has it.

At the Bronze, Xander plays pool alone, hitting the pool balls hard. Faith joins him and says he looks pissed. She guesses the group was talking behind her back about the glove. Xander tells her she's wrong, that Angel is still alive and he has the glove.

Faith: Guy like that, that kind of glove, could kill a whole mess of people.

Xander tells her Buffy didn't seem to care.

Faith: Buffy knew he was alive?

This realization doubles down on Faith's feeling that Buffy shuts her out. She and Xander agree you can't take a chance on whether Angel has changed or not.

Faith: I say I slay.

Xander: Can I come?

This is the worst Xander. Seen in the best light, he's fearful Buffy won't be careful and Angel will turn evil again. And Cordelia made a good point. Angel went after Buffy's friends, not Buffy. But urging Faith to kill Angel without knowing more is still awful.

At 27 minutes, in Giles's office, Post drinks tea and says she's knackered. Giles comments that it's her first Slayer. She asks if he's questioning her methods. I've read that's how you're supposed to deal with someone who is passive aggressive.

Confront the point directly. This shows Post's skills at countering the exact type of verbal attack she makes on others.

Earlier, though, Giles didn't confront her directly because he felt so vulnerable. Now he assures her he has respect for her methods in his "American way." And he also has the glove. It's with a friend of Buffy's. Giles agrees they need to get the glove right away. But when he adds that they need to destroy it, Post is surprised. Giles tells her living flame will destroy the glove.

At 28 and a half minutes, he turns to get his book to show her. She hits him on the back of the head with a statue, knocking him out. Now we know Post is evil, which could serve as the next major plot turn. It doesn't change Post's plans, though, so it doesn't radically change the story's direction. It does get Giles out of her way.

In the graveyard, Willow asks Buffy why she didn't ask Faith to come with her to look for Lagos.

Willow: Not to downplay my own slaying abilities, which in some circles are considered formidable.

Buffy says she tried calling Faith and got no answer. This quick exchange, with a little humor, is a great example of how to answer a plot question the audience might have about Buffy bringing Willow.

Now Buffy confides that she feels better with the secret about Angel out.

Willow: Sure, it's a big burden lifted. Keeping secrets is a lot of work. One could hypothetically imagine.

Willow asks if when Angel was a secret, it was sexier, which tells us another reason Willow may be drawn to Xander. She's always done the right thing and followed the rules. Along with having feelings for Xander for years, sneaking around adds to the excitement. But Buffy says for her it felt like more pressure. She wants to know why Willow is asking. Willow says she has something to tell Buffy, but the demon interrupts. Buffy fights and beheads it, very happy. When she asks what Willow was about to say, Willow chickens out and claims her secret was opening the SAT test booklet early.

Xander and Faith head to the library for weapons. They find Giles moaning. Xander calls 911. Faith assumes it was Angel. Xander's not so sure.

Faith: How much more proof do you need?
Xander: A bite would be nice.

But Faith's not going to wait. She takes off. This fits her character. She loves to fight, she's angry at Buffy, and she doesn't trust guys.

This moment also isn't the Three-Quarter Turn. As with Post earlier, Faith is only continuing with her plan to kill Angel. She just feels she has more justification now.

At 32 minutes, Angel stands before a cauldron of flames at the mansion.

The Three-Quarter Turn In *Revelations*

Paramedics are taking Giles out of the library when Buffy and Willow arrive. He struggles to talk but tells Buffy she must destroy the glove using living flame. Because he's weak, perhaps he can be forgiven for not telling her about Gwendolyn Post, and Buffy has no trouble figuring that out. But that is another minor question that undermines the story because it's important information Giles would want to tell her.

This interaction serves as the last major plot turn, shifting the story to destroying the glove and stopping Post. First, though, Xander tells Buffy Angel's not as cured as she thought. He admits, though, that he doesn't know for sure Angel attacked Giles. But Faith assumed it. Buffy tells Willow and Xander to figure out the living flame and bring it.

Isolation As A Theme: Angel And Giles

At the mansion, Post easily fools Angel, building on the theme of the problems isolation causes. In the past, Angel might have been with Buffy or heard from one of her friends. Now, alone, he knows nothing about the attack on Giles. And he doesn't know Buffy already killed Lagos. When Post says Giles sent her and she's there to destroy the glove before Lagos finds them, he has no reason to doubt her.

Similarly, Giles's isolation from the Council drives the entire story because he doesn't know Post's history. Post tells Angel if he does the flame wrong it can make the glove more powerful. He tells her the glove is in the trunk. The second he turns his back she knocks him out.

Post: I love this town. Everyone's so helpful.

As she's opening the trunk, though, Angel stands and goes into vamp face, surprising her. She had no idea Buffy's friend was a vampire. Post fights well, but Angel ultimately throws her against the wall. Faith comes in at that moment. Seeing Angel throw Post confirms everything she thinks she knows. Faith and Angel fight. She's got him on the ground, ready to stake him. Buffy arrives and intervenes.

In the library, Willow and Xander are ready to test the flames. But when they see what the glove can do in a book, they agree there's no time and rush out.

Post tells Faith that Buffy is blinded by love. I might've liked to see Buffy try to explain, but it would be difficult to do it as she and Faith fight. It's a long sequence, which raises another plot question. Where is Angel during their fight? Faith might have been able to knock him out since he's still not at full strength, but we didn't see that.

Buffy and Faith crash through large windows into the courtyard. Xander and Willow run in and see Post on the floor. She tells them the glove is in the trunk. She'll get it. They need to help Faith. Xander then tries to intervene in the fight, which is a bad idea. Faith easily throws him aside.

The Climax

The episode is nearing the Climax — that final confrontation between the opposing forces. At 37 minutes, 47 seconds, Willow watches Post put on the glove. The prongs grab onto her arm. She points at the ceiling. Lightning comes through the skylight. Faith and Buffy freeze and stare.

Post: Faith, a word of advice. You're an idiot.

Post speaks a spell in another language. Lightning shoots from the glove at Faith and Buffy, who dive away together. Angel dives in front of Willow, saving her when Post fires at her. Buffy tells Faith to draw Post's fire. Faith runs. As Post fires at her, Buffy finds a big shard of window glass. When Post points to the sky again, Buffy flings the shard. It lops off Post's lower arm above the glove. Lightning strikes Post and fries her into oblivion.

Buffy prevailed over Post, the antagonist of the episode. (And, once again where Buffy fights a human, she doesn't actually kill her. Here, the lightning does.)

Falling Action, Arcs, Bookends, And Subplots

At 40 minutes, the Falling Action, where we tie up loose ends and subplots, begins. Amidst smoke, everyone walks toward the spot where Post stood a moment before. On the ground, the glove releases its prongs from Post's severed arm.

At school the next day, Buffy's friends sit outside, commenting on the glove now being destroyed. Willow adds that Angel saved her from a horrible flamey death, which kind of makes her like him again. Buffy joins them and asks what they're talking about.

Oz: Oddly enough, your boyfriend again.

This serves as a bookend for that first conversation among the friends speculating about Buffy's behavior and possible new boyfriend. Buffy says he's really not her boyfriend. She's not sure what he is. She looks at Xander and asks if they are okay.

While it fits Buffy's character to make sure she's all right with her friends and to feel bad about lying to them, I really wanted Xander to apologize here, too. He had so much to do with Faith going off to kill Angel. But it fits his character to fail to recognize his errors or responsibility.

Buffy's apology adds to themes of guilt and isolation. Buffy feels guilty about lying and is unhappy with her isolation, which she wants to end. So she makes the first move. Xander does say they're okay, but seeing Angel and Buffy kissing he sort of leaned toward the postal, which is close to an apology for Xander. He adds that he trusts her.

Cordelia: I don't. Just for the record.

As I noted earlier, Xander doesn't seem to empathize with Buffy despite his own secret. Perhaps his guilt drives him to be harder on Buffy, though I don't think that's in the text.

Giles, head bandaged, joins them. He says Gwendolyn Post used to be a Watcher. The Council kicked her out a couple years earlier for misuse of dark power. There supposedly was a memo. Along with stressing Giles's isolation, this raises the question of how diligent the Council is.

After Buffy leaves, Willow says the Angel thing is so weird. Giles says they'll need to see how that unfolds. He's much calmer, but the bandage on his head emphasizes his vulnerability. It's one of the rare times we see the aftereffects of an injury.

Trust And Faith

We see physical injuries again when Buffy visits Faith. Faith answers the knock on her motel room door by saying "Come in" without looking to see who it is. It's an interesting character moment. It could signal Faith is too depressed to bother to look, that she has a death wish or wants someone to fight, or she simply doesn't think it matters one way or the other since she doesn't trust anyone anyway.

Her face is pretty swollen, which is especially unusual to see for a Slayer. Buffy looks fine. She tells Faith Gwendolyn Post fooled everybody, even Giles. That doesn't make Faith feel better. She says it just proves you can't trust anyone, something she should've learned by now.

Buffy: You can trust me.

Buffy adds that it might seem strange because she was just kicking Faith's face, which misses the point. Buffy gets a little closer to the issue when she says she knows she kept secrets, but she didn't have a choice. Buffy goes on to say she's on Faith's side.

Faith: I'm on my side. That's enough.
Buffy: Not always.
Faith: Is that it? (Buffy turns and heads for the door.)
Buffy. (Buffy turns back, looking hopeful.) Nothing.

Faith's almost-attempt to reach out leaves some hope that the two will connect again as the episode ends.

The writers drove this wedge between Faith and Buffy, but only part of it felt true to the characters. On first watch this last interplay between Buffy and Faith in particular didn't quite work for me. On the one hand, they are the only two Slayers. And I buy that Faith was starting to feel this strong bond with Buffy or to want that. Not only did she trust Post, she trusted Buffy, at least to a point, until she found out about Angel being back.

But along with not quite buying Faith being so upset when Buffy wouldn't talk about Angel early in the episode, I'm not sure I believe Buffy doesn't try harder to explain herself to Faith at the end. It fits Buffy's character to apologize to Xander, yet she seems to expect to heal things with Faith so easily. I needed her to go beyond saying she had no choice because she did have one, as Faith sees. Faith needs to hear that Buffy was afraid everyone would do exactly what Faith did — assume the worst and try to kill Angel.

Buffy claiming she had no choice also is out of character for her. Back in *Lie To Me*, Buffy told Ford, who was about to die a terrible death from cancer, that he didn't have a good choice, but he had a choice. It's been a theme for the series, and Buffy usually is the last person to dodge responsibility. Instead, she feels responsible for everything and gets overwhelmed by it. Yet now Buffy doesn't take responsibility for hiding Angel's return and doesn't try harder to make things right with Faith.

For all my questions, though, this episode shows why Season Three is amazing. Every time I watch *Revelations* I see different things in it. I feel for all the characters as their relationships break and partly mend. The themes of isolation and guilt create a strong undercurrent that binds all the stories together. And each plotline intertwines and affects the other, from Post's manipulation to Buffy's secret keeping to Willow's and Xander's guilt.

Spoilers And Foreshadowing

Faith, Buffy, And Willow

Post calls Faith's motel room Spartan. It's also dingy. This foreshadows what we'll learn about how the Council treats Slayers. It disregards them as people and views them as disposable. No thought was given to finding Faith a place to live, or to how any

Slayer can survive while slaying full-time if she doesn't have someone like Joyce to provide a home. Later we'll learn that Watchers get paid, though Slayers don't. And this season in *Helpless*, we'll see a ritual that seems designed to ensure any Slayer who lives to eighteen will be eliminated.

This episode also foreshadows a metaphor that comes out more in Season Six, which is Slaying as a stand in for all the unpaid labor many women do. In Season Six we'll see how Buffy's unpaid labor as a Slayer interferes with her ability to survive by making it next to impossible for her to take on paid jobs.

The motel room foreshadows Season Three developments, too. When Faith starts working for the Mayor, who is evil, one of the first things he does is move her out of the dingy motel. He gets her a nice apartment with beautiful furnishings. The Council doesn't pay Faith or care about her. The mayor does. We find out, too, that no one really took care of Faith even in her childhood. The mayor is the first one to do that. It goes a long way toward why he matters so much to her.

This episode foreshadows Faith making choices fueled in part by her resentment of all that Buffy has and she doesn't. Here, Faith feels excluded from Buffy's inner circle. Later in the series she'll tell Buffy she was jealous. Buffy has close friends, a mom, a home, and a great Watcher. Faith has none of those things.

Faith's last few words to Buffy foreshadow that the two will become close again this season. And the two actresses have great chemistry with each other. Which leads to a something I didn't see on my first watch of the series. It took until much later for me to consider that Faith and Buffy might have a romantic relationship. (In my defense, same gender romantic or sexual relationships weren't shown on network TV at the time, also a big part of why I didn't pick up on Willow and Tara until well into Season Four.)

Here, you can read Faith's anger and hurt as greater because not only did Buffy keep a secret, the secret involved the return of this great love of Buffy's life. The series did a great job of weaving that in and allowing the audience to fill in what else is going on under the surface.

Willow's comment about her slaying skills being in some circles considered formidable foreshadows her hurt feelings when the two Slayers begin hanging out all the time. Buffy no longer wants to bring Willow with her. She is mainly concerned for Willow. Now that there's another Slayer, there isn't as much reason for her friends to take so many risks to back her up. But Buffy feels great joy, too, at finding a friend who is like her and faces what she faces. She gets so wrapped up in that, she doesn't see that Willow feels hurt and excluded.

Willow's feelings also parallel how she might feel if Buffy found a new romantic partner and ditched her friends. That can be read as more support for Faith and Buffy as a couple, or as a metaphor. It works both ways and feels very real.

Future Watcher, Future Rebellion

Gwendolyn Post's lies and actions lay the groundwork for how negatively both Slayers react when new Watcher Wesley shows up. Giles, too, isn't thrilled, though he confirms that Wesley is legitimate. But no one is inclined to take what Wesley says at face value or to give him a lot of deference. Faith outright walks out on him. Buffy starts to rebel as well.

The Post experience foreshadows Buffy ultimately quitting the Council, too. She quits when the Council shows an utter lack of concern for Angel dying or for Buffy's feelings about him. And that utter lack of concern is made clear here. No one made sure Buffy and Giles knew about Gwendolyn Post, and it appears the Council did nothing to monitor Post. This omission echoes their failure to warn Giles when Kakistos killed Faith's Watcher. Or to tell Giles about Faith in the first place.

Questions For Your Writing

- Set aside your current work in progress for a week or two or ask someone unfamiliar with it to read it. What questions might the audience have about characters' choices or actions? Can you add a line or two to answer them?
- Is there any plot development in your story that feels forced? Do characters need to act inconsistently to make the plot work? How can you revise so that the plot feels natural and fits who the characters are?
- If you have multiple story lines, can you link them through a recurring theme or themes?
- Review Gwendolyn Post's early lines. What do they tell you about her? Now look at how you've introduced new characters in your story. Does their dialogue quickly convey key aspects of their personalities or backstories? If not, how might you revise it? Can you use conflict with other characters to do so?

The next chapter talks about *Lovers Walk*, where Spike returns to Sunnydale and takes Willow hostage.

CHAPTER 8
LOVERS WALK S3 E8

THIS CHAPTER TALKS about *Lovers Walk*, Season Three, Episode Eight, where Spike interrupts Willow's de-lusting spell, putting her and Xander in great peril. Written by Dan Vebber and directed by David Semel. Original air date: November 24, 1998.

Along with the episode breakdown, topics include:

- **Whether Willow is the protagonist**
- **A story that appears to be the main plot but a Climax in a subplot**
- **Using dialogue to link scenes and foreshadow later developments**
- **Spike as a layered, dramatic character who is evil, vulnerable, and emotionally healthy**
- **False vs. true conflict**

Okay, let's dive into the Hellmouth.

Opening Conflict

The opening conflict, for the second time this season, revolves around the SATs. While a story's opening conflict sometimes relates to the main plot, it can be any sort of conflict that draws the reader or viewer quickly into the fictional world.

Willow and Xander sit next to each other outside the school. Willow's distraught. She thought she would score higher on the SAT. Xander points out that her 740 on the verbal section strongly resembles his overall score, but she is not comforted. As Xander tells her she did amazing, he strokes her hair. But he leaps up when Cordelia and Oz join them. He babbles that he was comforting Willow, who was very sad.

Xander's actions and rushed words convey how nervous he feels, the closeness and chemistry between him and Willow, and that Xander does not want anyone else to know. Cordelia and Oz, though, don't notice. Cordelia's very happy with her scores. Xander jokes he's worried that word will get out that he's dating a brain.

Cordelia: Please. I have some experience in covering these things.

Oz looks at Willow's scores.

Oz: I can see why you'd be upset. That was my sarcastic voice.

XANDER: **It sounds a lot like your regular voice.**

Xander says they should celebrate by all going out together. He ignores Cordelia shaking her head and mouthing the word No.

Buffy joins them. She, too, looks distraught. Xander assumes she did badly. But Buffy scored 1430. They all think it's amazing. Oz tells her she can apply anywhere.

The high score fits what we've learned so far about Buffy. Her vocabulary, her literary references (in **Band Candy**, for example, she talked about going "all Willy Loman"), suggest that she's smart and does the reading when she can for school. Dr. Gregory in *Teacher's Pet* told Buffy she had a good mind. (Of course, he got killed after. But it meant a lot to Buffy.) Now we see she did well on the SAT.

But the score creates a dilemma. With these results, she has many options she didn't expect to have for college. She tells her friends she never thought about a future. She didn't really think she would have one. That fits her frustration in **What's My Line Parts One and Two**, where everyone's going to the career fair. Buffy feels angry and left out because being the Slayer determined so much of her life for her. Cordelia says how great this is. Now Buffy can get out of Sunnydale and never return. They all stare at her.

Cordelia: That's a good thing. What kind of moron would come back here?

At 2 minutes, 6 seconds, the scene cuts to a blacked out car driving over the Welcome To Sunnydale sign. Spike, drunk, screeches to a halt.

Spike (gets out of car): Home, sweet home.

He passes out in the street. And we go to credits.

A Spike Spark And A Story Spark

The episode is nearing the Story Spark or Inciting Incident, the event that gets the main plot rolling. Here, it could be Spike driving over the Sunnydale sign because in a lot of ways, Spike sets the main plot — where he kidnaps Willow and Xander — in motion. But right now, he has no plan to do that. Or to do anything specific. As the next scene shows, Spike is miserable because Drusilla broke up with him. At 3 minutes, 27 seconds, he enters the factory that got burnt out when Giles shot flaming arrows at Angel. It's where Spike and Drusilla lived happily for a long time. A very drunk Spike sings part of *My Way*, the Frank Sinatra version.

Spike: Drusilla, I'm home!

Spike veers between crying and violence. He talks to

himself and to one of the many dolls Drusilla left behind, asking why Dru left him. Then he vamps out and throws the doll on the ground. He grabs a shovel or something and beats the doll.

Spike: You stupid, worthless bitch.

Having a character talk to themselves can work in a movie, television show, or a play because the audience can't easily access the characters' thoughts. In novels and short stories, it feels a little more distracting and artificial because, at least if you're writing in third person point of view, as the author you can reveal any character's inner thoughts and feelings.

But even in those circumstances, the audience may believe it with a character like Spike. He is a dramatic character who in some ways is always performing. He might very well process his feelings by ranting and storming aloud to himself. Here when he does that, it provides a little backstory about why he came back so drunk and unhappy.

At 4 minutes, 44 seconds, right about the 10% mark, Cordelia is at her locker with Xander. She agrees to go bowling after a bit of arguing. I see this as the Story Spark because this impending double date is what prompts Willow to do her de-lusting spell. That brings her into Spike's path. Without it, Spike likely would never have involved Willow and Buffy might never know Spike returned to Sunnydale.

Xander sees photos of himself and Cordelia together taped inside her locker. He tells her he never knew he was locker material. She tells him he just barely is.

Cordelia: Besides, I look really cute in those photos.

In a moment of parallel storytelling, Oz gives Willow a present at her locker. It's a witch Pez dispenser, and she loves it. She says they have to get a little Pez werewolf to go with it, but Oz tells her they don't make them. Willow seems sad.

Willow: I don't have anything for you.
Oz: Yes, you do.

All of this conveys how much Willow means to Oz and how much he appreciates her. That makes Willow happy, and makes her feel worse about her attraction to Xander and kissing Xander. After Oz walks away, she looks down at that Pez witch, and we see all of it in her face. That moment, rather than Cordelia's decision, can be seen as the Story Spark if it's what puts Willow over the edge and causes her to choose to do the spell.

Suitcases are stacked on the table in the library. Giles is going to a retreat for a few days. Buffy teases him about his approach to packing, which she says is like hers.

Buffy: You're not going to settle there and grow crops or anything?

Giles tells Buffy her SAT scores are remarkable, and her mom must be thrilled.

Buffy: Yeah, she saw those scores and her head spun around and exploded.

Giles has been on the Hellmouth too long and feels the need to confirm that was metaphorical. Then he surprises Buffy by saying Joyce might be right in thinking Buffy ought to consider going away to college. She could have a first-rate education. Buffy pushes back about her Slayer role, and Giles says with Faith there, maybe Buffy can move on for a time.

This is the only mention of Faith in the episode. This offhand comment suggests that Giles almost sees her as a way to make Buffy's life easier. To be fair, Faith clearly loves slaying and did not like school. I don't have any sense that Faith as a character would specifically want the college opportunity Buffy may have. But it does seem dismissive of Faith as a person. I don't believe that Giles as a character disregards Faith as a person, so maybe the writers didn't see the implication of the line. Or they added it deliberately to show the way everything revolves around Buffy (and to include some reference to Faith). More on that in the Foreshadowing section.

Subplot, Exposition, And Theme

Buffy's not very excited about Giles telling her she could go away to school. This is one of the subplots. It's about Buffy moving on from Angel, Sunnydale, high school, or all three.

Giles now raises the topic of Angel, asking her not to do anything rash while he's gone. He specifically asks if she's planning to see Angel. She tells him yes, but they're friends. That's all either of them wants. She says nothing's going to happen between them.

The scene accomplishes so much through subtle conflict. The audience learns Giles is going away for a few days. There's the reminder that the high school is on a Hellmouth. Giles points out the dangers of seeing Angel. And Buffy's discomfort with the idea of going away is clear. In addition, a key episode theme or aspect of the subplot — the idea that Buffy and Angel are just friends — is introduced.

Dealing With Too Many Characters

The scene also shows a way to handle unneeded characters when you've established a strong ensemble cast. The technique can apply not only to television episodes but to novels within a series or sections of a novel where you don't need all the characters. Here, though the audience loves him, the story works better if Giles isn't there to help or give advice. So the writers send him off to a retreat, covering where he's going quickly through some light sparring about his overpacking.

Similarly, Faith gets a nod so the audience knows the show hasn't forgotten her. But she doesn't appear in the episode. And audience members who've watched in order know that she and Buffy are a bit on the outs, so it's believable that Buffy doesn't seek her help.

Linking Scenes

Buffy's assurance to Giles that nothing's going to happen between her and Angel provides a link to the next scene, which starts at about 8 minutes, 30 seconds with dialogue.

Willow: Something's going to happen.

As Willow and Xander walk outside the school, she worries about this double date. She's sure Oz will know something is off and goes on about bowling being all sexy, including the shoes.

Xander: You're turned on by rented shoes?

Xander's line is funny. And it's serious. It underscores that their attraction is so intense that Willow sees bowling as a sexy situation. Xander asks what Oz and Cordelia will know — just that he and Willow are good friends. And "maybe" kissed. Once or twice. But they almost kiss again as they talk. Willow shakes the witch Pez dispenser in Xander's face.

Xander: I wish I wasn't so attracted to you. I wish we could make it all stop.

Willow: Any suggestions?

Willow's line is a less obvious segue, but when we cut to Joyce, she's making suggestions about universities Buffy could attend.

Buffy: Can we talk about it another time? All day it's been like, "Congratulations, go away."

Joyce says she talked about this with Giles. She knows Buffy has slaying responsibilities, but Joyce is sure it can be worked out.

Joyce: Honestly, is there anything keeping you here?

On this line, the scene cuts to Angel, the answer to Joyce's question, sitting alone. I like this segue, particularly because we don't see Buffy with Angel. That stresses how important he is to Buffy's feelings whether she sees him or not.

This whole set up also is a great example of how fantasy and speculative fiction uses metaphor. Viewers and readers can identify with this situation. No, they have never been in love with a vampire they couldn't really be with because he could lose his soul if they have sex. But most people have gone through that feeling of their lives changing and fearing they'll lose someone because of it. Many people hesitate to go away to college when their boyfriend or girlfriend is not going with them because it will probably mean the end of the relationship. And this story deals with that in this almost epic way.

The scene cuts to Spike. He peers through the windows at Angel. Again speaking aloud to himself, he rants at Angel, saying he brainwashed Dru and everything is Angel's fault.

Spike: You're going down.

Spike then stumbles, falls, and passes out in the courtyard. In the next scene, when the sun rises, Spike's mostly in shadows. But the sun reaches his hand, and it bursts into flames. Spikes screams. He runs his hand under water in the courtyard fountain. But apparently it's holy water because his hand starts smoking more. He races into his blacked out car, drinks whiskey, then pours it over his hand. And screams again.

One story logic question here: Why does Angel never hear Spike ranting out in the courtyard at night? Or screaming in the morning? Perhaps he both reads and sleeps with earplugs.

The One-Quarter Twist Of *Lovers Walk*

The episode is nearing the One-Quarter Twist, the first major plot turn that typically occurs one quarter to one third through a story. Spike looks for ingredients and a spell book at the magic shop. He tells the proprietor he wants to curse someone and give him boils all over his face. Maybe also leprosy. The proprietor is a young woman in a flowing dress.

Proprietor: I'm hearing lots of negative energy.

She finally tells him they don't carry leprosy and turns away as Willow walks in. Spike steps out of Willow's sightline but listens as she shows the proprietor what she needs. The woman thinks Willow's getting ingredients for a love spell. But Willow says she knows how to do a love spell, but this is different. It's a de-lusting spell.

This dialogue brings out in a very natural way — through minor conflict over the type of spell so that the proprietor can help Willow — what Willow's planning. Unfortunately, because of it the proprietor becomes the second dead magic shop owner in the series because Spike just got a better idea. After Willow leaves, he says he doesn't need a spell book anymore and he kills the owner.

That was the first major plot turn. As it should, it comes from outside of the protagonist (Buffy or Willow) and spins the story in a new direction because now Spike's goal is to get Drusilla back by forcing Willow do a love spell. It raises the stakes, too, by putting Willow's life in danger.

The mayor hits golf balls in his office and says he would sell his soul for a decent short game, but it's a little late for that.

Mayor (glances at deputy mayor Allan): Oh, maybe I can sell your soul. (Allan looks worried.) Just kidding. So we have a Spike problem.

Allan says Spike killed someone in broad daylight. The mayor laughs about all the shenanigans Spike got up to last year, but they can't have that this year. It's an important year. The mayor calls Spike a loose cannon and says he'll rock the boat, then muses on whether that's a mixed metaphor. He and Allan agree that Allan will send a committee to deal with Spike.

This scene felt like a throwaway — filler that slowed the story — when I watched the episode the first time. I thought it was there to remind us the mayor was around. But it affects the plot because vampires later find Spike and confront him, and that will be key to how the story resolves.

This is a great example of why Season Three in many ways works better when you see it as part of a larger story. These small scenes about the mayor early on connect and build their own story that's key to the season arc. When you view it as a whole almost nothing is just a throw away.

Angel and Buffy: Real Or False Conflict?

In the next scene, Buffy tells Angel about her mom being excited about Buffy's chances to go away to college. She adds that she had a hard time coming up with an alibi for coming to see him. Joyce is having enough trouble processing Buffy being the Slayer. Buffy says her mother's not ready to deal with "that you and I are friends again." This line, too, at first feels a bit like a throwaway. But it will be key to a plot development later that Joyce doesn't know about Angel. Buffy continues that her mom has a point about Buffy getting out of Sunnydale, but there are reasons to stay too.

Angel: What are they?

Buffy looks taken aback that Angel would ask. After naming slaying, she asks what he thinks she should do. He tells her as a friend, he thinks she should leave. It's a good opportunity. Buffy starts packing her backpack.

Buffy: Yeah, it's not like there's any great thing keeping me here. Thanks for the advice. It's another perspective to consider.

As she puts her backpack on Angel says she just got here. But she tells him her mom worries a lot more these days. Her actions and the way she delivers the words tell us how hurt Buffy feels by Angel seeming not to understand that he's part of why she wants to stay. Then Angel feels hurt by her leaving.

This scene is an example of two characters not saying how they really feel, dancing around what they mean to each other, and then feeling rejected as a result. That can create strong tension and evoke deep emotion for the audience where it's true to the characters. But if there's no reason for the characters not to come out and say what they mean, that's false conflict — meaning the writers don't let the characters say what they feel solely to create conflict between them.

Given how much Buffy and Angel have been through together, part of me thinks that they would not hide their feelings from each other. On the other hand, Buffy at least is hiding from herself how she feels for Angel, which sets up a key arc for this episode. And Angel may be trying to do the right thing by encouraging her to go away to college.

Xander meets Willow at the science lab. She told him she'd help him with Chemistry. He's suspicious. First, he points out that it smells like church — evil church — inside the lab. But she says this will help him on the exam because he's struggling.

Xander: But that's why you love me, right? Academically dangerous.

Xander worries that this will make them late for their bowling double date. Willow reassures him Cordelia and Oz are meeting them here at the lab. Xander notices the spell book and ingredients. He thinks she's doing a love spell and reminds her how terribly that turned out when he tried it with Cordelia. (A fun callback to last season's *Bewitched, Bothered And Bewildered*.)

Willow tells him it's not a love spell, it's a de-lusting. She thought it would go better if he didn't know. When he protests, she reminds him he said he wished these feelings would just go away. And she says she can't do this anymore.

The Xander-Willow interaction clearly shows true conflict. They're both sharing how they feel honestly, but they're in conflict over what to do, or not do, about it. And while Willow held back from Xander until now that she planned to use a spell, she gave a plausible reason why.

When Xander moves to turn on the light, Spike enters the room and grabs Xander, who tries to fight. Willow also fights, and Spike knocks Xander out.

At the factory warehouse, Spike demands that Willow do a love spell for him. He veers between being distraught, drinking, crying, and threatening Willow. He wants her to make Dru love him again and to make Drusilla crawl. It's not that different from what Xander wanted with Cordelia, except that Spike does want Dru back and Xander only wanted Cordelia to feel bad.

Willow, nervous, tells him she's not a real witch but she'll try. He breaks a bottle and holds the broken glass to her face until she says she'll do it. Spike veers back to sadness. Drusilla wouldn't even kill him. She just left without caring enough to cut his head off or set him on fire or anything. All he wanted was some little sign she cared. Spike also tells Willow the truce with Buffy did it. Drusilla said he went soft. He was not demon enough.

Spike: I told her it didn't mean anything. I was thinking of her the whole time.

He adds that he caught Dru making out with a chaos demon. Spike asks Willow if she's ever seen one — they're all slime and antlers. And the worst part, according to Spike, was when Drusilla said they could still be friends. He's so unhappy Willow actually tries to comfort him.

Who Is The Protagonist?

The story is nearing its Midpoint. Usually here we see a major commitment by the protagonist to the quest or a major reversal of fortune. Which raises the question of who the episode protagonist is.

To sort that out, I look at three things: (1) who actively pursues a goal throughout the story; (2) who is the main point of view character; and (3) who has the most at stake.[1] Based on these questions, for the main plot about Spike wanting a love spell to get Dru back, I see it as Willow.

We are mainly in her point of view. Though Xander and Spike are mixed in, we feel the most for Willow. She has the most at stake, too, in terms of Spike threatening to cut her face, to kill her, and to kill Xander (whom he's also brought to the factory). Xander obviously has risk there, too, but it's up to Willow to save both their lives.

Finally, she is the one pursuing an active goal throughout the episode. From early on, she aims to deal with her feelings for Xander and eventually resorts to magic. Spike takes a little longer to settle on a goal, though he does actively pursue getting over Drusilla, which shifts to getting her back.

Buffy is the protagonist of the subplot about going away to college or not and how that affects her relationship with Angel. All of that subplot is told from her point of view. She has the most at stake with her happiness and her future. Angel's feelings are at stake, too, but he's going to live forever. Buffy's stakes are higher because she has limited time in her life. And while in the beginning she reacts more than acts, she is pursuing the goal then, too, as she tries to sort out what to do when her SAT scores open options for her.

Despite that, part of why I struggled a bit with this episode on first watch is that Buffy is not all that active in her subplot. Her part of the story works better seen as part of the season long Buffy and Angel arc. Also, you can see Spike as the overall protagonist of the episode. I'll talk more about that when we get to the Climax and Falling Action.

Midpoint Commitment: Willow Stands Up For Herself

As Willow comforts Spike, he starts sniffing her neck and talking about not having had a woman in weeks. Now Willow makes a commitment by drawing a line.

Willow: Hold on. I'll do your spell for you, and I'll get you

Drusilla back. But there will be no bottle in face and no having of any kind with me.

Willow recognizes that she has to push back against Spike if she's going to survive. And that she has some power here. Yes, he can kill her, but if he does, he won't get a spell. Then we see her fear and we see her discomfort with the idea of all this power, because she back pedals a bit.

Willow: All right?

He agrees. She tells him she doesn't know if the spell will work right the first time. Spike reverts to form and says if it doesn't, he'll just kill Xander and she can try again. Willow nonetheless tells him she needs other supplies and her spell book. When he asks where it is, she tells him it's at Buffy's, which is where he goes next. She may be purposely trying to let Buffy know what's happening because we last saw a spell book at the lab. But that's never clearly answered.

At 22 minutes, 54 seconds, Buffy jumps rope in the library. Cordelia and Oz rush in, worried because Willow and Xander are gone. They show Buffy the chaos in the science lab. Buffy tells them to find Giles and describes where his retreat is. Oz knows the place and says he'll drive there. This is another reason the writers sent Giles to a retreat. Now Oz and Cordelia go off on their own quest, getting them out of the way while Buffy deals with Spike.

Joyce calls Buffy at the library, hoping to schedule a college talk. Buffy hears Spike in the background.

Spike: Hello, Joyce.

On that compelling hook, we cut to a commercial. On return, Spike sits at the kitchen table and tells Joyce his sad tale of woe about the chaos demon and Drusilla. He's genuinely upset. Joyce makes hot chocolate for him and tries to empathize with him. She tells him people's lives take different paths. Like with her and Buffy's dad. But Spike insists she doesn't understand. His and Drusilla's love was literally eternal.

Then he asks if she's got any of those little marshmallows to go with the hot cocoa. She steps away to check the cabinet.

This scene further develops a connection between Spike and Joyce. She's really listening and offering him emotional support. And she has no reason to think Spike is a danger to her. The last she knew Spike was helping Buffy fight Angel.

Angel comes to Buffy's house and sees Spike and Joyce through the back window. He tries to storm in to help her, but he can't because Buffy revoked his invitation last year. He's stuck in the doorway. Joyce is understandably frightened. All she knows is how dangerous Angel is.

As in *Revelations*, this episode shows the peril of keeping secrets. Had Buffy explained everything to Joyce, Joyce would not be in as much danger. Now Spike stands behind Joyce, who threatens to stake Angel herself. Spike taunts Angel, telling him he's not invited and making little fang faces behind Joyce. He tells Angel he's "a very bad man." Buffy arrives, though, before he can hurt Joyce. She invites Angel in and pins Spike on the table. Joyce is confused by Buffy's action.

Spike (to Buffy): You do me now, you'll never find the little witch.

Joyce: Willow's a witch?

Angel and Buffy talk about how Spike has Willow.

Spike: And Xander.

Joyce: Xander's a witch?

Spike taunts Angel some more, asking when he became all soul-having again. He refuses to tell them where Willow and Xander are, but does agree Buffy and Angel can tag along while he gets his ingredients. Once the spell is done, he'll tell them where their friends are.

Buffy: You're not famous for keeping your promises, Spike.

Her line shows I was wrong about the end of *Becoming Part Two*. I thought Spike essentially kept his promise to help Buffy by taking out a bunch of the vampires and immobilizing Drusilla. Xander was able to get Giles out. While Spike left during that last fight between Buffy and Angel, I thought perhaps, to the extent she thought about it at all, she felt he pretty much kept up his end of the deal, despite that Spike originally said he wanted to put Angel in the bloody ground. Apparently, though, she does not feel that way.

The scene cuts to Oz driving the van with Cordelia. She's panicking. But he stops the van, sniffs the air, and says Willow is nearby. And she's afraid. He can smell her.

Cordelia: Is this some kind of residual werewolf thing?

This pays off that seed planted early in the episode where Willow talks about wanting to get Oz a Pez werewolf. That moment amps up tension because it stresses that Willow feels bad because she didn't get Oz anything. But it reminds the audience, too, that Oz is a werewolf, which makes his heightened sense of smell feel organic even for a brand new viewer.

Meanwhile, Spike, Angel, and Buffy walk through downtown Sunnydale. He's so sad that he wants to die. Buffy is quite ready to help him with that. But Angel stops her, reminding her they need Spike to find Willow and Xander. Buffy scoffs. She figures he's probably just got them locked up in the factory.

Spike claims he does not, then reminisces when they pass a bench where he and Drusilla killed a homeless man. He keeps talking at the magic shop where the three gather supplies, including rat's eyes. That sets him off on how he used to bring Dru rats for breakfast. Angel mumbles to himself, but loud enough for Spike to hear.

Angel: It's a lot of trouble for someone who doesn't even care about you. She really is just kind of fickle.

That completely fits what we saw of Drusilla in Season Two. Spike, though, says it's Buffy's and Angel's fault. It was because he helped them that he lost Dru.

Spike: I'm nothing without her.

Buffy tells him he's pathetic. Spike tells her she's one to talk and points out that the last time he saw them, they were fighting to the death. It makes him want to heave when they try to say they're friends.

Spike: You're not friends. You'll never be friends. You'll be in love 'til it kills you both. You'll fight and you'll shag and you'll hate each other until it makes you quiver, but you'll never be friends. Love isn't brains, children. It's blood. Blood screaming inside you to work its will. I may be Love's Bitch, but at least I'm man enough to admit it.

His speech calls back to previous episodes with Buffy and Angel fighting. It's a great way to explain the issue to new viewers and to remind current viewers of the past. It's also a subtle callback to this season's *Beauty And The Beasts* when guidance counselor Platt told Buffy that if you can't get past it, Love becomes your master and you are just it's dog. (And there's a lot of foreshadowing here that I'll cover in that section below.) The speech transitions us to another couple struggling with friendship, love, and attraction, though right now they're more worried about survival. At the factory, Willow goes upstairs and bangs on the door, trying to open it without success.

Xander wakes up. He's lying on the bed downstairs, dizzy and sick. Willow sits with him and tells him what happened with Spike. She reassures Xander he was real brave in trying to fight Spike. And she tells him they're in the factory, a burnt-out place in the middle of nowhere. Xander observes that they're "pretty much in a scream all you want scenario" and asks what their options are.

Willow: Well, I figure either I refuse to do the spell and he kills us, or I do the spell and he kills us.

She adds a third option. Spike's so drunk he forgets about them and they starve. Xander says if Spike gets that drunk he'll get sloppy and Xander will make his move. But when he tries, he can't even stand. He falls on the bed again. He and Willow move closer together, nearly kissing.

Willow: We're not supposed to.
Xander: Exception for impending death situation?

The Three-Quarter Turns And Twists

We're now about three quarters through the episode, where we usually see the last major plot turn. It should grow out of the Midpoint, yet take the story in another new direction. At the Midpoint here, Willow suffered a major reversal. Spike threatened her into doing the love spell. She also committed by standing up to Spike.

What happens next arises from the Midpoint if you see the turn as Willow and Xander almost kissing. But what really turns the story is that Cordelia and Oz get into the warehouse and, at about 32 and a half minutes, see Willow and Xander kissing. (That, too, comes out of the Midpoint Reversal in the sense that Spike kidnapping Willow and Xander sets the stage for all of it.)

The scene raises a question. Willow couldn't open the door from the inside. Yet it's not clear if it was locked because apparently Cordelia opens it so easily and quietly that Willow and Xander don't hear anything. But on the first few watches that never occurred to me because the emotional impact runs so high.

Cordelia: Oh God.
Xander: Oh God.
W: Oh God, Oz.
Oz: We have to get out of here.

These simple lines are such a great example of characterization. Oz is the only one who stays focused on the danger. Of course he must feel wounded, and we'll see later that he does, but right now he focuses on getting them all out of danger.

Cordelia runs up the stairs. And remember, this is the burnt-out factory, which was specifically mentioned in earlier dialogue — another example of simple dialogue that sets up later events. The stairs collapse. Cordelia plunges through. The others follow and stare down at her. She's lying on her back, impaled by rebar that has gone through her side.

It's very dramatic. It resonates with how awful Cordelia feels inside. But it also feels random despite the burnt-out factory setting. This late in a story, most key events ought to occur as a direct result of a character choice that came before. On the other hand, the factory is in bad shape. So perhaps my struggle is that most bad things that happen to the core characters occur as a result of more direct action by the antagonist or another foe. This event feels like pure bad luck.

At 33 minutes, Buffy's story turns as well. Vampires (presumably sent by the Deputy Mayor) surround Spike, Angel, and Buffy as they leave the shop with the spell ingredients. Spike knows one of the vampires, Lenny, who used to work for him. Lenny tells Buffy and Angel that they can just walk away. His group only needs to deal with Spike. But after Spike points out that if Buffy leaves her friends will die, Buffy says sorry, but she has to stay.

A Big Fight At The Climax

There's a huge fight. Buffy, Angel, and Spike are a bit overpowered. They try to barricade themselves in the magic shop. Vampires burst in and the heavy front door falls on Angel. They walk right over him. Normally, I don't think this would stop Angel, but we'll see later that he's still weak from everything that's happened to him.

We're near the end of the episode, but I have a little trouble sorting out where the Climax begins or what it is. Normally at a story's climax the opposing forces, the protagonist and antagonist, have their final clash and resolve the conflict between them.

This scene feels like a climax because it's a big fight scene. But Willow, who seems to be the protagonist in the main plot, isn't here. And she is already no longer in danger because we know Oz and Cordelia found her and Spike is too busy fighting to think of her.

Instead, this final confrontation involves the Buffy and Angel subplot and involves Spike wanting Drusilla back. During the fight, Lenny accuses Spike of going soft. This only energizes Spike. Angel gets out from under the door, but he's not up to full strength. All three temporary allies grab bottles of holy water. Buffy and Angel throw them at the vampires. Buffy and Spike coordinate their fighting, and ultimately they defeat all the vampires. That occurs at 37 minutes, 30 seconds, right about where the Climax often finishes.

Falling Action

There is some Falling Action, which is tying up the loose ends, for Buffy, Angel, and Spike.

Spike: Now that was fun.

Buffy says it wasn't, but Spike doesn't believe her. She helps Angel, who staggers a bit, putting her arms around him to help support him.

Spike: Oh, yeah. Just friends. No danger there.

They're ready to do the spell, but Spike doesn't care about it anymore. He tells them their friends are at the factory. And he says he's been going about this all wrong. Weeping. Crying. Blaming everybody else. He just has to be the man Dru fell in love with. So he'll find her, tie her up, and torture her until she likes him again.

Spike: Love's a funny thing.

Plot Or Subplot For Spike?

This episode features a strong subplot for Spike which, given that his plot turns are fairly clear, might actually be the main plot. Either way, Spike is definitely the protagonist of the story about resolving his grief and anger over Drusilla leaving him. He is the point of view character most of the time, though we see some scenes that address that through Willow's or Buffy's eyes. He has the most at stake emotionally. And he has an active goal throughout. Not only trying to get Drusilla back, but trying to find himself again and understand who is he without her. In fact, he says he's nothing without Dru, suggesting his true goal when he returns to Sunnydale might be to figure out how to survive without her.

And, interestingly, Spike deals with his feelings. He goes through grief and sadness. He rants about why it happened. He's angry at Drusilla, at Buffy, and at Angel. He's nostalgic. And then he finds himself through his own actions. He reaches the point where he realizes he stopped being who he was with Drusilla. Stopped being true to himself. Whether that's really why Drusilla left him or her not, we don't know. But that's what Spike believes, and it gives him strength. He moves out of grief and anger, chooses what to do next, and heads off to do it.

In contrast, Willow doesn't try to experience or deal with her feelings. She tries to short circuit them with a spell because she says she just can't deal with how she feels about Xander anymore.

Friends And More Falling Action

The next scenes can be viewed as part of the Falling Action, where loose ends are tied up and subplots are resolved, if the previous scene was the Climax. Or you can see these scenes as the Climax that resolves the plot about Willow's de-lusting spell and her and Xander.

At about 40 minutes, Xander holds Cordelia's hand under the broken stairs, pleading with her to hold on. Cordelia says his name, then tells him she can't see him. Her head turns to the side. It looks like she has died.

In the next scene there's a misdirect, though it plays fair with the audience. The scene cuts from Cordelia to the cemetery. A funeral is going on in the distance. The mourners wear their formal clothes, but we can't tell who they are. The minister says prayers.

Then the camera pans to Buffy and Willow walking in the cemetery past this funeral.

Buffy: So Cordelia is going to be okay?

I'm pretty sure the funeral did fake me out the first time around. But because a lot of *Buffy* scenes take place in the cemetery whether anyone died or not, and Buffy does talk with her friends there, it feels like a legitimate way to temporarily shock the audience. (In a show where the characters never hung out in cemeteries, I'd see that as a cheap way to get an emotional jolt.)

Willow tells Buffy Cordelia lost a lot of blood, but none of her vital organs were punctured. She couldn't have visitors until today. Buffy asks how Willow is doing. And Willow says she never knew she could feel this bad. For the longest time, she didn't know what she wanted. She wanted everything. And now she just wants Oz to talk to her again. So we do see a resolution combined with growth for Willow. She finds clarity when she's in danger of losing Oz. We don't know what will happen with Oz, but Willow at least knows what she wants.

Buffy tells her to give it some time and be prepared for some groveling. And Willow says she's ready. She's all over groveling.

Buffy: Good, because I hear sometimes it works.

Now the episode resolves the rest of the loose ends. The scene cuts to Xander bringing Cordelia this large bouquet of flowers. She is lying in a hospital bed looking at the far wall. He sits down.

Xander: Look, Cordy. I want you to know that I —
Cordelia: Xander. (Turns her face to him very slowly.)
Xander: Yeah.
Cordelia: Stay away from me.

Xander leaves. I give him a tiny amount of credit for that. He doesn't stay and try to change her mind. He leaves her alone.

At 41 minutes, Angel sits alone at the mansion. Buffy comes to see him, but tells him she is not coming back. He's okay now and doesn't need her.

Buffy: We're not friends. We never were. And I can fool Giles and I can fool my friends, but I can't fool myself. Or Spike for some reason. What I want from you I can never have.

Angel doesn't want to accept that. He says there must be some way that they can still spend time together.

Buffy: There is. Tell me that you don't love me.

She walks away and leaves him sitting alone, looking sad.

Now a montage set to very sad music conveys how each character feels and who they are. Willow sits on the floor of her room, her back against her bed, holding the Pez. Oz is in the Bronze, which is closed, alone. He holds his acoustic guitar, not playing it. Xander, alone, shelves books in the library. Cordelia lies alone in her hospital room, just staring at the wall.

Buffy is the only one outside. She's in the park. It's sunny. People are all around her, but they're walking past in slow motion, giving us an even greater sense of her isolation.

The scene cuts to cut to Spike. He's driving his blacked out car and singing *My Way* again, but this time the Sid Vicious punk rock cover. He seems victorious. Spike drives down the road and out of town. That ends the episode.

The Most Healthy Character?

An excerpt from an essay in the book *Fighting The Forces: What's At Stake In Buffy The Vampire Slayer*, edited by Rhonda V. Wilcox and David Lavery, goes to a question I raised in the beginning of this chapter. Is Spike healthier emotionally than Buffy, Angel, Willow, and Xander? I think so because he knows his feelings. He feels them and addresses them. And then he makes a choice. Buffy tries to do that at the end, but she and Angel mostly deny their feelings during the episode. Willow tries to do a spell to avoid hers. But Spike knows himself. And he's perceptive about other people.

The quote below is from *The Undemonization of Supporting Characters* by Alice Money on page 100 of the book. (This is not the entire quote. I'm leaving a few parts out here.)

...LOVERS WALK SHIFTS the character Spike not by making him a sweet, heartbroken, humanized lover but rather by showing his vulnerability in making him a rejected, drunken lover who will even to descend to compromising his depravity and dealing with humans in order to regain Dru. Any self-respecting vampire is totally amoral and ruthless, as evidenced by Spike's earlier cruelties, not to mention Angelus's acts of both gratuitous and calculated viciousness. But when Spike becomes an object of ridicule and a source of amusement, he loses some of his terror. Somehow it is difficult to maintain fear when the fearful creature turns sweetly nostalgic and weeps over the good times with Dru....

In a moment of epiphany, he realizes that each person —

Buffy, Angel, or he himself — can achieve fulfillment only by remaining true to his/her/its own nature....Amidst the carnage of helping Buffy and Angel defeat an attacking vampire gang in the magic shop, Spike is invigorated by the violence and determines a new course of action....The old Spike is back....Ironically, the episode ends with everyone except Spike made acutely miserable by love.

THE QUOTE FOCUSES MORE on Spike's epiphany about his true self, but he gets there through feeling his emotions deeply.

Spoilers And Foreshadowing

The Wish, The Mayor, And The Season End

Cordelia's comment at the beginning of *Lovers Walk* that Buffy can get out of Sunnydale and never come back strongly foreshadows the next episode, *The Wish*. There, Cordelia wishes Buffy never came to Sunnydale. The last scene of *Lovers Walk* sets up how devastated Cordelia will be in *The Wish*. She starts *Lovers Walk* happy and with photos of Xander in her locker. She agrees to go bowling with Xander, Willow, and Oz, despite all her comments about it being the least classy thing to do. All of that shows how much Xander now means to her. Then in the next episode all her old friends make fun of her for Xander cheating on her. We see how alone Cordelia feels, how devastated, and that drives her to make her wish.

The mayor needling and frightening Allan foreshadows Allan betraying him. (And it's a good metaphor for leaders of all types who motivate through fear and how it backfires.)

Spike's speech, where he tells Angel and Buffy they'll be in love until it kills them both but will never be friends foreshadows the end of the season. Angel will leave Buffy because he decides that he is bad for her and a danger to her. The physical danger becomes explicit when she forces him to drain her blood to save him from dying by poison and nearly dies herself.

Angel Crossovers

In *I Will Remember You*, when Buffy crosses over onto *Angel* the series for the first time, Buffy and Angel do get to be together. But for epic reasons, some of which echo the themes of Spike's speech, it cannot work.

Spike's comment on them being unable to be friends foreshadows what we see in other crossover episodes. Buffy expresses so much anger at Angel when Faith, after taking over Buffy's body in Season Four, ends up under Angel's protection. He responds in kind, wounded by learning Buffy has a new boyfriend when, in his memory, they so recently had one wonderful day together. Then Angel crosses over to *Buffy*, meaning to apologize. Instead, he terrorizes Riley.

Mortality And Magic

The magic shop owner's death foreshadows a third shop owner dying in Season Five. When the gang investigates, Giles sees the shop's books, notices how profitable the shop is, and buys the shop at a good price because of the high owner death rate. (I would love to know if the writers knew that was coming when they wrote *Lovers Walk*.)

The story of Willow resorting to a spell to avoid her feelings, and her willingness to affect Xander's emotions without his consent or knowledge, foreshadows her arc in the series. Willow will turn to magic more and more to avoid her feelings and to influence what other people do, feel, and think. This is especially so in Season Six.

At the beginning, Willow doesn't deal with her grief about Buffy's death because she focuses on a spell to bring Buffy back. Before the season starts, she tells Xander, Anya, and Tara about the spell because she needs their help. But she doesn't tell Giles, who she knows would try to stop her. She doesn't tell Spike or Dawn. And she doesn't tell anyone all the dangers of the spell.

Later in Season Six, Willow casts a spell on Tara to avoid conflict — specifically conflict over magic — and erases Tara's memory of a fight. She doubles down on that when Tara calls her on it, devastated that Willow messed with her mind. In response, Willow messes with all her friends' minds in *Tabula Rasa*.

And, of course, in Season Four's *Something Blue*, Willow tries to short circuit her grief. In the process she causes Giles to go blind, demons to come after Xander, and Spike and Buffy to fall in love.

What Else Spike Sees

When Spike taunts Buffy about how she does love the fight, which she denies, it foreshadows both Faith's and Buffy's conflicts and their bonding. Faith loves slaying and doesn't understand why Buffy says she doesn't like it and talks as if it's a burden. As Spike observes, that's Buffy denying a huge part of who she is. She loves many parts of slaying. And it's interesting that Spike sees that about her.

As *Buffy* goes on, Spike is often the person with whom Buffy is the most honest. She tells him things in Season Five that she doesn't tell Riley. And in Season Six she hides things from her friends — sometimes because she thinks they can't deal with them and sometimes because she can't — but tells Spike.

Spike also has great insight into Willow. When Oz leaves in

Something Blue, everyone else thinks she's dealing with it. Spike sees that she's devastated. Likewise, when Glory attacks Tara, Buffy thinks she talked Willow out of taking revenge until it's the right time. And Spike scoffs. He tells Buffy of course Willow's going after Glory, just as he would do for someone he loves (meaning Buffy). Spike is often the one who truly sees and understands other people's emotions.

On the other hand, sometimes he doesn't grasp things about himself. His story about Drusilla breaking up with him foreshadows the Season Five episode where Dru returns. She's distraught to discover Spike's in love with Buffy. But she says she sensed it back when she broke up with Spike. She saw Buffy all around him.

Questions For Your Writing

- Is your protagonist actively pursuing a goal? Are they the main point of view character? Do they have the most at stake? If not, why not?
- Does your Climax bring the antagonist and protagonist into direct conflict? Does it resolve the conflict? Who wins? Who loses?
- Is one of your subplots stronger than your main plot? If so, is that intentional? If not, how might you revise?
- Can you use dialogue to link the end of a scene to an action or dialogue line in the next scene? Ask yourself the same question for chapter endings and beginnings.
- Do you lay the groundwork for key plot developments early in your story? Are any important background facts your reader needs in the second half of the story missing?

- How is your antagonist vulnerable? Can you show that?
- Which of your characters are the most and least emotionally healthy? Does that work for your story?
- Examine the conflicts in your story. Do they ring true? Are there good reasons if one character holds back information from another or hides their feelings?

The next chapter talks about *The Wish*, an alternative timeline episode where Cordelia's wish that Buffy never came to Sunnydale is granted.

CHAPTER 9
THE WISH S3 E9

THIS CHAPTER TALKS about *The Wish*, Season Three, Episode Nine, where a demon grants Cordelia's wish that Buffy never came to Sunnydale. Written by Marti Noxon and directed by David Greenwalt. Original air date: December 8, 1998.

Along with the episode breakdown, topics include:

- A protagonist with strong goals and high stakes
- Alternate life events that could change an entire character
- Why *The Wish* is about Faith, who never appears in it
- An antagonist who pushes against the protagonist but might not set out to harm her
- What a character's appearance tells us about who they are

Okay, let's dive into the Hellmouth.

Opening Conflict

The episode starts, as it should, with plenty of conflict. A giant demon holds Buffy off the ground by her neck. She kicks wildly while calling for help. Willow finally tosses her a knife after first thinking Buffy asked for a "nerf." Xander helps, too, and Buffy kills the demon. Afterwards, Buffy tells them how grateful she is that the two of them were there. If they hadn't been, she doesn't know what she would have done.

She couldn't reach Faith. Buffy worries about that because slaying is a rough gig and Faith has been spending a lot of time alone.

When Xander asks if they're done for the afternoon, she asks if he has plans.

Xander: I cannot stress enough how much I don't have plans.

They talk about whether Cordelia will forgive him. He's left her a few messages — sixty or seventy. Xander goes on about how unfair Oz and Cordelia are because sure, he and Willow kissed. But it was the last time that was going to happen and they burst in rescuing them without even knocking. So it's really all Oz's and Cordelia's fault. Then we get one of my favorite lines in all of *Buffy*.

Buffy: Your logic does not resemble our earth logic.
Xander: Mine is much more advanced.

Willow expresses more distress and guilt than Xander. She says that it feels like all the air just goes out of the room when she thinks that she might not ever be able to be close to Oz again.

We're only about 2 minutes, 49 seconds in, and yet we have gotten so much already. There's the initial conflict with Buffy and the demon, which seems unrelated to the main story arc, but introduces it in a sense that I'll talk about later. Also Buffy's concern about Faith, who doesn't appear in this episode, but in a way the story is all about her. Plus through some minor conflict and conversation we learn about the Oz, Willow, Xander, and Cordelia conflicts and backstory.

The scene cuts to Cordelia sitting on her bed. She wears sweats and a tank top. We've never seen her in this type of comfortable, non-stylish clothing before. It tells us a lot about her frame of mind. She has a huge bandage around her midsection. As Xander's phone messages play, she engages in the time-honored tradition of cutting up and burning photographs with Xander in them. She cuts Willow and Buffy out of a photo and keeps only herself, which does a great job of introducing her motives in this episode.

And we go to credits.

Cordelia's Scary Story Spark

At 4 minutes, 17 seconds, Buffy and Willow stand near Oz's locker. Willow's upset that Oz has not visited his locker. He may need books in there, but still he doesn't appear. The two talk about Cordelia. They heard she was coming to school today. Willow adds that Amy saw Cordelia at the mall and she looked scary.

The scene changes to Cordelia getting out of her convertible. In contrast to the last scene, she wears a stunning form-fitting red dress and stiletto heels. Harmony and three other girls meet Cordelia outside the school. Harmony tells Cordelia she looks amazing. They do air kisses.

Now we are getting to the Story Spark or Inciting Incident. This next moment is a little past 10% at 5 minutes, 20 seconds (of a roughly 44 minute episode). But it sets off the main plot, which is what the Spark does. Harmony introduces Cordelia to Anya, who is new. Harmony adds that Anya's dad just bought a utility or something. Anya and Cordelia immediately bond when Anya admires Cordelia's bag and asks if it's Prada.

Cordelia: Good call. Most people in this town can't tell Prada from Payless.

Harmony says Cordelia was smart, faking an injury to be out of school.

Harmony: You take a week off, let everybody forget about the temporary insanity that was Xander Harris.

It's not clear how Harmony and her friends found out what happened. I doubt very much Cordelia told anyone. It seems unlikely Oz would. He's very closed mouthed generally. But perhaps Cordelia confided in someone or Willow talked to Amy.

Another girl with Harmony tells Cordelia what she needs to do is get back on the horse and start dating again. Cordelia agrees. Harmony has the perfect stallion for her. She leads Cordelia to Jonathan, who is sitting on a bottom step drinking a huge drink through a straw. He looks really confused when these pretty popular girls come up to him. Harmony tells Cordelia she's pretty sure he won't cheat on her, at least for a while.

Harmony: And he's got a killer moped.

Oz comes to his locker at last in the next scene.

Willow: Oz, wow. Look at us. Running into each other as two people who go to the same school are so likely to do now.

After saying "Hey," Oz turns to leave. Willow asks him to wait and apologizes. It's clear she's done this before, which Oz points out. But Willow says she really wants to make this up to him.

Oz: You can leave me alone. I need to figure things out.

Oz is very mature and emotionally healthy here. He's clear on what he needs. He goes on to express some understanding for how Willow feels when she keeps trying to talk to him. The acting and directing is perfect, because he delivers the lines in a quiet, almost compassionate way.

Otherwise, he could read as snippy, but that's not Oz's character.

Oz: Look, I'm sorry this is hard for you. But I told you what I need. So I can't help feeling that the reason you want to talk is so you can feel better about yourself. That's not my problem.

Callbacks And Building Toward The Twist

At about 8 minutes, the scene cuts to a different interior hallway. Cordelia sees Xander at the other end of the it. She stops John Lee, a football player, and asks if she has something in her teeth. He's facing her, somewhat blocking Xander's view. Cordelia moves her head from side to side. From Xander's perspective, it looks like they're kissing. He slinks away.

Cordelia flirts with John Lee. But he tells her the coach cut him back to second string. If he's seen hanging out with "Xander Harris's cast off," it will look bad for him. But he suggests they could go somewhere private, implying to make out. Cordelia's shocked and he walks off after telling her to think about it.

Now Cordelia runs into Anya and assumes she's going to pile on.

Cordelia: Go ahead, dazzle me with your oh, so brilliant insults.

But Anya doesn't want to do that. And when Cordelia mentions her hanging around with Harmony, Anya says Harmony follows her around and if she ever had an original thought her head might explode. The line calls back to Cordelia saying she was going to date whoever she wanted and telling Harmony she was a sheep who just did what everyone else did.

Not only is this a way for the writers to continue building Harmony's character, it may say something about Anya. We later find out she's a vengeance demon. The first scenes with her make me think she deliberately talked about things that would make Cordelia feel close to her quickly. First, recognizing Prada. Second, basically calling Harmony a sheep. The callback underscores Cordelia's humiliation, too. It reminds the audience that she felt she risked a lot socially to date Xander and now he repaid her by cheating on her.

Cordelia admires the pendant Anya wears. Anya says it's sort of a good luck charm. Cordelia thinks it would have been great if she had that pre-Xander. Anya empathizes and starts talking about how terrible Xander is and doesn't Cordelia just wish — but Cordelia cuts her off. She's going to forget all about Xander. She'll show how over him she is.

In the next scene Cordelia is doing exactly that. She laughs and talks at the bar area in the Bronze, appearing to have a wonderful time. Xander sits on a couch with Willow and Buffy. He does a very loud fake laugh and they stare at him.

Xander: I need to be both giving and receiving of mirth.

Buffy says she's support-o gal, but she doesn't feel good about the "us against Cordelia part." Willow points out that she and Xander are in the wrong. When Cordelia leaves the Bronze, Buffy follows her outside to talk to her. She promises Cordelia she's a free agent, Xander did not send her to beg for him as Cordelia suspects. At about 12 minutes, 49 seconds, Buffy tells Cordelia she knows what it's like when someone hurts you so badly and that talking to her friends helped her. The moment calls back to the pilot episode of Season Two. Cordelia followed Buffy out of the Bronze and gave her some advice about keeping her friends.

Now Cordelia looks like she is about to talk. But a vampire attacks. Buffy fights and stakes it.

The One-Quarter Twist Of *The Wish*

The episode is approaching the One-Quarter Twist, that first major plot turn that comes from outside the protagonist and spins the story in a new direction. It also often raises the stakes. Here it does all of that, though a little later than 25% through. (Usually in a novel it will be right at that one-quarter mark. In television, it varies more widely.)

Here, a number of moments could be this major turn. They all add up and prompt Cordelia's wish, though. First, Cordelia gets knocked toward a dumpster during the fight. She re-injures her side and gets trash on her. Then her friends come out and laugh at her. Cordelia says (to Buffy) that she's been asking herself why she's the one who gets impaled and bitten by snakes and dates incredible losers.

Cordelia: I finally figured it out —

At 14 minutes, 13 seconds, the scene cuts and Cordelia finishes her line in the sunny school courtyard as she talks to Anya.

Cordelia: — Buffy Summers.

Buffy sits across the courtyard talking with Xander and Willow. Anya notices Cordelia holding her side and asks her if she's in pain. Cordelia says she pulled her stitches last night and surprise, it was Buffy's fault. Harmony walks by again with her friends.

Harmony: Dumpster chic for the dumped.

Anya gives Cordelia her pendant for good luck and asks isn't it really Xander's fault? She agrees Buffy's a pain, but doesn't Cordelia wish....? But Cordelia says she never would have looked twice at Xander if Buffy hadn't made him "marginally cooler" by hanging around with him. Anya's surprised, but Cordelia finally makes a wish.

Cordelia: I wish Buffy Summers had never come to Sunnydale.

A little after 15 minutes, Anya turns into her demon face.
Anya: Done.

I see that moment as the first major plot turn for Cordelia. But because this story will also be Buffy's story, the One-Quarter Twist can be seen as the earlier moment when Cordelia decides that Buffy is the reason for all her pain.

On return, there's a white foggy screen, and then we see Cordelia in the courtyard alone. It's empty. Buffy and her friends are gone. Cordelia touches her side and feels no pain. She looks around. She's been on the Hellmouth long enough to get right away what happened.

Cordelia: Anya. "I wish Buffy Summers had never come to Sunnydale." She was like a good fairy. A scary, veiny, good fairy.

She laughs and goes inside.

In contrast to earlier, Harmony and her friends are thrilled to see Cordelia. They're all dressed in shades of gray. They compliment Cordelia's blue dress, saying it's so daring. John Lee pulls Cordelia aside to ask her to Winter Brunch. Cordelia says she'll get back to him. He's thrilled.

Harmony: Cordie, you reign.

In the next scene, the classroom is half empty. When the bell rings, the teacher grabs his books, reminds the students about the memorial tomorrow, and rushes out. Cordelia wants to know what the others are doing later. They remind her that curfew is in an hour, confusing her. Cordelia suggests going to the Bronze. Harmony takes her aside and asks what's wrong with her — wearing this come-bite-me outfit and joking about the Bronze. Cordelia claims she bumped her head. She's having trouble remembering things. Then she claims she doesn't care but asks:

Cordelia: ...in this reality, Xander Harris is miserable, right? And that Willow freak he hangs with is not even a blip on the radar screen?

Harmony (so much more serious than ever before): Well, yeah. They're dead.

Next, in a deserted parking lot with no cars in sight, Cordelia looks for her convertible. She is rude to this caretaker who walks by and he tells her she knows better — students aren't allowed to drive. Also, she better get home before sunset.

The scene cuts to Cordelia walking home in the dark. This seems not smart, and I was a little taken aback the first time I saw the episode. Though she doesn't know all the details of this reality, Cordelia certainly knows being out after dark alone in Sunnydale is a bad idea.

The DVD for this episode includes the shooting script. It says the scene is at dusk. That makes more sense. This is meant to be in December. The sun would be setting early. It's a little more believable that Cordelia is hurrying home at dusk, aiming to arrive there before sunset. The way it's filmed, though, it looks like it's already dark.

Businesses are closing their doors and pulling down grates. Cordelia runs into Xander. Both he and Willow (whom we'll see in a moment) look very different. Xander wears a black leather jacket over a crisp white T-shirt. His hair is combed back. He wears a chain around his neck. He looks good and exudes confidence. Cordelia doesn't notice the difference, possibly because she's shocked he's alive.

Cordelia: What is this? Some kind of sick joke? Harmony told me you were dead.

Xander: Now, why would she say something like that? Let's see.

Cordelia tells him they need to get Buffy. She was supposed to be here, and though Cordelia hates to admit it, she made things a lot better.

Xander: Buffy the Slayer?

Cordelia: No, Buffy the Dog Faced Girl. Duh. Who do you think I'm talking about?

Willow appears. She wears tight-fitting leather clothes.
Willow: Bored now.

Cordelia asks what's up with the leather. Willow talks about this part being less fun. There's no screaming. Xander puts his arm around her and says he appreciates her appetite.

Cordelia: No. No way. I wished us into bizarro land and you guys are still together? I cannot win.

Midpoint Of *The Wish*

Xander tells her probably not, but he'll give her a head start. He vamps out.

This is the Midpoint of the episode, as it's a major reversal for Cordelia. It comes about 20 minutes, 22 seconds in. Cordelia screams and runs. Xander leaps over a car, catches her, and throws her on the ground. But a van, driven by Oz, squeals down the street and pulls over.

Willow: Oh, swell. It's the White Hats.

Giles jumps out holding a giant cross. Larry, who we saw in earlier episodes (he was the football player who came out as gay), is with them along with another girl named Nancy. They hold off Willow and Xander and get Cordelia into the van.

At 21 minutes, 51 seconds, Cordelia, unconscious, is lying on the library table. One of the White Hats asks what Cordelia was doing — everyone knows vampires are attracted to bright colors. Like Cordelia's friends in the hall earlier, everyone in this group is dressed in shades of gray. Giles tells them to go watch the perimeter.

At the Bronze, humans are in cages. Some are tied up on pool tables. Discordant music blares. And we find out the Master is alive. This also could be considered a major reversal despite that Cordelia doesn't know about it. It's at almost exactly the episode midpoint at 22 and a half minutes in.

Story Questions

Xander and Willow go in the back. Xander tells the Master they just had a prime kill, an old crush of his actually, until that wanna-slay librarian showed up. He mentions that the girl kept talking about Buffy. The Master is angry that they didn't kill the girl who talked of summoning the Slayer when the plant will be operational in twenty-four hours. Willow pouts and says they had crosses.

This scene does a great job of raising story questions, which are questions that keep the audience watching so they can find out the answer. As viewers, we already wonder about this new world. But now there's something with a time limit — a plant that will become operational in twenty-four hours. That adds urgency and raises the question of what it's for. Also, when Willow and Xander back off so fast from crosses, I wonder if the vampires in the town have gone soft with no Slayer around.

In the library, Cordelia wakes up raving about making a wish. And she makes something of a commitment by insisting they need to get Buffy back. Giles tries to tell her to calm down and rest. But she tells him No, he has to get Buffy. Buffy changes everything. It was all better — including the clothes alone. Giles seems skeptical. Cordelia finally asks what he's doing there when Buffy's not. He was her Watcher. Giles is shocked. He doesn't see how she could know that, as he never told anyone.

Noises sound outside the library. Giles goes into the book cage to get weapons. But as he grabs a cross, Willow slams the gate and locks him in. Xander grabs Cordelia.

Xander: So you're a Watcher, huh? Watch this.

He and Willow stand on either side of Cordelia and bite and kill her. And we cut to a commercial. When we come back, Giles breaks out of the cage. Larry and Oz return and tell him the vampires killed Nancy. As they take Cordelia's body to the incinerator, Giles sees the pendant Anya gave her around her neck. He takes it off of her.

The scene switches to the Master taking a small cup from what looks like an espresso machine. I liked this transition because in the first moment of the new scene, I thought Giles was getting a cup of tea and instead it's the Master with Willow and Xander. They're all happy Cordelia's dead and the opening will commence as scheduled. Willow asks if she can go play with the puppy.

Giles talks on the phone in his office at night. He says it's imperative that he sees "her" and adds something like, "Well, when will you? You're her Watcher." All of it gives us the idea that Buffy's Watcher has no idea what Buffy's doing.

Giles: Just give her the message. If you ever see her again.

The scene cuts to the Bronze during the day.

Willow: Bored now. Daytime is the worst.

She goes into a cage where Angel is lying on the floor. She calls him the puppy and tortures him. Xander throws her a lit match. She drops more lit matches on Angel's bare chest. Xander says he loves watching her play.

At nearly 30 minutes in Giles finds the pendant in a book. He reads that it belongs to Anyanka, a demon who is a sort of patron saint to scorned women who grants wishes. The group figures out that Cordelia must have wished for something.

Oz: Well, if it was a long, healthy life, she should get her money back.

Giles tells them what Cordelia said about the Slayer. He has more volumes so he can research further and tells them to get some sleep.

That raises another question for me. Why are any of them at the library at night, given what's going on in this town? The answer may be that they're the only ones fighting the vampires, and vampires are out at night. So they gather at the library. It's their home base, much as it is in our usual universe. But it seems so dangerous. Maybe that tells us what desperate times these are. Giles is allowing regular students who have no particular powers to risk their lives helping him fight vampires.

Giles drives toward home but pulls over when he sees vampires herding humans into the back of a giant truck. Using his cross, Giles scares a number of the vampires off. Some humans get away. But then a few vampires overpower him. He's on the ground.

We're now reaching the Three-Quarter Turn. This is the last major plot turn, and instead of coming from an outside force (as the One-Quarter Twist usually does), it grows from the Midpoint. Here, it arises directly from Cordelia's Midpoint Reversal when the vampires killed her. It also arises from her commitment to getting Buffy back.

At 31 minutes, 45 seconds, someone we don't see at first fights off the vampires and helps Giles. When we do see her, Buffy looks different. Her hair is pulled back in one long braid down her back. She wears cargo pants, flat shoes, and a gray tank top. Somewhat like Cordelia in the opening, she's dressed and done her hair for practicality, not style. This Buffy has no time to care about appearances. A scar over her lip shows she's been injured more seriously than our Buffy. Injured permanently.

Buffy: Want to tell me what I'm doing here?

In Giles's apartment Buffy is impatient as Giles looks through his books. He's excited when he discovers that they need to destroy Anyanka's power center. Buffy rains on his parade immediately because she asks what the power center is. When the book has no answer, Buffy wants to just put a stake through Anyanka. Giles protests that she's not a vampire.

Buffy: Well, you'd be surprised how many things that'll kill.

But Giles doesn't want to kill Anyanka. He wants to reverse the wishes. Now Buffy is really skeptical.

Buffy: You're taking an awful lot on faith here, Jeeves.
Giles: Giles.

Giles tries to convince her without much luck.

Buffy: World is what it is. We fight. We die. Wishing doesn't change that.

Giles; I have to believe in a better world.

Buffy: Go ahead. I have to live in this one.

Giles explains what Cordelia said, including that Giles was meant to be her Watcher. But Buffy thinks Cordelia is probably just a big fan. Giles tells Buffy the Master sent his most vicious disciples to kill Cordelia. Buffy's shocked that no one has tried to take out this Master when they know where he is. Giles points out that they have tried to kill him.

He doesn't want Buffy to go off on her own to face the Master. But she says she wouldn't be much help anyway with research. Then he wants to try to get others to go with her.

Buffy: I don't play well with others.

Buffy goes to the Bronze alone. It's deserted other than Angel, still in his cage. He calls her by name and tells her he waited there for her.

Angel: The Master rose. He let me live...to punish me. I kept hoping maybe you'd come. My destiny.

Buffy: Is this a get-in-my-pants thing? You guys in Sunnydale talk like I'm the Second Coming.

Angel finally convinces her that he wants to help her, but while she's unchaining him, her cross nearly burns him. He jerks away. Buffy thinks Angel's trying to lead her to the Master so the Master can kill her. But he opens his shirt — so we get to see his chest yet again, of course — and shows his wounds. He tells her if she doesn't believe he wants to help her, believe he wants the Master dead. All this conflict brings out backstory for both characters and fills the audience in on the new world.

At the factory, a large group of humans is penned in a cage. The Master gives a speech in front of a large machine that includes a conveyor belt. He tells them the detractors say death is a vampire's art and this machine goes against their nature. But he sees it differently. They've always been bound by the mindless routine of the predator. It's impractical. They spend all their time hunting and killing. In the meantime, humans have brought the world a truly demonic concept: mass production.

We switch to Giles, alone in his apartment. He does a spell besieging Anyanka to appear in the name of all women scorned. Suddenly and silently she appears in the shadows. She's got her demon face on and speaks in her gravelly scary demon voice, startling Giles (and the audience).

Anyanka: Do you have any idea what I do to a man who uses that spell?

The scene cuts back and forth to the factory throughout this part of the episode.

At the factory, a girl is brought out of the cage. It's not Harmony, but is one of the girls who was mean to Cordelia. She's put on the conveyor belt, which starts moving. The Master comments that she's still alive for the freshness. A dozen mechanical arms with needles go right into her body at different spots. Red blood flows through the clear tubes.

Buffy's in the crowd with Angel.

Angel: What's the plan?

Buffy (handing him a stake): Don't fall on that.

The Master holds up the first glass of blood.

The Climax Begins

At 40 minutes, 12 seconds, the Climax begins. That's where the opposing forces have their final clash and the main conflict resolves. The Master lifts his glass in a toast. Buffy raises her crossbow.

The Master: Welcome to the future.

Buffy fires. The arrow would have hit the Master's chest, but he grabs Xander and puts him in the way. The arrow hits Xander's shoulder. Angel starts letting the humans out of the cage. Larry and Oz are among those who were rounded up. They join the fight. The scene cuts to Giles's apartment.

Giles: Cordelia Chase. What did she wish for?

Anyanka: I had no idea her wish would be so exciting! "Brave new world." I hope she likes it.

Giles tells her Cordelia is dead, but that's just the way it goes in Anyanka's view. Giles insists she must change it back. He also says he's not afraid of her.

Giles: Your only power lies in the Wish.

Anyanka: Wrong.

She grabs him by the neck and shoves him against the wall, lifting him much like the demon lifted Buffy in the beginning of the episode.

At the factory, Angel is about to punch Xander, but Xander stakes him. Angel turns and says, "Buffy," and dusts. The scene cuts back to Giles's apartment.

Anyanka: This is the world we made. Isn't it wonderful?

Buffy fights on, staking Xander, her face stoic. She doesn't know him, so there's no reason that she would particularly react. But the Buffy we know has feelings, even about staking vampires. She's not flat. But she moves on with no change of expression. That moment, too, is so striking compared to her comment in the beginning of this episode about how much Willow and Xander mean to her.

The action slows to slow motion. Buffy and the Master shove other vampires out of the way to move towards each other. Buffy kicks a vampire in the face. We see her shoe hitting, which is a telling moment. We normally don't see that kind of shot. We see her stake vampires and fight them, but something about the boot or the shoe in the face is visceral and tells us so much about Buffy in this universe.

Giles sees Anyanka's pendant around her neck and it glows. He grabs it. She's shocked, and he punches her.

The Master and Buffy reach each other.

Giles has the pendant on the desk and holds an object in his hand to break the pendant.

(One thing about the Giles and Anya interaction that confuses me is that he grabs the necklace from Anyanka's neck, but he already had the necklace she gave Cordelia. I think that's a flaw in the story logic. But as a viewer I don't care because I love this story.)

Anyanka: You trusting fool, how do you know the other world is any better than this?

Giles: Because it has to be.

Giles brings the object down on the pendant. It shatters.

The Master snaps Buffy's neck. She starts falling toward the ground. There is still fighting around her because to everyone there it's not even a big event. They don't know who Buffy is. The Master knows, but they don't.

Before Buffy hits the ground, the scene fades to that white foggy screen that we saw before. Everything switches. Cordelia is back in the courtyard, outside the school. It's sunny. Buffy, Willow, and Xander sit together again.

Cordelia: I wish Buffy Summers had never come to Sunnydale.

Anya turns around, but her face doesn't turn into a demon. It stays normal. There's no scary voice.

Anya: Done.

I see that moment as the end of the Climax because Giles changed the world back. Cordelia returned. She doesn't know about what happened, and she's back at the moment where she makes a wish.

The Falling Action

Now we're at the Falling Action. This is where the writers tie up loose ends in the main plot and end any open subplots.

When Anya says "Done," Cordelia talks about how cool that would be. She then runs through other wishes, including wishing Buffy had never been born. She eventually gets to Xander, wishing he'd never know the touch of a woman. Anya keeps saying "Done" and being confused that it's not working. That part makes me wonder what she's unclear about. My sense is that Anya knows what happened and remembers the alternate universe. But maybe she didn't realize that not only would Cordelia's wish be reversed, she would not be a demon anymore.

Buffy (wearing her usual stylish clothes again), Willow, and Xander laugh and talk in the background and Giles joins them. That ends the episode.

Can Your Protagonist Die Mid-Story?

It's unusual to have a protagonist die during the story. Sometimes a protagonist dies at the end, during the final conflict, or in the Falling Action. But rarely mid-plot. I can think of one movie where it happens, which I won't name here just in case anyone hasn't seen it despite how old it is.[1]

Despite Cordelia's death, which occurs past the Midpoint of the episode, I see her as the protagonist. An ideal protagonist should:

1. be the main point of view character
2. actively pursue a goal throughout the story
3. have the most at stake

Here, up until she dies, we see the story mainly through

Cordelia's eyes, with just a couple scenes from Willow's point of view. After Cordelia is killed (at 26 minutes, 30 seconds out of a 44-minute episode) in a way we are still in her point of view because we are in the world that she created. When Anyanka says, "this is the world we made," it appears she means she and Cordelia. Mostly it is Cordelia's story, and we return to her, alive, at the end.

Cordelia also has an active goal. From the beginning, she wants to get over Xander and cut him out of her life. She wants Willow and Buffy gone, too. She sees them as a group. The group that caused her problems. So she has an active goal she pursues before making the wish, and she doubles down on it by wishing Buffy never came to Sunnydale.

After the wish, she lives in this world she's excited about. The changes make her happier. Then her goal shifts as she starts dealing with the harmful consequences of her wish. Her goal becomes to get Buffy back. And even after she dies, that commitment to get Buffy back propels the story. Finally, Cordelia has the most at stake. First, her social life and her happiness. Next, her life, which hangs in the balance as Giles strives to right the world.

For all those reasons, I see her as the protagonist.

Faith, Buffy, And Theme

This is my favorite *Buffy* episode in large part because I'm so intrigued by the idea of what makes Buffy who she is. And what makes any of us who we are for that matter. **The Wish** asks what things, if changed, would drastically alter who Buffy is and how she lives. From the moment we saw her in the pilot, she's been committed to having a normal life. But here we see Buffy without that. Buffy who has everything stripped away.

On that note, I don't think it's an accident that Buffy tells Giles, with a lot of skepticism, that she's taking an awful lot "on faith." While Faith doesn't appear in the episode, in many ways it is about her as a character.

What we know of Faith at this point in the series is that she's isolated. She rarely talks of family. She's living in this motel room by herself. At the beginning of *The Wish*, Buffy worries because Faith's not hanging out with anyone. Faith's first Watcher got killed in front of her, her second turned out to be a fraud who tricked her and then tried to kill her. Right now, she has no Watcher of her own.

This episode puts Buffy in Faith's circumstances. No friends, no mom (at least we don't see Joyce and Buffy doesn't mention her), no close relationship with her Watcher. Buffy's line about not playing well with others speaks to her isolation. And her view that we fight and we die and wishing doesn't change it strongly suggests a lot of loss. Taken to this extreme, Buffy becomes flatter in effect, more fatalistic, and loses her trademark humor and desire for a normal life. Perhaps that's why this Buffy doesn't survive her clash with the Master when the "real" Buffy did — eventually and with the help of friends.

Faith as a concept also plays a role in the episode. Cordelia has faith that the world will be better if Buffy comes to Sunnydale. Her commitment to that idea leads her to tell Giles he was meant to be Buffy's Watcher. That in turn gives Giles the faith to hunt Buffy down. His faith leads him to confront Anyanka, too, and to smash the pendant. His reasoning that the old world had to be better requires a certain amount of conviction and faith. Things can always be worse, and he doesn't have the close tie to Buffy that he did in the real world. But he believes.

In contrast, Buffy in this episode has no faith. She doesn't believe that anything really makes a difference in the big picture.

The Antagonist In *The Wish*

This episode prompted me to look more closely at what makes a character an antagonist. In essence, the antagonist is defined only in relation to the protagonist. And the antagonist has only one key job: to oppose the protagonist.

My initial thought was that Anyanka must be the antagonist. But in the beginning, she's not opposed to Cordelia. She befriends her to manipulate her, but at least ostensibly she is there to help and avenge Cordelia.

Even when she grants the wish, she doesn't know what Cordelia will wish for or what will happen. In fact, she tells Giles she had no idea the wish would be so exciting. Once the world changes, it's a terrible place for Cordelia. And Giles must defeat Anyanka to right the world again. That suggests though she might not start out intending to harm Cordelia, she is the antagonist throughout.

Also, she does oppose Cordelia in one way early on. Anyanka wants Cordelia to focus on Xander and make a wish about him. Cordelia resists until the very last moments of the episode when it no longer matters.

Another option is to see evil, or the way the world works, as the antagonist. That could work because the story clearly is about being careful what you wish for. Anyanka represents or embodies that concept.

More thoughts on that in the foreshadowing section.

Insights From The Script About Anya And Story Structure

When Giles reads about Anyanka, he says not only that she was a sort of patron saint for scorned women, but that she was a human who raised a demon to curse her lover. The demon did her bidding, but turned her into a demon as well. As I'll talk about in the foreshadowing section, though, we later get a slightly different story of Anya becoming a demon.

The script addresses my question about Giles already having the pendant Anyanka gave Cordelia, but then we see Anyanka wearing it and he yanks it from her neck. The script says she is wearing a pendant identical to Cordelia's. That doesn't quite explain how that works, but I liked knowing that the writers did recognize that there were two pendants.

The script also shows the act breaks. It uses a three-act structure. When plotting that way, the first act is generally about one quarter to one third of the story, the second act spans what I think of as the second quarter and third quarter of the episode, and the third act is roughly the last quarter. There's no act break at the midpoint.

Here, Act One ends where Anya shows her demon face, which is what I saw as the likely first major plot turn. The next act break, which begins the third act, occurs when Buffy's on screen and rescues Giles. That's what I saw as the last major plot turn (the Three-Quarter Turn), as it grows from the Midpoint, spins the story again, and drives it toward the Climax.

This breakdown illustrates why I like looking at the plot in quarters rather than three acts and focusing on a strong Midpoint. While there is a solid Midpoint here, many novels sag in the middle as writers struggle with how to keep the momentum going during the long stretch between the act breaks. In my view, the three-act structure makes it harder to focus on the Midpoint and to recognize how important it is to your writing.

Spoilers And Foreshadowing

Future Anya And Willow

In Seasons Five, Six, and Seven, we learn more about Anya as a human woman. Her lover cheated on her. She did a spell to curse him and turned him into a troll. The demon D'Hoffryn was so impressed by all the chaos she caused that he offered her a job as a vengeance demon. She went on to relish that role.

These later developments don't depart too much from what Giles tells us in *The Wish*. It's a good example of taking a character you may have meant to appear once or twice in your series and expanding their backstory to add nuance and make them more engaging. This more involved history for Anya creates options for other subplots, such as D'Hoffryn returning to the Buffyverse to interact with Willow, Anya's failed and later successful attempts to become a vengeance demon again, and Anya's struggles to deal with relationships, humanity, and her own mortality.

This episode foreshadows *Doppelgangland*, too. There, Anya tries to get her pendant back. In so doing, she inadvertently brings Vampire Willow into this world. Cordelia and Vampire Willow interact, which is really fun when Cordelia thinks she's talking to human Willow.

As to Willow, it's striking that the first thing we hear Vampire Willow say in *The Wish* is "bored now," which Willow echoes in Season Six just before killing Warren.

Faith And Buffy

This entire episode foreshadows the Faith and Buffy story arc. Seeing alternate universe Buffy helps the audience feel sympathy for when Faith gets angry at Buffy and jealous of all she has that Faith doesn't. The episode shows the effects of Faith's isolation compared with Buffy's connections. In many ways, Buffy and Faith are mirrors of one another.

Further, though Buffy has no memory of *The Wish* universe, later in the series we'll see that she often understands Faith's choices and actions because she senses how life would be for her without Giles, her friends, and her mother. And Buffy goes to some dark places in Season Six when her mother and Giles are gone and she feels cut off from her friends.

Evil As The Antagonist

While probably the true antagonist is Anya, not evil in general, we'll see an amorphous antagonist in the next episode, *Amends*. There, the antagonist is The First Evil. It exists and influences everything, but is not corporeal. The Bringers work for it and represent it to some extent in *Amends* and later in Season Seven.

The First takes the form of people who are dead. It primarily appears as Jenny Calendar in *Amends* when manipulating Angel. But the antagonist itself is this primal force of evil in the world. And you could view The First as influencing the events of *The Wish*. Perhaps it is why Cordelia's wish is twisted to create such a dark universe.

The Wish hits a related theme that arises again in *Gingerbread*. In that episode, Joyce (under the influence of a demon) says Buffy has no plan and what she's doing — slaying a few vampires or demons at a time — is kind of fruitless. Buffy kills them but there are always more, and Joyce asks if Buffy really changes anything on a fundamental level. *The Wish* preemptively answers that question. Yes, it does make a difference.

Questions For Your Writing

- What are the stakes for your protagonist? Can you raise them? How?

- Do your protagonist's goals change during the story? Why or why not?
- In your fiction, what events in a main character's backstory truly shaped who they are as a person?
- Does your main plot or one of the subplots shed light on a separate character's life or story? Could it?
- How do your main characters dress, style their hair, and otherwise present themselves to others? Are there points in your story where that might change? Why or why not?
- Does your antagonist start out aiming to help your protagonist or block or defeat them? Does that change?
- What are your antagonist's intentions toward the protagonist? And what does your antagonist want that puts them at odds with your protagonist?

The next chapter talks about *Amends*, where The First Evil tries to turn Angel into Angelus again. (It's also the only Christmas episode in ***Buffy***.)

CHAPTER 10
AMENDS S3 E10

THIS CHAPTER TALKS ABOUT *AMENDS*, Season Three, Episode Ten, where The First Evil torments Angelus during the Christmas season. Written and directed by Joss Whedon. Original air date: December 15, 1998.

Along with the episode breakdown, topics include:

- How *Amends* tracks Dickens' *A Christmas Carol*
- Whether the episode serves as a series pilot for *Angel*
- Flashbacks and dreams that move the story
- When a *deus ex machina* ending might satisfy your audience
- Sorting out overlapping protagonists and antagonists and the challenges of an incorporeal antagonist like The First
- Creating a well-structured subplot

Okay, let's dive into the Hellmouth.

Opening Conflict

Before I get to the plot, I need to confess that I've never loved this episode. But as I watched it more analytically for the *Buffy and the Art of Story* podcast, I grasped why so many people love it. And gained a better sense of what it does to set up *Angel* the series.

The opening conflict here directly relates to the main plot. A subheading tells us it is Dublin, 1838. A young man, Daniel, hurries across the snow. Angel grabs Daniel in an alley. Daniel whimpers when he sees Angel with his full vampire face on.

Angel: Be of good cheer. It's Christmas.

Angel lunges and bites Daniel. In the present, Angel awakens in a sweat.

The choice to start with a flashback within a dream is probably part of why it's not my favorite. I don't love most flashbacks of Angel either when he was human or in his early vampire days, and usually I don't love dreams for storytelling.

But, as always, *Buffy* uses both very well. We've often seen Buffy's dreams be prophetic and help her answer questions and unravel mysteries. They drive her actions and choices. For that reason, the dreams in *Buffy* move the story, which is the ideal way to use a dream rather than including one just to convey information or be artsy.

Here, too, and perhaps more so than in previous episodes, the dreams and flashbacks will be part of the story, as opposed to pausing or stopping it.

Next, Angel walks through the streets of Sunnydale. It's dark. Holiday lights and decorations are everywhere. Angel runs into Buffy. They have a stilted conversation. We get the sense they have not seen each other since the end of *Lovers Walk* where she told Angel she couldn't see him anymore. Buffy's shopping for presents for her friends and asks without thinking if he's shopping.

Buffy (awkward): Vampires. Probably not that big on Christmas.

As they talk, Angel, distracted, looks across the street. At 2 minutes, 30 seconds, he sees Daniel standing there, which really spooks him. Buffy asks what's wrong. And we cut to the credits.

On return, the school bell rings as Buffy, Willow, and Xander walk out of class. Buffy explains that Angel just bailed and says it was weird. Willow suggests talking to Giles, but Buffy doesn't want to. Giles is still kind of twitchy about Angel.

Xander: Oh, it must be that whole Angel killed his girlfriend and tortured him thing. Yeah. Giles is pretty petty when it comes to stuff like that.

Buffy tells him that's enough already. This scene illustrates a good use of conflict, as we so often see in *Buffy*, to get across some backstory. It reminds viewers exactly what happened and why Giles will be so hostile to Angel in later scenes.

I love the bell ringing, too, as our friends exit the classroom in the middle of a conversation. It does a couple things. One, Buffy doesn't repeat everything that we just saw, but we know she told it to her friends. Two, the bell ringing as they leave class gives the viewers a sense of them being in school without having to sit through classes with them. Using this type of exit moment is a great way to show your characters in a setting like work or school without slowing your story.

Now Buffy, Willow, and Xander sit in one of the school's lounging areas talking about the Christmas break. Buffy says hers will be quiet — just the tree, nog, and roast beast. She asks what Willow's doing and Willow reminds them she's Jewish and not everyone worships Santa. (This tells us people have been saying this to her a lot.) Buffy says she just meant for vacation. Xander tells them he's doing his annual sleep outside in his sleeping bag to look at the stars.

Story Spark And Subplots

We're over 4 minutes into the episode. Normally, a Story Spark or Inciting Incident appears by 10% through any *Buffy* episode. Here, the main plot turns out to be The First Evil manipulating Angel, so I think the Story Spark occurs when Angel sees Daniel across the street at 2 minutes, 30 seconds. That's when he knows he didn't just dream about this horrible thing he did in his past as a vampire. It's intruding into real life.

There also are some very clear subplots. One thing I loved on rewatching for the podcast was seeing the clear turns in each one. That makes *Amends* a great episode to watch for how to weave subplots into your main plot.

The Willow and Oz subplot will start soon. But first, at 5 minutes, Cordelia overhears Xander's comment about sleeping under the stars. She says she thought Xander slept outside to avoid his family's drunken Christmas fights. Xander thanks her for sharing that information he told her in confidence. She tells them she'll be skiing in Aspen with actual snow, and it must be a drag to be stuck here in Sunnydale.

After she leaves, the others comment on Cordelia reverting to form but Willow says they should cut her some slack. She's had a rough time. Willow adds that she herself is pretty big on forgiveness as a theme this year because of — and Oz walks up and says "Hey." That happens at 6 minutes. It's the Story Spark for Oz and Willow.

In the next scene, the two talk in an empty classroom. Oz talks about seeing her with Xander.

Oz: I never felt that way before when there wasn't a full moon.

That line tells us that despite how calmly Oz reacted in the moment, he experienced violent emotions.

Oz: I know you guys have a history.

Willow: But it's a history that's in the past. Well, I, I guess most history is in the past, but it's over.

Oz: Well, I don't know. I don't know that it ever will be over between you two.

Oz is very perceptive here. But he adds that what he does know is that he misses her.

Oz: Like every second, almost like I lost an arm or worse a torso.

Oz says he's willing to give it a shot. Willow's thrilled, and they hug. This dialogue shows Oz's maturity. He recognizes a bond between Willow and Xander. While he may very well be convinced nothing sexual or romantic will happen going forward, he understands he needs to be able to live with this bond.

The next scene is at a Christmas tree lot. In one part of the lot the trees are all dead. But the rest look good, including some with fake snow on the branches, which Joyce says is very Christmasy.

Joyce suggests that Buffy invite Faith for Christmas Eve. Buffy's not so sure. She and Faith haven't really been hanging out lately. Or talking or making eye contact. But Joyce asks if Buffy really wants to leave Faith to spend Christmas Eve in that dingy little motel. Buffy comments on her mom laying on the guilt, but agrees to ask Faith. Joyce prompting Buffy to issue this invitation is the Story Spark for a minor subplot about Buffy and Faith reconnecting.

Subplots generally use the same types of major plot turns in the same order as a main plot, though sometimes the one-quarter and three-quarter plot turns are skipped. You can fit the subplot in so that it complements the main plot.

For example, you can cut to a subplot when you need a break from intense main plot action. Or switch right after a cliffhanger in the main plot that will keep your audience eager for more. (I just finished recording the Season Six musical episode for the podcast. It's an excellent one to watch for how to use subplots to enhance the whole story.)

Buffy suggests that they should invite Giles, too. Joyce immediately says she's sure he has other things to do. When Buffy presses, Joyce just tells her No and suggests they split up. This moment calls back to when (unknown to Buffy) Joyce and Giles had sex in **Band Candy**. It's another example of how Season Three rewards ongoing viewers over those who jump in here and there (which was still fairly common for viewers to do when the series first aired).

At about 9 minutes, 20 seconds, the scene shifts. It's dark. Guys with no eyes who wear monks' robes chant. Angel wakes up in a sweat.

The scene cuts again, this time to Faith's hotel. Buffy invites her to Christmas Eve. Faith guesses that Joyce made her, which Buffy denies. But Faith claims she's busy. She was invited to this big party. Buffy says okay, but if she changes her mind — Faith reiterates her party claim. Before she leaves Buffy admires the holiday lights Faith strung around the room.

Faith: 'Tis the season. Whatever that means.

I see this as a Midpoint Commitment in the Buffy/Faith subplot. When Buffy asks Faith, she tries to convey that she personally wants Faith to come. Though Faith doesn't buy it, Buffy committed to trying to repair the damage she caused by not telling Faith about Angel's return in the earlier episodes.

Now we are approaching the One-Quarter Twist in our main plot.

Setting, Character, And The One-Quarter Twist

The first major plot turn occurs right about one quarter through the episode at almost 11 minutes. Giles is cooking on his stovetop, pausing to taste the food. He's also making tea. Giles's apartment is always this wonderful place to be. It's homey and comforting.

He cooks good food. He makes tea for himself or others. I love that because it goes against the stereotypes of single people, and single men in particular, which say they can't have a "real" home or cook for themselves. (As someone who lives alone, I always dislike the implication that you can't enjoy your home if you live by yourself.)

A knock on the door interrupts Giles. It's Angel. Giles freezes and stares at him.

Angel: Um, I'm sorry to bother you.

Giles (laughs): "Sorry." Coming from you, that phrase strikes me as rather funny. "Sorry to bother you."

Angel: I need your help.

Giles: And the funny just keeps on coming.

Angel says he has nowhere else to go. Giles tells him okay, but he walks away. Angel reminds him he can't come in without an invitation. Giles says he's aware of that and returns with a crossbow he points at Angel before inviting him in.

This action tells us a lot about how Giles feels about Angel, regardless that Buffy told him Angel was better and that Angel saved Willow from Gwendolyn Post.

Angel is breathing hard, obviously distressed. He tells Giles he's been dreaming about the past, but it's like he is living it again. He needs to know why he is back on earth because he should be in a demon dimension. Giles asks if knowing why he's back will bring Angel peace of mind. When Angel says it might, Giles suggests that might not be such a good thing. The last time Angel became complacent about his existence it turned out rather badly.

These lines explain something I struggled with. I understand Giles's visceral reaction to seeing Angel again. This person killed Jenny and tortured Giles. Giles almost wouldn't be human if he didn't react badly to seeing Angel. At the same time, I thought Giles might make a distinction between Angel the person (or the vampire with a soul) and Angelus.

But the comment about when Angel got comfortable before tells us Giles is not only reacting emotionally to what Angel did to him but is concerned about him becoming Angelus again. As Giles talks, Jenny Calender appears and stands near Giles. She touches his shoulder.

Angel: Don't you see her?
Giles: Who?
Angel (clearly very spooked): I can't.
Angel races out of the apartment.

Dreams And Ghosts Of Christmas Past

This is where I see parallels to *A Christmas Carol*. Daniel seems like the ghost of Christmas Past, taking Angel on this journey through his life. We will continue to see that, and it sets up the ending that prompts or leads into *Angel* the series. Jenny acts as a sort of ghost of Christmas Present. She emphasizes where Angel is right now, the turmoil he is in.

In the next scene, Angel tosses and turns in bed. Then, in another dream or flashback at a holiday party, Angel corners a serving maid under the stairs. He doesn't have his vampire face on yet. She tells him she really needs to go back to work, begging him to leave her alone.

Maid: I can't lose my job. I'll get put out on the street.
Angel: Well, go ahead, call your mistress for help. I'm sure she'll believe you.

Angel vamps out and starts to bite her. But he looks up and Buffy is there. She's lit so that she almost glows. As she stares at him, Angel wakes up. Then Buffy wakes up. They shared this dream. And we cut to a commercial.

This is another example of using dreams and flashbacks that don't stop the story. Whether you see Angel's experience as ghosts haunting him or his internal struggle, it drives the story.

And Buffy appearing in and seeing Angel's dream will be key to everything that happens.

Angel gets out of bed. Jenny is there. He asks what she wants.

Jenny: I want to die in bed surrounded by fat grandchildren, but I guess that's off the menu.

Angel apologizes, but she tells him if he wants to feel sorry for someone, he can feel sorry for himself, "but I guess you've got that covered." She morphs into Daniel.

The Gang Comes Through And A Subplot Twist

The scene cuts to Buffy at the library telling Giles she was in Angel's dream. Giles is skeptical. Buffy insists something is wrong with Angel. Giles finally says he knows. He saw Angel. And he's been looking into how to find out why Angel is back. Yay, Giles. Despite everything he said, he won't let his feelings about Angel keep him from helping, which could be a serious mistake because Angel could become a danger again.

Buffy says she's not seeing Angel anymore, but she can't put him behind her if they're doing guest spots in one another's dreams. As they agree they'll help Angel, Xander appears in the doorway and asks where they start. He adds that he knows he hasn't been Buffy's bestest friend about Angel, but maybe he finally got the Hanukkah spirit. Buffy asks Xander if it's really how he wants to spend his Christmas vacation. He tells her it's the most exciting thing he has planned, and who else can claim that pathetic of a social life?

Willow (entering): Hi guys, what are we doing?

After a short montage of everyone reading and studying, Willow and Buffy pause to talk. Oz is coming over to Willow's on Christmas Eve when her parents are out of town. But Willow says things are still awkward between them.

Buffy: Xander has a piece of you that Oz just can't touch. I

guess now it's about showing Oz that he comes first.

That serves as a One-Quarter Twist in the Willow and Oz subplot. It comes from outside of Willow. And Buffy's comment spins the story because it gives Willow an idea.

Angelus And Christmas Past

At about 19 minutes another man tells Angel how he felt when he found his children after Angel slaughtered them. He says Angel arranged them so artfully. The man morphs into the serving maid who tells Angel that others kill to feed, but he took more kinds of pleasure in it than any other beast.

Each of them haunts him again much like the ghost of Christmas Past showing Scrooge scenes from his life. Though, here, past and future are less defined. Angel tries to argue that it wasn't him, it was the demon. He was a man once.

Jenny: Oh yes. And what a man you were.

We see a quick scene of Angel drinking, almost falling over, and grabbing a girl. Different ghosts cycle through and taunt him about how worthless he was. It ends with one telling him that cruelty is the only thing he ever had a true talent for and it's not a curse. It's his destiny.

In the library, Xander yawns. Upstairs, Buffy falls asleep on the floor near some books and papers. Angel, too, is sleeping in the mansion. Now we are coming to what I see as the Midpoint turn in the main plot.

The Midpoint Of *Amends*

Usually at the Midpoint protagonists make a major commitment to the quest or suffer a major reversal or both. Here, at about 21 and a half minutes, we see a dream Buffy and Angel both experience. They're kissing in her bedroom. They start making love. The lighting is soft, similar to that in flashbacks of their lovemaking in earlier episodes. A Bringer, one of those eyeless beings, appears in the room. Angel sees it and bites Buffy.

Angel wakes up. Jenny urges him to take Buffy, to pour all his anger and frustration into her. Then he'll be free. He can't live for eternity with all this pain.

Jenny: This is why we brought you back....Then you'll be ready to kill her.

This scene touches on present and future. In *Becoming Parts One and Two*, learning about Buffy pushed Angel to want to help people and be more human. Now he's lost Buffy, yet he can't be the demon that he was. He doesn't want to be. So in the present he's tormented by being unable to be a human or a vampire.

Jenny plays on his pain, suggesting it'll be endless unless he acts. She offers him a future free of torment. If he does this thing, goes to Buffy and turns into Angelus again, he can be the monster he was once more. It will be a relief.

I see the dream as a reversal for both Buffy and Angel. For Angel because he is horrified at the thought of doing this, yet it speaks to him and haunts him. And for Buffy, of course, this is her greatest fear about Angel.

She reaffirms her commitment here, too, to do something to help Angel no matter what.

The Protagonist And Antagonist

The ideal protagonist should be the main point of view character, have a goal and actively pursue it, and have the most at stake. Here, while we do get a fair amount in Buffy's point of view, a large part of the story is told through Angel's point of view.

Angel, too, has the more active goal. Initially, he's reacting to his dreams and to seeing Daniel. But he quickly shifts to trying to sort it out. He goes to Giles and asks for help though he has every reason to think Giles might try to kill him on sight. His goal is to find out why he was brought back and what to do about it.

Buffy, in contrast, is troubled in the beginning, but not enough to go to Giles. She doesn't become very active until she is in Angel's dream.

Angel also has the most at stake. His fight is for his soul, for who or what he will be. A vampire with a soul on the side of the good? Or a monster again? Or will he end his own existence? While Buffy is in danger from Angel, at least in this episode she seems so much stronger than him. Based on all of this, Angel has more at stake.

The antagonist isn't clear at the beginning. The main job of the antagonist is to push against the protagonist, pulling out all the stops to keep the protagonist from achieving their goal.

Here, at first, we don't know what exactly is going on with these people, who may be ghosts, from Angel's past. Jenny hints at a purpose when she says "that's why we brought you back," but we don't know what the "we" is.

It's possible Angel is imagining all of this, making his own psyche the opposing force. By the end of *Amends*, though, it becomes clear The First Evil a/k/a The First is manifesting as all these different ghosts. It attacks Angel throughout the episode. Because its goal is never defined, we can see it as pushing primarily against Angel (if he's the protagonist) or primarily against Buffy (if she's the protagonist). But The First is the antagonist.

After several rewatches, my view is that Angel is the protagonist. His goal is to find out why he was returned from Hell. The First is the antagonist set on thwarting Angel and destroying him again. Buffy is a protagonist, too, but in a subplot where she aims to help Angel and keep him alive. He, as the subplot antagonist, resists.

While I don't think a story has to be totally clear throughout on protagonist and antagonist, I tend to like stories that are clearer than this one and that have more defined major plot turns. In the end, though, I do think it is a well-structured story. But as this analysis shows, it's one where much of the structure is not apparent the first time around.

Buffy wakes up in the library. Giles found information on The First Evil, an ancient evil that is powerful enough to have brought Angel back. He shows Buffy a drawing of those eyeless guys and tells us they are called Bringers or Harbingers. They're high priests of The First Evil. They can conjure spirit manifestations to haunt people.

Giles explains that The First can't be fought directly because it is not physical. Buffy says she can fight the priests if she can find them. She and Xander go to Willy's bar, hoping he has information. Holiday lights hang all around the bar.

Willy (very loud): It's the Slayer. What brings the Slayer down here?

The vampires at the bar slink away. Xander and Buffy question Willy, and Xander keeps interrupting with threats. Buffy tells him maybe he shouldn't help. Willy finally says he has heard a few things. There's lots of migration out of Sunnydale by the lower inhabitants, and these are things that are not easily scared. He doesn't know where the Bringers might be, except somewhere underground. As they leave, Willy tells Xander he did great. Willy was very intimidated by him.

Willy (to Buffy): Hey, Kid. Merry Christmas.

The scene includes lots of Christmas references, which is part of why I link the episode to *A Christmas Carol*. On the street, though, Buffy and Xander talk about the sweltering heat, emphasizing the contrast between Sunnydale and what's thought of as traditional Christmas weather (snowy and cold).

Buffy is frustrated. Learning that these Bringers are underground doesn't help because they're in a town with all these sewer tunnels. Xander mentions there are cave formations, too. He reassures Buffy, though, that they will figure it out, adding that maybe she should go home and deck the halls. I like Xander here. He's encouraging, and he reminds her to enjoy the holiday.

Oz And Willow Subplot Midpoint And Turns

At 28 minutes, 45 seconds, Oz walks into Willow's house. He has videos for them to watch. He's a bit stunned to find her sitting in a lovely dress by the fireplace, candles burning all around. Barry White plays on the stereo. I see this as a Midpoint Commitment for Willow.

Oz: You ever have that dream where you're in a play and it's the middle of the play and you don't know your lines and you kind of don't know the plot?

Willow tells him she just wants to make tonight special.

Oz: How special are we talking?

Willow struggles to convey what she means.

Willow: We're both mature younger people. And so we could, I — I'm ready to — with you. We could do that thing.

Oz, sitting next to her, very kindly tells her she looks great, everything is wonderful, but he's not ready. Willow asks if he's scared, because she thought he did this before. He has, but he says this is different.

Oz: And when it happens, I want it to be because we both need it too. For the same reason. You don't have to prove anything to me.

Willow tells him she just wanted him to know. He tells her he got the message. They kiss. It calls back to that scene in the van when Willow wanted him to kiss her, and he thought she was doing it to get back at Xander. It's clear that now they communicate well, feel good about their relationship, and are back together.

Right after Willow's commitment to show Oz she put him first, the subplot took a major turn when Oz responded. His answer spun their story in a new direction — tonight is not going to be the night that they make love — and arose from Willow's commitment. Then there was a resolution or Climax. Willow and Oz are back together.

This scene illustrates how the major plot points and turns in a subplot typically happen in the same order as in the main plot, but they may be compressed and occur more quickly. (They also may stretch out across the entire story.)

From a thematic perspective, it's striking that Willow talks about wanting Oz to be her "first." I'm not sure how that relates to The First Evil. But I don't think it could be accidental that this scene occurs in an episode about The First.

At home, Buffy enjoys trimming the tree. As at Willow's, a fire burns in the living room.

Buffy: Nothing like a roaring fire to keep away the blistering heat.

The doorbell rings. It's Faith. She brings gifts wrapped in newspaper though twice she says they're crappy. Joyce is really happy that she's there. So is Buffy. Faith admits that she didn't really have a party to go to. Buffy says she'll go upstairs and get her gifts. The episode moves toward the Three-Quarter Turn in the main plot.

Plot and Subplot Three Quarter Turns

At 31 minutes, 2 seconds, Buffy enters her bedroom and Angel jumps out from behind her door, startling her. He struggles to speak. He's breathing hard. We mostly see the scene through his point of view. Jenny hovers behind Buffy. The camera angle tells us Angel is focusing on Buffy's neck. He says Buffy has to stay away from him.

Buffy: You came to see me to tell me that I can't see you?

Buffy tells him something is doing this to him. As he moves closer, his manner threatening, Jenny urges him on. But Angel yells at her to leave him alone and dives out the window.

Here, as it should, the Three-Quarter Turn arises out of the Midpoint and spins the story yet again. The Midpoint Reversal was the dream where Angel and Buffy made love and he bit her. It led to this moment where he came to her room, likely telling himself he was going to warn her away, but really because he wanted to act out that dream. Now he's having this fight with himself.

Buffy understands how far over the edge Angel is and how dangerous. She runs downstairs and asks Faith to stay and watch out for her mom. She promises she'll fill Faith in on what's going on later. And Faith is okay with that.

There also was something of a Three-Quarter Turn in the Faith and Buffy subplot. Earlier, Buffy made a commitment by asking Faith to come over. Faith made her own commitment by refusing. But later she showed up at the Summers' house. That's a pretty big turn in the Buffy/Faith relationship. Faith is willing to be part of this evening with Buffy and her mom.

Now there's a resolution or Climax of that subplot because Faith is willing to trust Buffy that something is really wrong and Buffy needs to handle it right now. Faith doesn't argue. She stays to protect Joyce. And she trusts that Buffy will fill her in despite that a lot of her mistrust of Buffy, and her anger, related to Buffy not telling Faith about Angel.

Buffy goes to Giles's apartment and tells him to find her these priest guys because Angel is slipping. Giles warns her she may have to kill Angel. Again.

This is the third time Buffy and Giles have this talk. First, she told him she was in Angel's dream and they needed to help Angel, and Giles agreed. Then in the library she woke up from a more vivid dream. That's when Giles found out about The First and the Bringers (the priests). Buffy said if she could find the Bringers she could fight them. Now she tells Giles things are really, really bad and she really, really needs Giles to find her the priests.

The repetition probably is intentional. It may be meant to echo the three ghosts in *A Christmas Carol* or to invoke the feel of stories and fairy tales where three is a magical number. But it feels slow to me. Though the intensity of Buffy's feelings increases, nothing new occurs.

The slower pace may be because the story is more Angel's than Buffy's. Also, for Buffy the high stakes involve what all this means for her feelings about Angel, not fighting The First. But *Buffy* works best for me when both the emotional conflict and the evil-fighting conflict have well-structured, escalating plots.

After Giles points out that Buffy may need to kill Angel again, the scene cuts to Angel telling Jenny, "I can't do it." The audience knows Jenny is The First, but Angel doesn't. Jenny tells him he has to do it and adds that he was never a fighter, so don't start trying now. Sooner or later, she says, Angel will drink Buffy. As long as he's alive, that is what he'll end up doing.

Angel says then he'll die. When Jenny tells him he's not strong enough to kill himself, he responds that all he needs is for the sun to rise. He heads for the courtyard. Jenny tells him he's not supposed to die. That isn't the plan.

Jenny/The First: But it'll do.

If we see *Amends* as primarily Angel's story, this is a major turn for him. It arises from that Midpoint (Angel's dream that he makes love to and then bites Buffy) but takes the story in a completely new and unexpected direction.

The First's Goals

It's not clear what The First's plan is throughout the episode. It seems to be to turn Angel evil again and/or for him to kill Buffy. But when Angel threatens to kill himself, Jenny says that works.

All of which suggests that the goal is to devastate Buffy emotionally, making her a less effective slayer. After all, if Buffy dies, a new slayer might take her place. (It's unclear how Buffy's previous death as well as the current existence of two slayers affects the succession.) But if she's a wreck emotionally because Angel's evil again or dead, she won't fight as well. The First's goal also might be to take Angel out of the equation as a force for good one way or another.

The lack of clarity about The First's goal makes this a tough episode for me as a viewer (and writer) who likes fairly linear stories. What exactly The First wants doesn't truly matter for the emotional plotlines. Yet I want to know.

Returning to Buffy and Giles, he reads prophecies that all sound like riddles. He finally finds something that says the Bringers are harbingers of death and nothing shall grow above or below them. Buffy connects it to those dead Christmas trees. I love that she's the one who makes that connection. As is so often the case, her strength is not only physical strength and mystical ability but using her mind. That is contrary to the Buffy we saw in *The Wish* who said she'd be no good to Giles on the research or strategy fronts.

Buffy goes to the Christmas tree lot and finds the dead trees. She hacks into a cave below with an axe. The Bringers chant among lit candles.

Buffy: All right, ten more minutes of chanting and you guys have to go to bed.

There's a huge fight. Jenny appears and gives a long dramatic monologue that Buffy interrupts.

The First: I'm not a demon, little girl. I am something that you can't even conceive. The First Evil. Beyond sin, beyond death....I am the thing the darkness fears. You'll never see me, but I am everywhere. Every being, every thought, every drop of hate —

Buffy: All right, I get it. You're evil. Do we have to chat

about it all day?

The First tells her that Angel will be dead by sunrise. Buffy's Christmas will be his wake.

Jenny/The First: You have no idea what you're dealing with.

Buffy: Let me guess, is it evil?

The First transforms into a large, scary monster.

The First (shouting): Dead by sunrise.

The Climax, An Incorporeal Antagonist, And The Pilot

That last scene escalated the conflict and moved the story toward the Climax, where the opposing forces clash one last time and resolve the main conflict.

The scene also highlights a major challenge of The First Evil as an antagonist: it is incorporeal. That's particularly difficult here because so much of series includes physical fighting, often as a metaphor for resolving other issues. The First is an entity Buffy can't physically fight. Another issue with The First is that its main power is to haunt and influence people by talking to them. That doesn't allow for much action.

Finally, The First isn't very effective when directly attacking Buffy. She's good at trading quips with villains and fairly easily deflects attempts to throw her off guard emotionally. If Buffy is our protagonist, The First mainly acts against her through its effect on Angel. If Angel is the protagonist, and he probably is for the reasons I covered earlier, The First acts on him by pushing him to harm Buffy or kill himself. The First is far more effective against Angel than Buffy. Angel is already suffering over the guilt he feels, and The First knows how best to attack him verbally.

But we don't see The First in the actual Climax, which occurs in a scene between Buffy and Angel. All the same, I see the Angel verses The First main conflict playing out there.

Angel, in essence, takes over The First's viewpoint, saying the words and taking the actions (or trying to) based on what The First said to him. Buffy steps in as antagonist, fighting The First when Angel has given up.

Buffy finds Angel on a hill, looking down at the town a few minutes before sunrise. She begs him to get inside. Something evil is haunting him. He tells her he knows. But Angel insists it wasn't haunting him, it was showing him what he is.

Buffy: Some great evil takes credit for bringing you back and you buy it? You just give up?

This scene provides a great example of two characters with opposing viewpoints who feel deeply that they are right and who, depending upon how you look at it, both could be right. It's a much more complicated, nuanced conflict than pure good versus pure evil. While Angel has been influenced by evil, there are reasons what he says makes sense. As Giles emphasized throughout the episode, Angel could become Angelus again. Angel's unwilling to risk it.

Buffy tells him it's the evil talking, but Angel says he wanted to do what The First told him to do. He wants her so badly, wants to take comfort in her, though he knows it'll cost him his soul. Angel tells her he has always been weak.

Angel: It's not the demon in me that needs killing, Buffy. It's the man.

Buffy tells him everyone is weak. Everyone fails. But she says if this evil brought him back, it means it needs him, which means he can hurt it.

Her words have so much power because Buffy doesn't try to deny Angel's fears or his feelings or tell him he doesn't mean it. Instead, she reassures him that everyone struggles. She also tells him he has done terrible things, but he has the power to make amends, giving us the title of the episode.

Buffy: But if you die now, then all you ever were was a monster.

I see this entire scene, and especially Buffy's line above, as the theme for the series *Angel*. So much of it is about Angel trying to balance the scales or make amends for his centuries as a vampire.

Buffy and Angel do have a physical fight.

Angel: Am I a thing worth saving?

She yells at him that she can't lose him again.

Buffy: I love you so much. And I tried to make you go away. I killed you and it didn't help. And I hate it. I hate that it's so hard and that you can hurt me so much.

Sarah Michelle Gellar does a fantastic job of conveying the emotion in these lines. The lines themselves, though, never quite work for me because I never saw Buffy as killing Angel to make him go away. She killed him to save the world and she paid a huge emotional price for that, for all of it. For loving Angel, for having a part in him turning into Angelus, for being unable to kill him sooner.

Amends was written and directed by Joss Whedon. He certainly knows what Buffy as a character feels and means. So I wonder, is this how he sees it for Buffy? Or is it how he felt he needed it to be seen to launch *Angel* the series? From outside, to me it feels like Whedon shifted gears and stepped out of Buffy's world and into Angel's world. Buffy's words are, perhaps, how Angel sees it. Angel believes Buffy killed him not only to save the world but to get Angel and Angelus out of her life for good.

Buffy goes on to tell Angel that what's weak is giving up. He tells her to let him be strong for once, but she's not buying it. She tells him it's not strong to give up or end his life. Strong is fighting. But if he's too much of a coward to do it, then burn. The sun begins to rise.

Buffy: If I can't convince you that you belong in this world, then I don't know what can.

Snow starts to fall. They both look up in wonder. Clouds

and snow block the sun. There is no sunrise and Angel can't die. At least not today.

Deus Ex Machina?

Until I watched *Amends* for the *Buffy and the Art of Story* podcast, I did not get this ending. I saw it as *deus ex machina* - where a god comes down from on high and conveniently fixes everything. That always bothered me because if Angel is our protagonist, he doesn't reach a resolution. He doesn't make a choice. He is saved out of nowhere. If we see Buffy as the protagonist, she at least fought hard. But all the same, the resolution doesn't arise from her actions.

The ending worked better when I looked at the whole episode closely through the lens of how well it sets up, or perhaps serves as a pilot for, *Angel* the series. Angel grapples with what The First Evil tells him throughout the episode. He reaches a conclusion that the best thing to do is remove himself from this equation so he poses no threat to the world.

But an opposing force, a force of good, appears at the end (and may have been operating behind the scenes throughout). The force for good takes the option of self-destruction off the table for this one day. The day corresponds, as we'll see in the Falling Action, with Christmas and beauty and being with Buffy. That gives Angel a chance to get out of that terrible emotional place, which the end of the episode implies he does, and he chooses to go on.

The Falling Action

The story shifts to tying up loose ends in the Falling Action section. At 42 minutes, 10 seconds, Willow and Oz lie on Willow's bed, which is still made. They're dressed. (Willow may be in pajamas). Maybe they're watching those videos Oz brought over. They go to the window and look out in wonder at the snow, a rare occurrence in their part of California.

Joyce and Faith walk outside together. Faith holds out her arms and hands to feel the snow. She looks so relaxed and happy. That one gesture expresses her sense of wonder. Outside his house, Xander is sleeping in his sleeping bag. Snow blankets him and drifts down all around him. This is about the healthiest we've seen Xander in an emotional sense. He chose to step away from whatever chaos is going on in his family and created his own ritual to mark this holiday. The snow adds a sort of blessing for his tradition.

Snow blankets the Sunnydale sign, too, and from a TV in a store window a weather guy says it's the first time snow has ever fallen on Christmas in Sunnydale. He adds that they shouldn't expect to see the sun at all today.

Angel and Buffy hold hands and walk down the street, looking up at the sky and snow. Snow covers the street and sidewalks. Due to the low budget, the snow looks terrible — like a bunch of cotton. All the same, there's a storybook snow globe feel to it. It's a mythic ending, suggesting Angel will survive this day and beyond.

Forces For Good And Evil

In the essay *Prophecy Girl And The Powers That Be: The Philosophy Of Religion In The Buffyverse* (in the book *Fear and Trembling in Sunnydale: Buffy The Vampire Slayer And Philosophy*, edited by James B. South), Wendy Love Anderson argues on pages 223-224 that it's hard to say precisely who or what governs the Buffyverse. That's so partly because the powers of evil get a more thorough introduction than those for good. But the naming of the evil in *Amends* "The First" confirms for her that "evil precedes good...." Evil also is powerful and ever present, as shown by The First/Jenny stating, "I am everywhere. Every being every thought, every drop of hate."

I found that point compelling, especially because no one names or refers to specifically the force for good in *Amends*.

Spoilers And Foreshadowing

The Series *Angel*

Angel expresses the mission statement of *Angel* the series when he says they fight not because they're going to win but because there are things worth fighting for. In subtle ways, this is different from *Buffy* the series. Buffy also fights because there are things worth fighting for. But while she does not always win, for the most part good prevails. And in her final battle at the end of Season Seven, Buffy, the team, and all the new Slayers win. In contrast, the *Angel* series finale ends with Angel and company poised for an apocalyptic fight.

The First's taunts about Angel feeling sorry for himself and posing a danger to others foreshadow developments of his character. In his own series, Angel at times becomes mired in self-pity, loss, and depression, and sometimes as a result does terrible things. On the other hand, The First tells Angel in *Amends* that he was never a fighter, so he should give up. But he does the opposite, dedicating himself to fighting for good.

When Angel tells Buffy he wants to lose himself in her even though he knows he'll lose his soul, that foreshadows Angel trying to do exactly that with Darla in *Angel*. He's so angry, frustrated, and depressed that he has sex with her thinking that he'll lose his soul. It doesn't happen for other reasons, but the choice weighs on the side of why Angel saw his continued existence as a grave threat to the world.

Which brings me to another way *Amends* serves as a pilot for Angel. It emphasizes that Angel is almost a fulcrum. The forces of evil are always trying to turn him to have a warrior on their side or to take him out of the equation in case he stays good. And sometimes he dives into his dark side on his own.

As to those forces, Wendy Love Anderson points out on page 224 of the essay quoted earlier that in both shows, myriad vampires, demons, and sometimes humans represent evil. But other than Buffy, Angel, and their friends, supernatural forces for good are absent. Anderson continues: "...on *Angel*, the Powers That Be are not only inscrutable and impersonal, but also unapproachable, and the 'channels' by which Angel approaches them tend to undercut their authority."

In addition, while most faces of evil are forbidding, the ones representing the good lean toward comical at times. For example, channels to the good on *Angel* include the Oracles, Lorne (the green karaoke-singing demon), and a giant plastic hamburger that Wesley talks to about a key prophecy. And in *Buffy*, direct messages from the powers for good are rare to non-existent.

Oz, Willow, And The Wolf

Oz says when he saw Willow and Xander kissing he "never felt that way before when there wasn't a full moon." This single line foreshadows much of his arc in Season Four. Before that, it appears Oz poses a threat only three days out of the month, during which he can lock himself up. But when he realizes Tara and Willow are together, he becomes the wolf in daytime. I had no idea that anger as a trigger for his transformation was foreshadowed so early on.

Angel And Buffy

The First warns in *Amends* that sooner or later Angel will drink Buffy. I never focused on that line until I outlined the episode for the podcast. Yet it foreshadows what happens at the end of Season Three. Angel does drink Buffy, and it's sooner rather than later. He does it at her urging to save his life, but comes close to killing her. I see that action as being, more than anything, what drives him to leave Sunnydale.

The Final Villain

Introducing The First Evil foreshadows Season Seven, where The First will be the season-long Big Bad. Here, The First seems equally happy to devastate Buffy emotionally as to kill her. That sets up Season Seven, which likewise shows throwing the Slayer off balance could turn the tide in the epic good and evil struggle. In addition, Season Seven morphs that theme into the storyline that Buffy's return from the dead throws the Slayer line itself out of whack, giving The First the chance to take over once and for all.

The challenges of The First as a villain in *Amends* return in Season Seven. Because The First can't directly act in a physical way, the writers use many types of characters to act for it. Ubervamps, the Bringers, humans who volunteer or whom The First takes over (though that power is somewhat inconsistent), and Caleb, the preacher. But mainly The First appears as people who died, as it does here when it appears as Jenny. And it taunts people.

We'll see when I get to Season Seven in the podcast, but I recall finding The First a bit flat as a villain because of that. In *Amends*, its focus on Angel creates a greater sense of menace because we know how much harm Angel can do to Buffy and to everyone. In Season Seven it's harder to sort out what The First is doing or why, leaving me less engaged.

Questions For Your Writing

- Is there a work of fiction that inspires you the way *A Christmas Carol* seems to have inspired *Amends*? How does it influence your story or your writing in general?
- What did you learn from *Amends* about how to resolve one story while hinting at or sparking conflicts that will appear in future works?
- If your story includes flashbacks or dreams, how do they move the story forward? If you took them out, would your story work just as well?
- How does your final conflict resolve? If it's through *deus ex machina*, what have you included to be sure your protagonist fights hard enough and your readers will be satisfied?
- Look at the major turns in your subplot. Which ones did you include? Are you satisfied with the order?
- Do you know who your protagonist and antagonist are? If not, take some time now to sort out the three protagonist prongs and to be sure your antagonist has a strong reason to push against the protagonist.
- If you are writing an incorporeal antagonist, does it pose a strong enough threat to keep your audience on edge? What characters act on behalf of or represent the antagonist?

The next chapter talks about *Gingerbread*, where the adults in Sunnydale, including Joyce, are ready to watch their children burn.

CHAPTER 11
GINGERBREAD S3 E11

THIS CHAPTER TALKS ABOUT *GINGERBREAD*, Season Three, Episode Eleven, where a demon in disguise causes adults in Sunnydale to turn on their children with near-fatal consequences. Written by Jane Espenson and Thania St. John and directed by James Whitmore, Jr. Original air date: January 12, 1999.

Along with the episode breakdown, topics include:

- Drawing from a fairy tale to tell a literal story about a witch hunt
- Recurring series themes about the dangers of too-hands-on parenting and vigilante justice
- Dialogue lines that show Angel is a good friend and partner to Buffy
- The mission statement for *Angel* the series
- Extreme behavior and statements that are nonetheless grounded in Joyce's character and deepest concerns

Okay, let's dive into the Hellmouth.

Opening Conflict

The opening conflict relates to an episode theme. Buffy patrols in the park at night. Joyce, bearing snacks, surprises her. She wants to show interest in what Buffy is doing and thought it was about time she saw first-hand what slaying is like. Buffy, not thrilled, tells Joyce slaying is kind of an alone thing. She tries to convince Joyce that it's dull. Just then a vampire attacks. Joyce cheers Buffy on until she sees a vampire she knows.

Joyce: Oh my God, it's Mr. Henderson from the bank.

Buffy chases after Mr. Henderson after telling Joyce to stay there. But Joyce wanders the park alone and sees the bodies of two little kids, a blond boy and blond girl, slaughtered on the merry-go-round. Symbols are drawn on their hands. And at 2 minutes, 8 seconds, we go to the credits. On return, the police swarm the park. Joyce is extremely upset.

Joyce: Buffy, they were little kids. Did you see them? So tiny.

Buffy very much takes the role of the grownup, hugging Joyce and trying to comfort her.

Buffy: I'm so sorry that you had to see that.

In another type of episode, the Story Spark or Inciting Incident, which often occurs around 10% through a story and gets the main plot rolling, would be the murder of the children. But the plot here is about how the townspeople react to that murder and the resulting mob mentality. For that reason, I see the Spark as occurring later.

First, Buffy tells Joyce it'll be okay. She'll find whoever did this. Joyce, though, points out that Buffy can't make it right because she can't bring the children back or change the fact that they were killed. That could be a Story Spark. But it's not clear yet that Joyce's response is unusual or signals a sea change in how the town will see the murders.

A Different Story Spark

Buffy tells Joyce to try to calm down, but then we cut to her talking to Giles in the library at 4 minutes, 28 seconds.

Buffy: Don't tell me to calm down.

Buffy goes on to say that these are little kids, and her mom can't even talk. I see Buffy's reaction as the Story Spark here, and it's right around ten percent through. Joyce's fear and panic and her comments that anything Buffy can do is not enough causes Buffy to respond in this intense way. Then when Giles tells her that this may have been done by humans (based on the mark on the kids' hands), she shifts almost out of character. She tells him to find a loophole in that Slayers don't kill people rule.

That shift is so striking because we've never seen Buffy budge on that point. She was so hard on herself in *Ted*, when she thought he was human and she'd killed him, despite that he hit her very hard. Buffy knew she went beyond what she needed to defend herself and was devastated at killing a human being.

Giles tells her he knows it was a dreadful crime, but he's shocked at her asking for a loophole. He says she's taking it personally. Buffy agrees that it is completely personal and tells him to find the people who did this. It's not clear if Buffy is still looking for the loophole or has calmed down a bit and wants to stop but not kill the people who did this. But she is on the edge in a way that we have not seen before.

Next, there's some comic relief. In line in the cafeteria, Xander makes awkward conversation with Oz about getting a burrito. This is one of the first times we see these two together since Oz walked in on Willow and Xander kissing.

Amy sits at the lunch table with Willow. Oz comments that he hasn't seen Willow all day and asks where she's been. His tone isn't accusatory. But Xander responds as if it were.

Xander: Not with me. No sir. Ask anyone.

There's an awkward silence, broken only when the group starts talking about Buffy's birthday next week. They cut off when Buffy approaches. She tells them about the murder of the children and that her mom found them. When she explains that Joyce came out to watch her slay, Willow is envious that Joyce tried to bond with Buffy. Her words make clear that her mother shows little interest in Willow.

Right then, Joyce walks up. Buffy is taken aback by seeing her mom at school. Joyce asks if Buffy talked to Giles yet about the kids. Buffy says Giles thinks it might be ritual or occult. When Joyce links the occult to witches, Willow chokes on what she's eating. Joyce says she knows the kids think that the occult is cool and that Buffy told her Willow dabbles.

Willow: Yes, I'm a dabbler.

In the hall, Buffy tries to convince Joyce that Joyce is about home and this is school and it's not good to mix them. But Joyce says she has to help. She called everyone she knows in town and told them about the kids' murder. They're all just as upset as she is. And they set up a vigil for tonight. The mayor will be there. Buffy appears deeply concerned as she tells Joyce they keep these things quiet when working on them. Joyce apologizes.

Joyce: Well, there probably won't be that many people there.

The scene cuts to a very crowded town hall meeting. At about 10 minutes in Buffy looks around.

Buffy (to Willow): This is great. Maybe we can all go patrolling together.

But Willow again comments that at least Joyce is there and interested, unlike Willow's mom. Except that Willow's mom (Sheila) is there. She says hi to Willow and "Bunny" and notices that Willow cut her hair. Willow responds that she did it on a whim —two months ago. Joyce joins them, as does Giles.

He and Joyce barely meet each other's eyes and have an awkward conversation, fallout from them having sex in **Band Candy**. Giles once again proves that poker is not his game in an exchange with Willow's mother.

Sheila: There's a rumor going around.
Giles: About us? Uh, um, about what?

Sheila tells him the rumor is that witches are responsible, which she doesn't find strange. She recently co-authored a paper and was shocked at the statistics. The mayor takes the microphone and starts to speak.

The One-Quarter Twist

I see the moment after the mayor's speech as the One-Quarter Twist. It comes from outside Buffy, spins the story in a new direction, and definitely raises the stakes. First the mayor talks about what a tragic crime this was, but what a caring community Sunnydale is. He says it's a good town. He says, "Never Again," the slogan on posters and signs the townspeople hold that include photos of those children.

But at 12 minutes, 34 seconds, the twist occurs when Joyce takes the microphone.

Joyce: Mr. Mayor, you're dead wrong. This is not a good town.

As misguided as Joyce turns out to be, she's a great speaker. She grabs their attention right away. She plays off what the mayor said, contradicting him and shocking everyone. Then she heads right to the point. She asks how many people there have lost someone who disappeared or died with neck trauma. She comments on how everyone is too afraid to speak out. She says she was supposed to lead them in a moment of silence, but silence is the town's disease. For too long unnatural evil has plagued the town so that it's not their town anymore. It belongs to the witches, monsters, and slayers.

She utters that last line at 13 minutes, 23 seconds. There's ominous music. Buffy's face shows how shocked she is. Joyce's speech puts the entire town at odds with Buffy, Willow, and the forces of good. This is huge and it raises the stakes. Literally, as we'll see. It ends with Willow, Amy, and Buffy tied to giant stakes about to be burned to death. Joyce then issues a call to action — the town needs to find whoever did this and make them pay.

The next scene is a bit of a mislead though it is explained later. At almost 14 minutes, three students in black hooded robes surrounded by candles do a spell. One pushes her hood aside. It's Willow. The symbol that was on the murdered children's hands is in the center of the circle. And there's a cut to commercial. That was a great hook, making the audience wonder what Willow's role could be in all this.

On return, students attack a boy from that circle, Michael, when he's at his locker. A bully says people like Michael need to learn a lesson. Amy tries to intervene but they threaten her, too. When Buffy appears, though, the lead bully looks at her and lets go of Michael.

Bully (to Buffy): No problem. We're walking.

Michael rushes off. Cordelia tells Buffy that she's going to be busy if she's protecting witches. Buffy doubts there'll be any more trouble.

Cordelia: I doubt your doubt....If you're going to hang with them, expect badness, because that's what you get when you hang with freaks and losers. Believe me, I know. (She walks away, but turns back.) That was a pointed comment about me hanging with you guys.

Buffy says she got that, but witches didn't do this. Then Giles, who has come up behind her, tells her that witches probably did. His research keeps coming back to that symbol, and witches use it. To verify the meaning, he needs to check a book

Willow borrowed. He asks Buffy to try to find Willow and the book.

Buffy finds Xander. When she asks if Willow's around, we get a little more comic relief. He rants over everyone assuming he knows where Willow is.

Buffy: Aren't these her books?

Xander: Yeah, she's in the restroom.

Still, he argues a man should be innocent until proven guilty. When Buffy points out he is guilty, Xander claims he means future guilt. Everyone keeps thinking he'll mess up again, including Oz, who is now so quiet around Xander.

Buffy: Sure. Right. Because usually Oz is such a chatterbox.

Xander claims it's more of a "verbal non-verbal," and Oz speaks volumes with his eyes. Like Buffy, I don't see anything suggesting Oz is waiting for Xander to screw up again. But the exchange tells us a lot about Xander's psyche. I suspect his feeling that everyone thinks he'll mess up relates less to Willow and Oz and more to how he feels throughout life and probably to how his parents treat him, though that's not explicit in this episode.

That, in my view, is an ideal way to use comic relief. Not only does it provide a break from the story's tension, it uses conflict to add to what the audience knows about a key character.

Buffy sees Willow's notebook where she's drawn the symbol. She's a bit accusatory when she asks Willow what it is. That leads to one of my favorite Willow lines.

Willow: I doodle. I do doodle. You too. You do doodle too.

Buffy tells her this is the symbol that was on the kids' hands. Before Willow can answer, police start breaking open student lockers to look for occult supplies.

Xander worries about the Playboys in his locker. Cordelia's

mad when they take her imported hairspray. Amy has to go to Snyder's office because of what they found in her locker. They find something in Willow's as well. Willow quickly tells Buffy the symbol was for a protection spell for her. It's nothing dangerous and it was for Buffy's birthday.

Willow: Only now it's broken because you know about it. So Happy Birthday.

Snyder tells Willow to come with him. Buffy surreptitiously takes Willow's books and notebook and disappears into the crowd. So despite that Willow has this symbol and could offer only a hurried explanation, Buffy immediately believes her.

Major Midpoint Reversal And Theme

At the Midpoint of an episode, we typically see either a major commitment by the protagonist or a major reversal. Here, there's a Midpoint Reversal. When Buffy goes to the library to talk to Giles, she finds police filling boxes with books they're confiscating.

Off to the side, Buffy explains to Giles about the protection symbol and says something odd is going on. But they can't research because all the books are being taken away. Principal Snyder enters, amused by Giles's anger and panic. Buffy's also angry. Snyder tells her if she has a problem, she can take it up with MOO — Mothers Opposed to the Occult. Buffy asks who came up with that acronym.

Snyder: That would be the founder. I believe you call her "Mom."

That moment, at about 21 minutes into the episode, serves as a true reversal. While the police confiscating books is bad, finding out that her mother is behind it is a very personal (and dangerous) reversal for Buffy.

The scene cuts to Willow and her mother, Sheila. Sheila is not too worried about Willow having magical supplies. She says it's a classic adolescent response to the pressures of incipient adulthood. She talks about the psychology of girls Willow's age. Willow strives to get her mom to see her as an individual. When Willow starts talking about doing spells, Sheila worries that she's delusional. Willow argues her mom can't know what she can do because the last long conversation they had was about the patriarchal bias of the Mr. Rogers show. That leads to another favorite line of mine:

Sheila: Well, with King Friday lording it over all the lesser subjects....

One thing finally shocks Sheila —Willow's dating a musician. All the same, Sheila grounds Willow because she talked to Joyce, read articles, and consulted with colleagues and she sees this as a call for discipline. Willow feels that's unfair because she never did anything wrong before. Sheila also tells her she has to stop speaking to "Bunny Summers." Willow, angry, starts claiming she can call out the devil and asks if her mother sees any goats. Willow says there are none because she sacrificed them.

At about 24 minutes, just after Sheila tells Willow to stop seeing Bunny, Joyce tells Buffy she doesn't want her seeing "that Willow." She had no idea Willow's forays into the occult were so serious.

The two sit in a side room Joyce made into an office. Posters of the two children hang all around. Buffy's angry about the books being taken. Joyce asks if Buffy understands how much it scares her that any student can go in and get ideas from those books. Buffy tries to convince Joyce to let her handle everything. It's what she does. But Joyce questions whether Buffy does any real good. Evil pops up and Buffy fights, but is Sunnydale getting better? Are they running out of vampires?

Joyce: It's not your fault. You don't have a plan. You just react to things. It's bound to be kind of fruitless.

These lines are ironic because, though neither character

knows it, we saw in *The Wish* what Buffy reacting without a plan really looks like, and it got Buffy killed. The Buffy in this world (what I think of as the real world) does have a plan. Maybe not the way Joyce sees it, but she does.

Buffy: Okay, maybe I don't have a plan. Lord knows I don't have lapel buttons. And maybe the next time that the world is getting sucked into hell, I won't be able to stop it because the anti-hell- sucking book isn't on the approved reading list.

Buffy's words go to a clear episode theme about the danger of suppressing ideas and how fear drives that. We've already seen police confiscating books. Joyce's organization set approved reading lists. Later we'll see book burning leading to burning girls at the stake. (The books are used as kindling, emphasizing the point.)

Joyce expresses fear to justify the censorship. She doesn't want kids to access these materials. Buffy gives the counterpoint, which clearly in the Buffyverse is the right answer. They need the books and information, including about evil, to fight evil.

After Buffy leaves to go react to some vampires, the boy and girl appear. They reassure Joyce she's doing the right thing. She's making things better. But they tell her there are still bad people out there and they can't rest until Joyce hurts them. The way they hurt the children.

Reuniting And A Mission Statement

Angel joins Buffy at the playground. Candles burn on the merry-go-round near photos of the kids. Angel tells Buffy he's doing all right, maybe better than she is. This is the first time we see them together after the events of *Amends*. He tells her he heard about the murders. Buffy says people die in Sunnydale all the time, and she never saw anything like this.

Angel: They were children. Innocent.

Buffy: And Mr. Henderson from the bank had it coming?

This statement, especially so close to the middle of an episode that's mostly a one-off, speaks volumes about how society looks at crime. We prioritize certain victims or feel that certain deaths or certain crimes are more heinous depending on the victim.

Buffy also tells Angel what her mother said about it being fruitless and asks if Sunnydale's any better than before she got there, another echo of *The Wish*, which answered that question. Buffy adds that they fight but never win. Not completely.

Angel: We never will. That's not why we fight. We do it because there are things worth fighting for.

Also very striking lines. And I don't think it's too much of a spoiler to say that in essence that is the theme of *Angel* the series.

Angel then gives Buffy an idea. When he talks about what's worth fighting for, he mentions the kids and their parents. That prompts Buffy, as we'll find out in the next scene, to realize that she knows nothing about these children.

I love that Angel offers emotional support and by simply talking it through helps her begin to unravel what's truly happening. It shows once again Angel being a good partner and friend to her.

At nearly 29 minutes, Giles swears at the computer as he tries to get information without his beloved books. Buffy enters and asks what they know about these kids. What school did they go to, who are their parents, what are their names?

Xander: Well, sure, we know their names.

But nobody does. Oz says Willow is the best researcher. She's not allowed to come to the phone, but he uses the computer to contact her. (That was very new and exciting at the time.) In her bedroom, Willow uses her laptop and finds articles going back every fifty years showing these same two children. Each time, they're killed and they have this mark. And the town goes vigilante. She finds references all the way back to 1649 and the Black Forest.

Sheila And The Three-Quarter Turn

The Three-Quarter Turn here grows out of Buffy's Midpoint Reversal where Joyce turned out to be behind MOO. The turn also spins the story in yet another new direction and raises the stakes. At 31 minutes, 23 seconds, Sheila enters Willow's room, shuts the laptop, and says Willow is not minding her. She doesn't want Willow communicating with her cyber-coven. She adds that she believes Willow now about her witchcraft.

Sheila: And all I can do is let you go with love.

More ominous music plays as Sheila locks Willow in her bedroom.

A continuity issue here bothered me even on my first watch of this episode. In *Lie To Me* in Season Two, Willow's bedroom had patio doors. Angel knocked on one and Willow let him in. When Sheila locks Willow in, Willow could just walk out onto the patio. Except in this episode, those doors don't exist. We just have to accept that now there's no outside door to Willow's room.

Back at the library, Giles explains a fringe theory that some fairytales have real incidents at the heart, which makes this all make sense.

Buffy: Yeah, it's all falling into place. Of course, that place is nowhere near this place.

Giles adds that some demons feed us our darkest fears and watch us destroy ourselves. Here, the kids' names are very close to Hansel and Gretel. The friends talk about Hansel and Gretel running home raving about witches, leading to thousands of women being persecuted and burned at the stake. This conversation makes explicit the themes about what fear can do to a community.

Buffy says she needs to talk to her mother. But Michael, that boy the bullies cornered early in the episode, runs in. He was attacked. But not by the bullies, by his parents. He tells the gang there's a trial at city hall and they got Amy. Oz worries about Willow in particular. The scene switches to Sheila telling Willow to get her coat. It's time to go. She has a group of people with her. Willow tries to block the door.

In the meantime, Buffy and Giles go to the Summers home. Joyce is there with another group of people. They seem to be talking reasonably. But when Buffy draws Joyce aside to talk, Joyce and another group member overpower Giles and Buffy with chloroform.

In other circumstances I might not believe anyone could sneak up on Buffy. But it works here because she trusts her mom. That makes her vulnerable. As Buffy lies on the floor, the little boy and girl appear on the stairs. They tell Joyce they're still scared of the bad girls. Joyce has to make them stop, to make them go away forever.

Oz and Xander rush into Willow's bedroom. The chaos tells them there was a fight.

At the town hall, at 35 minutes, 14 seconds, Willow, Amy, and Buffy are tied to giant stakes on top of piles of books. Buffy is still knocked out. Townspeople gather around with torches.

This scene raises the question of why the townspeople do this inside. Not a great place to start a giant fire. Apparently, the demon can influence people, but can't make them do things a certain way. Either that or the writers are showing that the mob mentality includes lack of concern for the mob's own well-being. It adds to the idea that people take leave of their senses in that circumstance. Or perhaps the writers just wanted this symbolism of it taking place in the town hall.

Minor Character Arcs

At the Summers home, Cordelia slaps Giles in the face until he wakes up and then complains that her hand hurts. She tells him things have gotten way out of control. Her examples mainly involve herself. But she adds that she came there to tell Buffy that she had to stop it. Then she pauses to ask how many times Giles has been knocked out.

Cordelia: I swear, one of these days you're going to wake up in a coma.
Giles (staggering to his feet): We need to save Buffy from Hansel and Gretel.
Cordelia: Now let's be clear. The brain damage happened before I hit you.

In the town hall, Oz and Xander try to get the townspeople to let them in to join the mob. The townspeople are not fooled, partly because Oz can't help himself from commenting on how out there they all are. Inside, Buffy wakes up and tries to persuade Joyce that she doesn't want to do this. Joyce says it doesn't matter what she wants.

Joyce: I wanted a normal happy daughter. Instead, I got a Slayer.

This is such an awful thing to say. Though she's under a spell, I find it so disturbing. I hate thinking Buffy's mom would say these things, spell or no spell. But they echo some comments Joyce made when not under a spell, so we know deep down this is partly how Joyce feels. Buffy and Joyce never deal with that in the episode.

Amy does her go-to spell asking the goddess to let the unclean thing crawl. I don't think this was her intent, but it turns her into a rat. She runs away.

Buffy: She couldn't do us first?

Willow and Buffy try to bluff. They claim they, too, have this power. Willow says it's a really big power. Buffy threatens to turn the townspeople into vermin. And then there's another line I love.

Buffy: And some of you will be fish. Yes, you in the back there, you'll be fish.

One guy says that maybe they should go, but then the little kids appear and beg everyone for help.

At about 38 and a half minutes, as he drives toward the town hall, Giles gives Cordelia instructions. She crushes herbs as he tries to recall a German incantation about lifting a veil. The trouble is, he doesn't have his books. Cordelia's grossed out when he tells her to put a toadstone into the mixture.

Cordelia: It doesn't look like a toad.

Giles: There's no reason it should. It's from inside the toad.

Cordelia: I hate you.

These scenes move character arcs in a small way. Amy turns into a rat as a result of her inexpert use of magic. Cordelia is drawn back into the Scooby gang. She's helping Giles, grossed out or not. And Xander continues to be more active. At the town hall, he and Oz hear Willow scream and climb into a space between the ceiling and the drop ceiling. (I always wonder how many buildings really have this. It's such a trope in horror and action movies.)

The Climax

Now we are reaching the Climax where our opposing forces confront one another for their final clash to resolve the conflict. At about 39 and a half minutes, the books are on fire. The flames come very close to Willow and Buffy. Buffy tells Joyce she won't be able to live with herself if she goes through with this. But Joyce tells Buffy she earned it by toying with unnatural forces.

Giles and Cordelia burst into the village hall. Giles grabs a hairpin from Cordelia's hair and picks the lock to the main room.

Cordelia: God, you really were the little youthful offender, weren't you?

Buffy struggles with her bonds and apologizes to Willow when she can't free herself. Then she sees Cordy and Giles. Cordelia breaks the glass, gets out a fire hose, and sprays the townspeople, really angry at them. Buffy yells at her to put out the fire. And she does.

In that sense, Buffy and Cordelia both save the day. Oz and Xander are still up in that drop ceiling, but the flames are out. There's smoke everywhere. Giles does the incantation and throws the mixture of herbs and toadstones. The two little kids hug each other, then grow. They turn into a giant ugly demon that towers over everyone.

Cordelia: Okay. I think I like the two little ones more than the one big one.

Buffy keeps struggling. She finally wrenches that giant stake out of the pile of books, but she is still tied to it. She bends over so that her back is flat. The stake sticks out straight and the demon runs right into it and is impaled. Buffy can't see because she is looking down at the ground.

Buffy: Did I get it? Did I get it?

Her voice is squeaky. I don't know why, but I've never loved that line or its delivery, probably because I am rarely a fan of goofy Buffy. Many people are, though, so I don't see that as an issue with the writing, directing, or acting. It's just personal taste.

The Falling Action

Now the episode ties up loose ends, though there aren't many. At 42 and a half minutes, Oz and Xander fall through the ceiling. (So there is a little nod to reality, as that drop ceiling can't hold them up forever.) Oz says his next line, which I love, amidst all the dust and debris.

Oz: We're here to save you.

In the next scene, Willow and Buffy sit on the floor in Willow's room near a rat cage. Willow says her mom is doing that selective memory thing Joyce used to be so good at. The only thing Sheila remembered is that Willow is dating a musician. Oz has to come to dinner next week.

Willow: It's sort of like taking an interest in me.

They then try a spell, hoping to bring Amy back. It's clear they've tried several times before.

This time, too, fails. Amy the rat just sits there on her hind legs, squeaking. Buffy suggests that they could get her one of those wheel thingies. And the episode ends.

The Effect Of *Gingerbread*

I struggle with this episode. While I think of it as a one-off that could be lifted out of the season, it includes a ton of foreshadowing, which I'll talk about below. Yet much of it barely affects the season, and some key moments are ignored within the episode. Buffy and Joyce don't discuss Joyce's actions or words. We don't know what Joyce remembers or doesn't.

There is some movement for Angel and Buffy. They seem very natural with each other. But that, too, doesn't quite work for me. In *Amends*, that snowfall kept Angel from killing himself, but nothing showed he changed his mind or why. It feels strange that now he appears completely at peace. While he tells Buffy he's still figuring things out, he was so distraught last episode that, even for Angel, it seems there ought to be more fallout.

It also troubles me that Faith is absent. I don't recall her being mentioned, and an extra Slayer would be super handy when the townspeople all turn on Buffy. I am sure there were production reasons why Eliza Dushku, who plays Faith, isn't in the episode. And perhaps it was written to be dropped in wherever it fit, so the writers didn't know what Faith's status would be when it aired. But from a storytelling perspective, at this point in the season the audience needs some nod to why Faith can't help.

I do like the strong themes. Along with the book burning and censorship, **Gingerbread** echoes themes from the third episode of the entire series, **The Witch,** which included Amy as well. That episode compared Amy's mother to Buffy's, suggesting strongly that perhaps a lack of interest, or at least some distance, is better. Here, Willow complains about her mother being uninterested. She envies Joyce coming to school out of concern about Buffy and the other students. But when Sheila takes an interest, she tries to kill her daughter. And Joyce does the same. Though it's due to the influence of the demon, Joyce wouldn't have been involved in the first place except that she joined Buffy while she was patrolling.

The idea that it's better when parents don't really know what their kids are doing may be an unintentional result of telling a story about mob mentality. But given the very personal things Joyce says to Buffy about getting a Slayer when she wanted a normal daughter, it seems the writers to some extent meant to include that theme.

That scene, and Buffy's wish for a loophole that allows her to kill humans early in the episode, touch on another theme. Fear for her mother's well-being drives Buffy to make that comment to Giles. Joyce and Sheila both feel first afraid for their daughters and then of them, prompting them to do and say awful things. The story shows the powerful and dangerous way fear motivates people.

Finally, the theme about the dangers of vigilante justice underscores why Buffy is adamant about not killing humans. In the beginning she's tempted to break that rule. But the result is disastrous here when people take justice into their own hands and instead engage in evil acts.

Spoilers And Foreshadowing

Change Or No Change

This episode doesn't change the Buffyverse very much, with one exception.

Willow's mother, Sheila, never appears again in the series, though the characters occasionally mention her. Nothing suggests the events of *Gingerbread* had a lasting effect on Willow's relationship with her mother.

The protection spell returns in a minor way in *Bad Girls*. Willow becomes quite sad after she gives Buffy a protection spell or amulet for her birthday. Buffy at first seems pleased, but she quickly abandons Willow to take off with Faith. Willow is left feeling her attempts to protect Buffy are meaningless compared to what Faith can do as another Slayer. That scene, though, plays out the same way with or without the spoiled spell in *Gingerbread*.

Amy, on the other hand, does remain a rat for much of the series. And, as I'll talk about below, that's significant for Willow's journey. In that sense the episode changes the world of *Buffy*.

But I'm not sure the Amy who returns in Season Six fits with Amy as shown in *Gingerbread*. While she helped with the protection spell, at the end she apparently wasn't able to loosen the ropes, put out the fire, or influence the townspeople. Instead, she turned herself into a rat. That saved her from being burned at the stake. But if she had other options, it seems she would have tried them, as once Amy's a rat she's stuck there.

When she is changed into a human again in Season Six,

though, Amy knows all kinds of spells and has great command of her powers.

Amy The Rat And Willow

From *Gingerbread* on, deratting Amy becomes a running theme that reflects Willow's power — and her doubts about it. In Season Four (in *Something Blue*), Willow comments morosely that she can't even derat Amy. Unknown to her, though, in that episode she brings Amy back for a moment, having cast a spell to do her will. As Willow rambles to herself, Amy briefly appears behind her. But Willow's next words turn her into a rat again, and Willow never knows what happened.

In Season Six, Willow becomes so powerful and skilled that she figures out, almost as an afterthought, how to bring Amy back. Amy's return causes Willow's friends to worry about her having a powerful magical playmate right when her overuse of magic is causing problems in her life. (Another great example of the writers giving a character what they want at the worst possible moment.)

Willow's later choice to stop doing magic angers Amy. Amy tries to undermine it, and Willow tells her to stay away. Then in Season Seven, Amy casts a spell that turns Willow into Tara's killer — Willow's worst nightmare. I'm not sure *Gingerbread* foreshadows any of the events of Season Six or Seven. But in earlier episodes Amy comfortably used magic to serve her own ends (such as to improve her grades). So it makes sense she resents Willow choosing to abstain from magic, perhaps seeing Willow as judging her.

More On Willow's Magic

Willow's growing power is foreshadowed in a minor way in this episode. Willow hyperbolically tells her mother that she sacrificed goats. And she will sacrifice a similar animal (a fawn) and drain its blood in Season Six in a very emotional scene. That detail shows how far Willow traveled. She engages in an act she once saw as outlandish and dangerous, and that she used to pretend to her mother that she worshipped Satan.

Notably, Willow doesn't tell Tara what she's done, claiming instead that she got the blood she needed on the black market. And that alone worries Tara.

Bad Girls

The demon here repeatedly calls Buffy, Willow, and Amy "bad girls." The repetition foreshadows Episode Fourteen of the season: *Bad Girls*. There, Buffy grows closer to Faith and adopts some of her freewheeling "we can do whatever we want" approach to slaying. Unfortunately, this means Buffy's there when Faith kills a human being, though perhaps one who is on the side of evil, and covers it up.

Gingerbread lays the groundwork for *Bad Girls* and the next episode, *Consequences*, by underscoring what happens when good people (symbolized by Joyce) decide that killing human beings is necessary or acceptable to stop evil.

Class Protector

Finally, this episode foreshadows one of the most moving moments in all of *Buffy*. Here, the bully at the locker lets go of Michael and takes off as soon as Buffy steps in. It's clear he knows who Buffy is and knows she can easily win a fight with him.

This brief interaction sets up the end of the season, when Buffy gets the Class Protector award. The students formally recognize her for all she's done to protect them. The one-time award they create comes with a custom gold umbrella she clearly loves. The recognition to that point has been denied Buffy as a Slayer, a role that otherwise often isolates her from typical high school activities and friendships.

Questions For Your Writing

- What themes might you like to write about? Do they spark any story ideas?
- If thinking about theme first doesn't work for you, examine the consequences of your characters' actions. Do any themes emerge? Are they themes you want to include?
- Do you think the writers here aimed to write a plot that included themes about mob rule, fear, parenting, and the dangers of vigilante justice? Or did they emerge from the story?
- What fairy tale or childhood story spoke to you? Can you draw from it as you write your own fiction?
- How can you show through dialogue, without directly stating it, that two characters have a solid friendship, are good partners, or have a solid romantic relationship?
- If your protagonist needed to craft a mission statement, what would it be? How about your antagonist?
- If events drive your characters to extreme behavior, did you sow seeds of it earlier in the narrative? If not, can you?

The next episode of the series is ***Helpless***, where on her 18th birthday the Council puts Buffy through a dangerous test. That episode starts the second half of Season Three and will be covered in the next *Buffy and the Art of Story* book.

To get notice when it releases, and get free story structure worksheets to use with your own writing, visit LisaLilly.com/Worksheets.

CHAPTER 12
RESOURCES

I HOPE you found the analysis of the *Buffy* episodes in the first half of Season Three and the related questions fun and helpful. I learned so much about fiction writing from watching, rewatching, and now podcasting about *Buffy the Vampire Slayer,* and I love sharing that with readers and listeners.

If you're a writer or storyteller, in addition to the free story structure template (also known as worksheets, but you don't want to think of writing as work, do you?) at WritingAsASecondCareer.com/Worksheets, you may find the rest of my Writing As A Second Career series useful.

The books on plot include *Super Simple Story Structure: A Quick Guide To Plotting And Writing Your Novel*; *The One-Year Novelist: A Week-By-Week Guide To Writing Your Novel In One Year*; and, for middle school children, *How To Plot Your Novel: Grades 6-8.*

Learn more about characterization in *Creating Compelling Characters From The Inside Out.* If you're struggling to get a novel or story started, or to finish once you've begun, you may want to look at *Write On: How To Overcome Writer's Block So You Can Write Your Novel.* My books on the writing life include

Happiness, Anxiety, And Writing: Using Your Creativity To Live A Calmer, Happier Life and *Fiction Writing As Your Second Career*.

You can find a full list of my books for writers, which include the other *Buffy and the Art of Story* books, in the Also By section at the end of this book. And you can find more content about *Buffy* and about fiction writing at Patreon.com/LisaMLilly.

Thank you for taking this journey deeper into *Buffy* with me. Good luck with your writing!

DID you enjoy this book and find it helpful? Please write a review to help other writers find it, too. Even a sentence or a few words can make a difference.

NOTES

5. Homecoming S3 E5

1. I'm a particular fan of this line, and I borrowed from it when I started my creative publishing company Spiny Woman LLC.

8. Lovers Walk S3 E8

1. I first heard about these three factors for identifying the protagonist of a story from Lani Diane Rich in her podcast *How Story Works*.

9. The Wish S3 E9

1. The movie where the initial protagonist dies partway through is Alfred Hitchcock's *Psycho*.

ABOUT THE AUTHOR

An author, lawyer, and adjunct professor of law, L. M. Lilly's non-fiction includes **Happiness, Anxiety, and Writing: Using Your Creativity To Live A Calmer, Happier Life**; **Super Simple Story Structure: A Quick Guide to Plotting & Writing Your Novel**; **Buffy And The Art Of Story Season One: Writing Better Fiction By Watching Buffy**; and **Creating Compelling Characters From The Inside Out**.

Writing as Lisa M. Lilly, she is the author of the best selling **Awakening supernatural thriller series** about Tara Spencer, a young woman who becomes the focus of a powerful religious cult when she inexplicably finds herself pregnant, and of the **Q.C. Davis mystery series**. She is currently working on the latest book in that series.

Lilly also is the author of **When Darkness Falls**, a gothic horror novel set in Chicago's South Loop, and the short-story collection **The Tower Formerly Known as Sears and Two Other Tales of Urban Horror**, the title story of which was made into the short film Willis Tower.

Lilly is a resident of Chicago and a member and past officer of the Alliance Against Intoxicated Motorists. She joined AAIM after an intoxicated driver caused the deaths of her parents in 2007. Her book of essays, **Standing in Traffic**, is available on AAIM's website.

Visit her website LisaLilly.com for more information, to listen to the Buffy and the Art of Story podcast, or to join her email list.

ALSO BY L. M. LILLY

The One-Year Novelist: A Week-By-Week Guide To Writing Your Novel In One Year

Happiness, Anxiety, and Writing: Using Your Creativity To Live A Calmer, Happier Life

Super Simple Story Structure: A Quick Guide to Plotting and Writing Your Novel

Creating Compelling Characters From The Inside Out

How To Write A Novel, Grades 6-8

Write On: How To Overcome Writer's Block So You Can Write Your Novel

Fiction Writing As Your Second Career

Buffy And The Art Of Story Season One: Writing Better Fiction By Watching Buffy

Buffy And The Art Of Story Season Two Part 1: Threats, Lies, and Surprises in Episodes 1-11

Buffy And The Art Of Story Season Two Part 2: Writing About Love, Loss, and Betrayal in Episodes 12-22

As Lisa M. Lilly:

The Awakening (Book 1 in The Awakening Series)

The Unbelievers (Book 2 in The Awakening Series)

The Conflagration (Book 3 in The Awakening Series)

The Illumination (Book 4 in The Awakening Series)

The Awakening Supernatural Thriller Series Complete Omnibus/Box Set

When Darkness Falls (a standalone supernatural suspense novel)

The Tower Formerly Known As Sears And Two Other Tales Of Urban Horror

The Worried Man (Q.C. Davis Mystery 1)

The Charming Man (Q.C. Davis Mystery 2)

The Fractured Man (Q.C. Davis Mystery 3)

No Good Plays (A Q.C. Davis Mystery Novella)

The Troubled Man (Q.C. Davis Mystery 4)

The Hidden Man (Q.C. Davis Mystery 5)

The Forgotten Man (Q.C. Davis Mystery 6)

Q.C. Davis Mysteries 1-3 (The Worried Man, The Charming Man, and The Fractured Man) Box Set

www.ingramcontent.com/pod-product-compliance
Lightning Source LLC
Chambersburg PA
CBHW071957110526
44592CB00012B/1117